Beholding Salvation

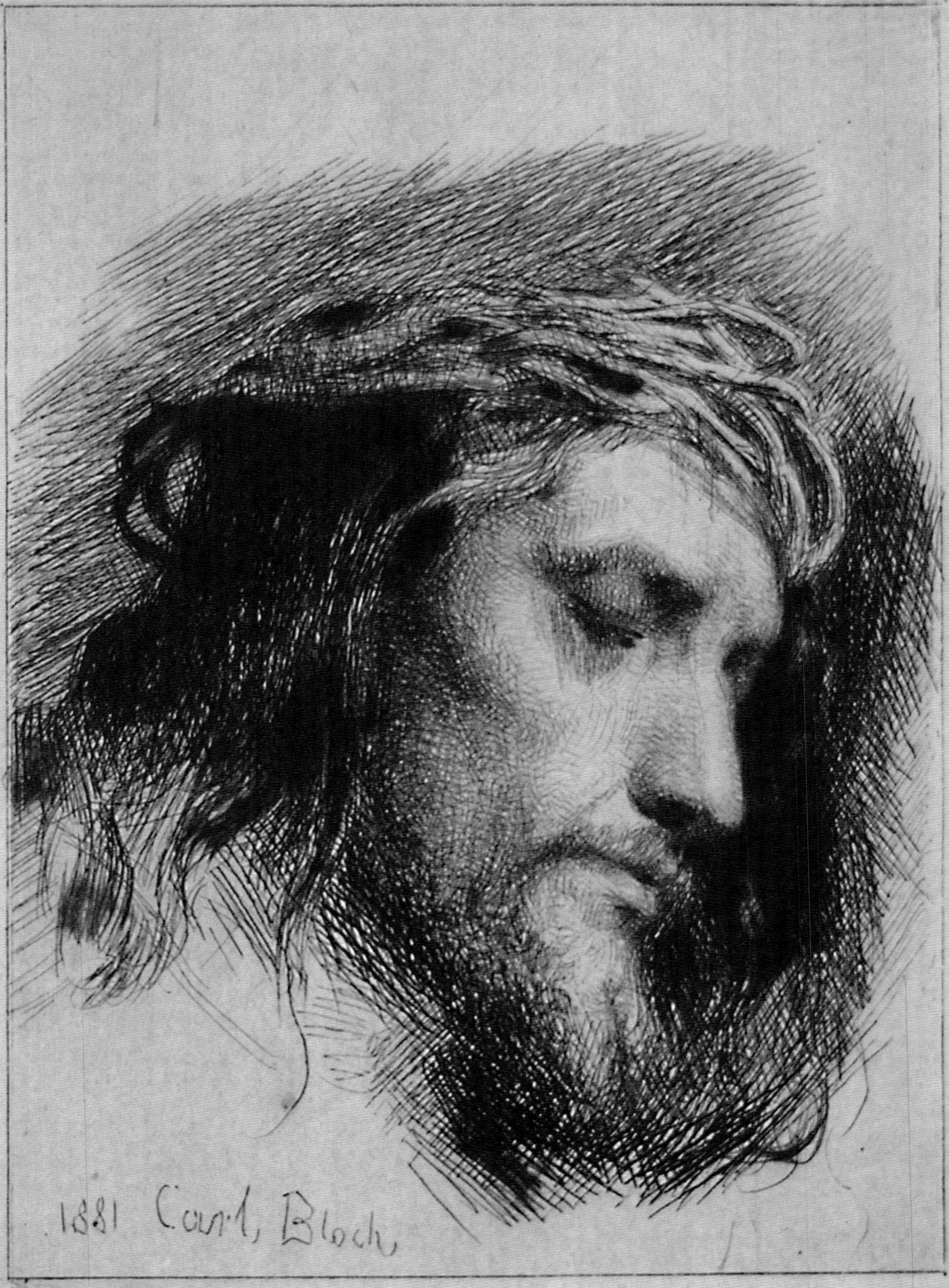
1881 Carl Bloch

BEHOLDING SALVATION

The Life of Christ in Word and Image

S. Kent Brown
Richard Neitzel Holzapfel
Dawn C. Pheysey

with Nicole Cannariato

Deseret Book
Salt Lake City, Utah

DESERET BOOK

BRIGHAM YOUNG UNIVERSITY
MUSEUM OF ART

Carl Heinrich Bloch (1834–1890), *Christ with a Crown of Thorns*, 1881, etching, 3 1/4 x 2 7/8 inches. Brigham Young University Museum of Art, purchased with funds provided by Robert and Lisa Wheatley.

Visit us at deseretbook.com

Library of Congress Cataloging-in-Publication Data

Brown, S. Kent.
Beholding salvation : the life of Christ in word and image / S. Kent Brown, Richard Neitzel Holzapfel, and Dawn C. Pheysey.
p. cm.
Includes bibliographical references.
ISBN 10: 1-59038-614-0 (hardbound : alk. paper)
ISBN 13: 978-1-59038-614-9 (hardbound : alk. paper)
1. Jesus Christ—Biography. 2. Jesus Christ—Art. I. Holzapfel, Richard Neitzel. II. Pheysey. Dawn III. Title.
BT301.3.H65 2006
704.9'4853—dc22 2006010429

Printed in the United States of America
Inland Press, Menomonee Falls, WI

10 9 8 7 6 5 4 3 2

Contents

	Foreword	vi
	Acknowledgments	viii
	Introduction	ix
	"What Beholdest Thou?"	xi
Chapter 1:	Annunciation	1
Chapter 2:	Birth	7
Chapter 3:	Youth	19
Chapter 4:	Baptism and Temptations	25
Chapter 5:	Sermons and Teachings	31
Chapter 6:	Miracles	37
Chapter 7:	Notable Moments	43
Chapter 8:	In Jerusalem for the Last Time	51
Chapter 9:	The Last Supper	57
Chapter 10:	Gethsemane	63
Chapter 11:	Trials	71
Chapter 12:	Crucifixion	77
Chapter 13:	Anastasis	91
Chapter 14:	Resurrection	95
Chapter 15:	The First Vision	103
Chapter 16:	Christ As Judge	109
	Further Reading	114
	Index	115

Foreword

Even a cursory review of the world's greatest art collections reveals how extensively the life of Jesus Christ has been featured in these noteworthy works over the centuries. This publication, and the exhibition *Beholding Salvation: Images of Christ* that it accompanies, are the first treatments of Christian art at Brigham Young University Museum of Art that focus wholly on the ministry of the Savior as portrayed across the broad sweep of Christian art.

S. Kent Brown and Richard Neitzel Holzapfel, both professors of religion at BYU, initiated this project in collaboration with Dawn C. Pheysey, curator of religious art at BYU Museum of Art. Brown and Holzapfel contributed the scriptural discourse for this publication. Their insightful commentary on the seminal themes represented by the artworks contextualizes the spiritual significance of the works in this collection. These seasoned writers also bring new life to a retelling of the sacred events that comprise the Savior's life and ministry. Their insights not only draw us closer to the Savior but also enliven our understanding of the eternal truths upon which these artworks are predicated.

The artworks reproduced in this volume also serve to increase our appreciation for the talent, devotion, and inspiration of artists, who across the centuries have contributed to the great body of Christian art.

Dawn C. Pheysey and her talented assistant Nicole Cannariato have contributed a cogent and highly informed analysis of the signs and symbols as well as the socio-historical context of the artworks reproduced in this volume. Rather than regarding the works as merely illustrative of theological subjects, their text explores symbolism and other pictorial conventions that religious artists have used over the ages to convey the central themes and doctrines of their faith.

When engaging an inspired work of sincere devotion, viewers can experience both an aesthetic response and an even more powerful spiritual recognition. George Ferguson, an art historian who has made a study of this phenomenon, describes it as "the never-ending experiences man has with truth, beauty, and goodness. There is a language for these experiences. It is a very simple and beautiful language which man has known and used since the beginning of time. It is called the language of the sign and the symbol, the outward and visible form through which is revealed the inward and invisible reality that moves and directs the soul of a man. A single tear coursing down the cheek reveals what words could never express. These signs and symbols are the language of the soul."[1]

The study of these signs and symbols in visual art, known as iconography, has made a profound contribution to our understanding of the concepts that inform devotional imagery.

Although first codified as a field of investigation by French scholars in the seventeenth century, it was not until writers such as Émile Mâle and Erwin Panofsky wrote on the subject in the early twentieth century that modern readers took note of the value of iconography in interpreting Christian images. Their scholarship has changed the way we view religious artworks, allowing us to make distinctions between iconic, narrative, and devotional images; where the iconic image's function is to stand for the object of prayer, the function of the narrative and devotional forms are for purposes of devotion or for "contemplative absorption."[2]

Because these distinctions are often not clearly defined, the original context or intended setting of the artwork is an important factor in determining the artist's intended reception of the image. This aspect is often overlooked when works are taken out of their original ecclesiastical, social, cultural, and spiritual settings and transplanted into the "aestheticized" environment of the art museum or the neutrality of the printed page. Thus, though the artworks in this volume, and its associated exhibition, encompass a wide range of styles, attempts have been made to indicate each work's originally intended viewing context. To this end, Pheysey and Cannariato's text situates examples of Catholic, Protestant, and Latter-day Saint religious artwork within the domain of devotional practice and the spiritual world of their artists, while simultaneously revealing the works' universal religious truths.

The exhibition of more than 170 artworks and the narrative in this companion book encompass the full cycle of Christ's ministry in both the Old and New Worlds, beginning with poignant portrayals of the Annunciation and the domesticity of the Savior's early childhood, before moving with awesome inevitability toward His supreme sacrifice and supernal act of redemption—the Atonement. The exposition culminates with triumphant portrayals of the Resurrection and the serene majesty of the postmortal ministry of the Savior. Visitors to the BYU Museum of Art are afforded opportunities in a conducive and sensitively ordered viewing environment to reflect on these truths and ponder the "solemnities of eternity"[3] invoked by these masterful works.

In a publication of devotional art such as this, it would be remiss not to draw attention at the outset to the profound impact that iconoclasm, in one form or another, has had on the production of Christian images.

There were few pictorial representations of Christ until the beginning of the second century due to a fear of violating the second commandment, which prohibited the making and worshipping of graven images. In the eighth century, another controversy erupted over the use of religious imagery, resulting in the destruction of many Christian icons, mosaics, and sculptures. Again, nearly eight hundred years later, Protestant reformers condemned the use of religious images in devotional practice as idolatrous.

It was not until 1563 that the Council of Trent decreed for all Catholic believers that images were useful "for educating the illiterate, as a stimulus to memory, and as a catalyst for devotion."[4] Thereafter, in the Western world, the representation of Christ was legitimized by the fact that, although divine, the Savior had taken upon Himself a mortal form and consequently His body became both the subject and the validation of images by mortal means. The injunction against depictions of sacred subjects became a thing of the past in most Christian communities. Religious artworks, once considered heretical, were now lauded, prompting one seventeenth-century scholar to declare that the "highest end" of the painting of sacred images was "to unite men with God."[5]

This publication speaks powerfully to believers and nonbelievers alike, in acquainting and reacquainting all with the reality of the Savior's ministry, through Christian devotional art; it is also an eloquent validation of the image as a tool for deeper inquiry and spiritual understanding in a world often limited by exclusive reliance on textual analysis. Through both word and image, this creative project reaffirms and bears witness to the divine mission and ministry of a living Savior who invites all to come unto Him and receive His image in their countenances.

Herman Carel du Toit
Head of Museum Research
Brigham Young University Museum of Art

1. George Ferguson, *Signs and Symbols in Christian Art* (Oxford: Oxford University Press, 1959), 45.
2. Erwin Panofsky, "'Imago Pietatis': Ein Beitrag zur Typengeschichte des 'Schmerzensmann' und der 'Maria Mediatrix,'" in *Festschrift für Max J, Friedländer zum 60* Geburtstag (Leipzig, 1927), 261–308, quoted by James Clifton, in *The Body of Christ in the Art of Europe and New Spain 1150–1800* (Houston: The Museum of Fine Arts, 1998), 14.
3. Doctrine and Covenants 43:34.
4. James Clifton, *The Body of Christ in the Art of Europe and New Spain 1150–1800* (Houston: The Museum of Fine Arts, 1998), 13.
5. "El arte de la pintura" in Enggass and Brown, *Italian and Spanish Art, 1600–1750: Sources and Documents* (Evanston, Ill.: Northwestern University Press, 1970), 162–65.

Acknowledgments

Many hands have touched the words and images of this book.

We thank Sheri Dew, Jana Erickson, and Richard Erickson, at Deseret Book for their assistance and expertise. We especially appreciate and value the skill and patience of our editor, Richard Peterson.

We especially acknowledge the generous donation of the George S. and Dolores Doré Eccles Foundation in assembling the exhibition.

The support of our colleagues at the Brigham Young University College of Religious Education and the Museum of Art has been vital. We express appreciation to administrative assistant Joany Pinegar of the Religious Studies Center for her conscientious attention to detail as she made changes and corrections to the manuscript. Our thanks go to Ted Stoddard and Alison Coutts, who contributed their fine editorial skills and provided critical proofreading. We acknowledge the support of Museum Director Campbell Gray, who has given consistent encouragement. We are grateful also to designer Brian Bird for his diligent work on the layout of each page, responding tirelessly to unending requests to alter minute details on texts and images. We especially thank Herman DuToit, lead educator on this project, for his foreword and insightful comments and editorial suggestions. Christopher Krause contributed his fine photographic skills.

Research assistants Lindsay Davidson, Reed Larsen, Elizabeth Pinborough, Erin Tanner, and Stanley Thayne from the Religious Studies Center have also contributed much to the development of this book. Likewise, the Art History area of the College of Fine Arts and Communications provided several student interns—Nicole Cannariato, Julianne Gough, Rebecca Lloyd, and Lisa Mortensen—who were involved in the research for the exhibition and the book. A research grant from the Religious Studies Center provided moneys for graduate assistant Nicole Cannariato to continue work on the project for an additional two years. With her excellent writing skills and sensitivity to the project, she made significant contributions to the book and exhibition.

We also thank those institutions, artists, and individuals who kindly loaned their works to this book's associated exhibition and provided images of those works included in this volume: James Clifton, the Sarah Campbell Blaffer Foundation; Craig Galli and Clark B. Hinckley, Salt Lake Bonneville Stake of The Church of Jesus Christ of Latter-day Saints; Derek Jensen and Russell Taylor of the L. Tom Perry Special Collections, Harold B. Lee Library, Brigham Young University; Joseph and Jan Cannon; Maria Peterson and Dr. Robyn Roberts, East High School, Salt Lake City School District; Laurie Olson Lisonbee and Shawn and Andrea Merriman; The Metropolitan Museum of Art; Gary Boatright, Robert Davis, Gloria Scovill, and Carrie Snow, Museum of Church History and Art; Flemming Friborg and Tine Blicher-Moritz, the Ny Carlsberg Glyptotek; Itiel Pann; Marilyn Palmeri, Charles E. Pierce Jr., and William Voelkle, Pierpont Morgan Library; J. Kirk Richards; Charles R. Loving, Robert Smogor, and Stephen Spiro, Snite Museum of Art; Madelyn Garrett and Luise Poulton, Rare Books Division, Special Collections, J. Willard Marriott Library, University of Utah; Kathleen Carricaburu, David M. Carroll, and David Dee, Utah Museum of Fine Arts; and Walter and Mary Whipple. We also thank researcher and author Roger Cooper for sharing his vast knowledge about the artist Bernard Sleigh.

We also gratefully acknowledge all those who have gifted or generously provided funds for the purchase of the religious art reproduced in this book. These benefactors are noted in the captions below the images.

Introduction

Joining image to word creates a rich tapestry of meaning not always visible in text alone. For example, what might it have been like for a shy, young shepherd to stand behind his friends when they finally found "the babe wrapped in swaddling clothes" (Luke 2:12) and paid homage to Him? Luke's report of the shepherds' visitation does not offer up such detail, but the artist, while being true to Luke's words, is free to show such a shepherd in the background, just out of the glow of the celestial light radiating from the Christ Child. The scene, in effect, becomes vivid and whole in the artist's hands. The exhibition *Beholding Salvation: Images of Christ,* and this accompanying volume, illustrate this point. The narrative and art historical texts set out the interpretive framework for both the life and ministry of the Savior and for the imagery that illuminates His life. The images offer a palpable grace and visual depth.

The story of Jesus as Messiah, of course, started eons before He was born to Mary, in a distant era "before the world began" (3 Nephi 26:5). His promises for our eternity thus came with Him, and artists have tried to portray the continuity between the mortal infant and His former life in glory by combining light, texture, and form in a manner that affirms His divinity. Because of heaven's high expectations for the Savior, even His youth has come under the ever-sharpening focus of both author and artist who recreate scenes, reported or imagined, from Jesus' early years in attempts to grasp how He came to fit within our recognizable world.

The Gospel accounts bring together a rich set of incidents from Jesus' life that have inspired believing, devoted minds ever since the incidents happened, whether miracles or teaching moments or personal interactions. These events hand to us lively moments that broaden our view of who Jesus is and establish principles of truth. We must understand that such events were powerful enough to lift Jesus out of history's slipstream and cause a wake of their own that affected people irreversibly for centuries after His mortal life and ministry.

As striking as these occurrences are, they retreat in the face of the towering events of the last day of Jesus' mortal life. More than any other moments in His life and ministry, except possibly His birth, the events of Jesus' final twenty-four hours have drawn to themselves pen and ink, brush and paint, imagination and contemplation. Just as compelling for believers, however, are Jesus' redeeming visit to the realm of the dead, His triumphant resurrection from death, and His subsequent multitude of appearances to faithful disciples—upwards of 550 known witnesses in the Old World and many more than this number in the New.

After the long sleep of apostasy, wherein the gifts of the Spirit and the powers of heaven were lost to mortals, the gates of heaven once again opened wide, and both the Father and the Son passed through them on Their way to Upstate New York to visit the young Joseph Smith to whom They then entrusted the task of restoring the saving gospel. That appearance, known in Latter-day Saint parlance as "The First Vision," has itself acted as a magnet for authors and artists who have sought to lay bare its meanings in word and image.

At the end of this earth's run as a dwelling place for mortals will come the final judgment, an event long prophesied in sacred writ. In the wide prophetic eye, the Savior is portrayed variously as "a refiner's fire, and like fullers' soap," as one "with healing in his wings," and as one "red in [his] apparel . . . [he having] trodden the winepress alone" (Malachi 3:2; 4:2; Isaiah 63:2–3). In the words of the Apostle Paul, "We shall all stand before the judgment seat of Christ" at the end (Romans 14:10). As one judged contemptible and deserving execution in this life, He shall pass a just judgment on all in that coming sphere by bringing together, in a grand scene, "all things . . . which are in heaven, and which are on earth" (Ephesians 1:10).

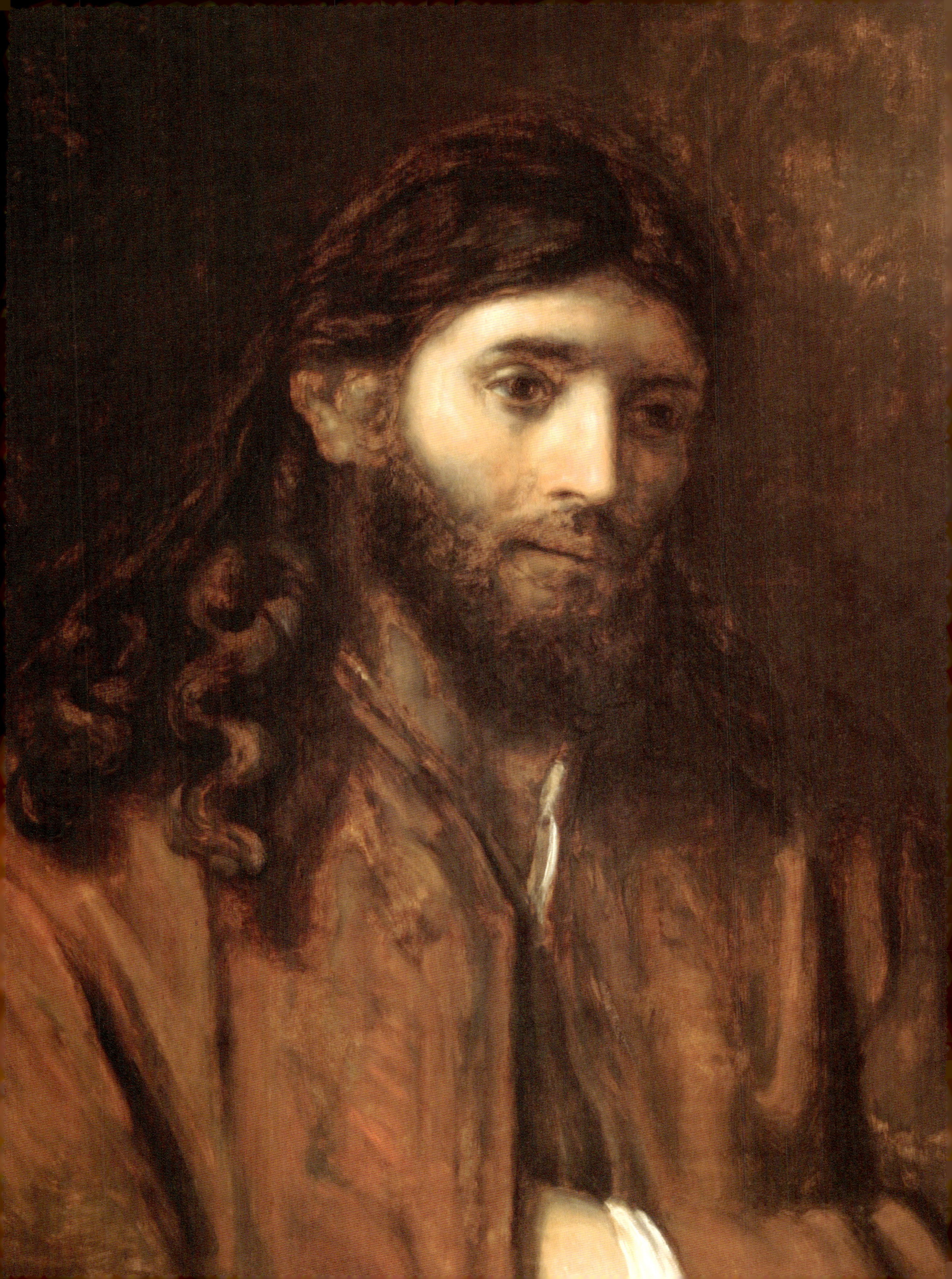

"What Beholdest Thou?"

When the Book of Mormon prophet Nephi saw his vision of the life of the Savior, the angel asked him not only to look, but to "*Behold* the Lamb of God, yea, even the Son of the Eternal Father!" (1 Nephi 11:21). A similar charge was voiced in John the Baptist's exclamation "*Behold* the Lamb of God, which taketh away the sin of the world" (John 1:29). *Beholding* requires more than merely looking; it involves considering and pondering, understanding and interpreting, receiving knowledge and holding in remembrance.

Likewise, viewing religious works of art calls for more than simply recognizing familiar figures, places, and narratives; it entails *beholding* profound principles, deep doctrines, and veiled meanings. Over the centuries Christian artists have developed certain conventions that convey significant concepts to the minds of prepared viewers. These canons of representation encouraged reflection on the life of Christ and solidified religious doctrines. The purpose of the historical text in this book is to explore some of these conventions and to interpret their use in sensitizing viewers to the historical and spiritual realities of the Christian faith. We hope that today's viewers will be edified and inspired to greater devotion through contemplating these images of Christ in much the same way that previous generations of faithful observers gained a heightened reverence for the Savior and His ministry in their day.

Many of the works in this collection were produced by European artists working in former times under the auspices of the Catholic Church, a powerful patron of the arts for many centuries. Others were created to advance the teachings of the Protestant reformers. Still others are the result of modern-day revelation. By presenting numerous works from diverse Christian faiths, this text seeks to engage readers in a search for that which is uplifting, truthful, and meaningful. We can learn much about the divine nature of Christ's ministry from the works of these artists—Catholic, Protestant, and Latter-day Saint—as we study the iconography and conventions that facilitate communication of these hallowed events and ideas. Whether mandated by a religious institution, commissioned by a wealthy patron, or motivated by personal beliefs, these images teach and reinforce sacred doctrine and promote private contemplation. Regardless of the specific tenets that these artworks were intended to express, viewers can ascribe personal understanding to the images that transcend doctrinal differences. As you ponder these pages of both word and image, we invite you to discover deeper meaning and achieve greater understanding as you *behold* salvation.

Circle of Rembrandt (ca. 1650), detail of *Head of Christ*, 17th century, oil on panel, 24 3/8 x 19 3/16 inches, Brigham Young University Museum of Art, gift of Vivian Vicondo.

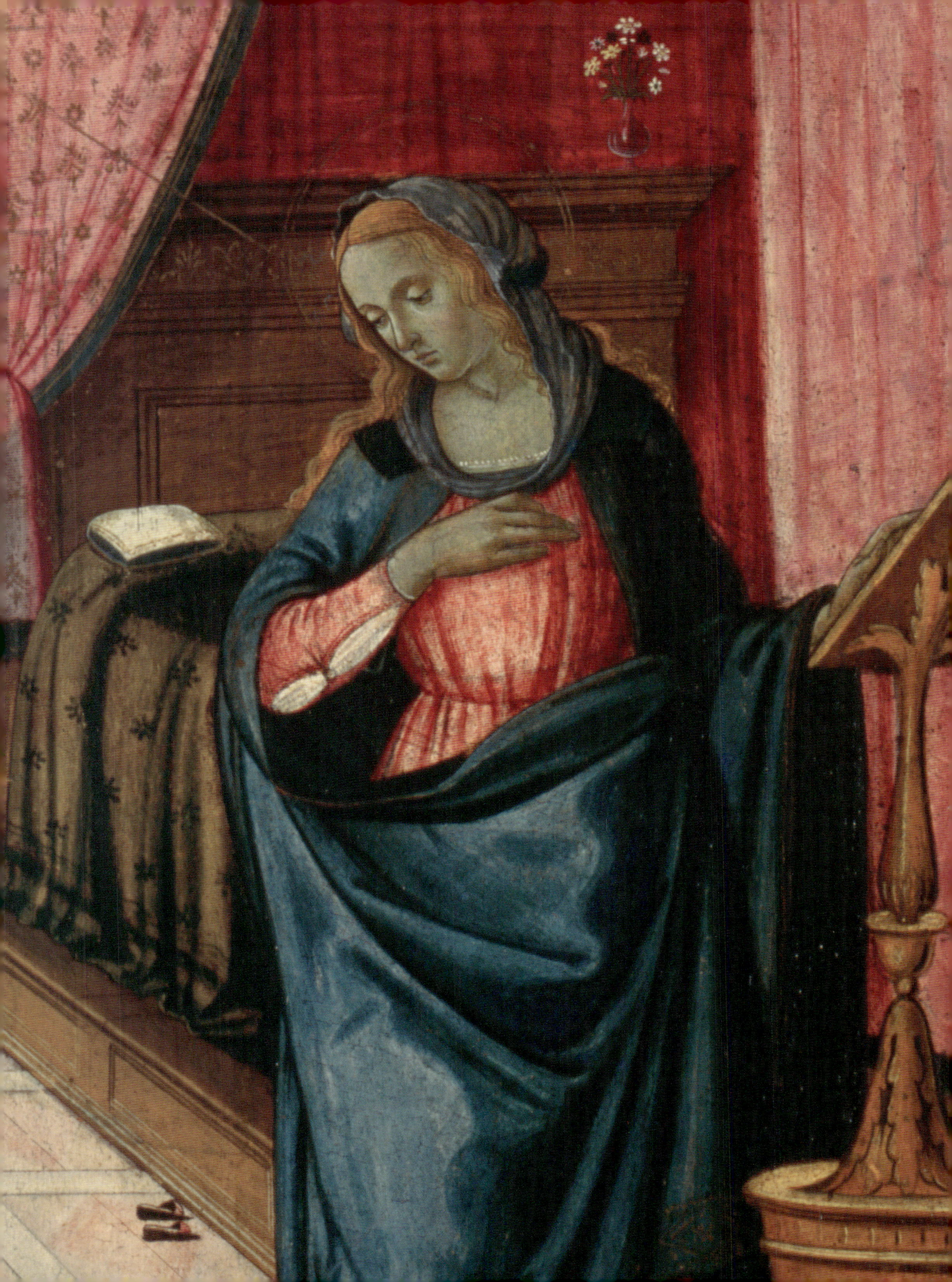

Chapter 1

ANNUNCIATION

Grand moments in scripture always begin with a voice, a divine voice, which brings news or instruction to the earth. So it was with the approach of the Son of God and His herald. The voice this time first pierced the quiet sanctuary of the temple where the aged priest Zacharias was stretching forth his hand to light the incense on the golden altar, which stood directly in front of the temple's veil. Although art cannot capture the sound of that voice, it can depict the sudden surprise that enveloped the priest. It can represent the happy consequences of the voice's promise to Zacharias that a son, to be called John, was to be born and grow to manhood.

Zacharias, a literal descendant of Aaron, had come to this sacred moment with high anticipation because, typically, priests were chosen only once in their lives to light the holy incense. Standing at the altar, next to the veil, beyond which lay the Holy of Holies, Zacharias was as close as he would ever come to God's presence. Then the voice of an angel, and then his fearful presence, changed everything for this priest and for Elisabeth, his wife.

The angel, named Gabriel, brought important news and an era-making prophecy. A child would be born to Zacharias and Elisabeth, a son who would go as a forerunner of the long-awaited Messiah. It would be a miracle. Why? Because this couple had lived into their "old age" without children (Luke 1:36). Both Zacharias and Luke the Gospel writer call them "well stricken in years" (Luke 1:7, 18). Their childless situation, in fact, had brought a palpable "reproach," especially upon Elisabeth (see Luke 1:25).

But Zacharias doubted. "Whereby shall I know this?" he asked boldly, "for I am an old man, and my wife well stricken in years" (Luke 1:18). At this moment and in his own way, Zacharias stood for many religious officials of his day: upright yet unbelieving, exacting yet skeptical, faithful yet spiritually impotent. The response of the angel was swift and decisive. He declared: "Thou shalt be dumb, and not able to speak, until the day that these things shall be performed, because thou believest not my words" (Luke 1:20). As a result, Zacharias was left speechless before "the people [who] waited" for him to come out of the temple (Luke 1:21). In addition, he lost his ability to hear, as the account of the naming of his son John indicates (see Luke 1:59–66). Thus, he was entombed within his own mind, his thoughts being his only companion, his communication limited to gestures and writing (see Luke 1:22, 62–63). Doubtless his limited state led him to reevaluate his relationship to God and to make efforts to harmonize his life with the Divine, as the later outpouring of the spirit of prophecy shows (see Luke 1:67–79).

The annunciation to Mary, one of the most beloved themes in art, bears none of the magnificent temple setting that surrounded Zacharias. Instead, the same angel who came to the priest found Mary in her home, as the expression "came in unto her" suggests (Luke 1:28). In fact, her fear at the angel's appearance hints that she was in a place where she did not expect to meet a stranger. The news was both disquieting and enlivening. The youthful Mary, likely not yet fourteen years old, and perhaps younger, betrays in her words—"be it unto me according to thy word"—that she grasped in an instant the daunting consequences that would roll through her life because of the angel's promise that she would "conceive" by "the power of the Highest" before her betrothal was complete.

Master of Apollo and Daphne (active 16th century), detail of *The Annunciation*, early 16th century, oil on panel, 35 3⁄8 x 22 1⁄4 inches. Gift of Mr. Val A. Browning, from the Permanent Collection of the Utah Museum of Fine Arts.

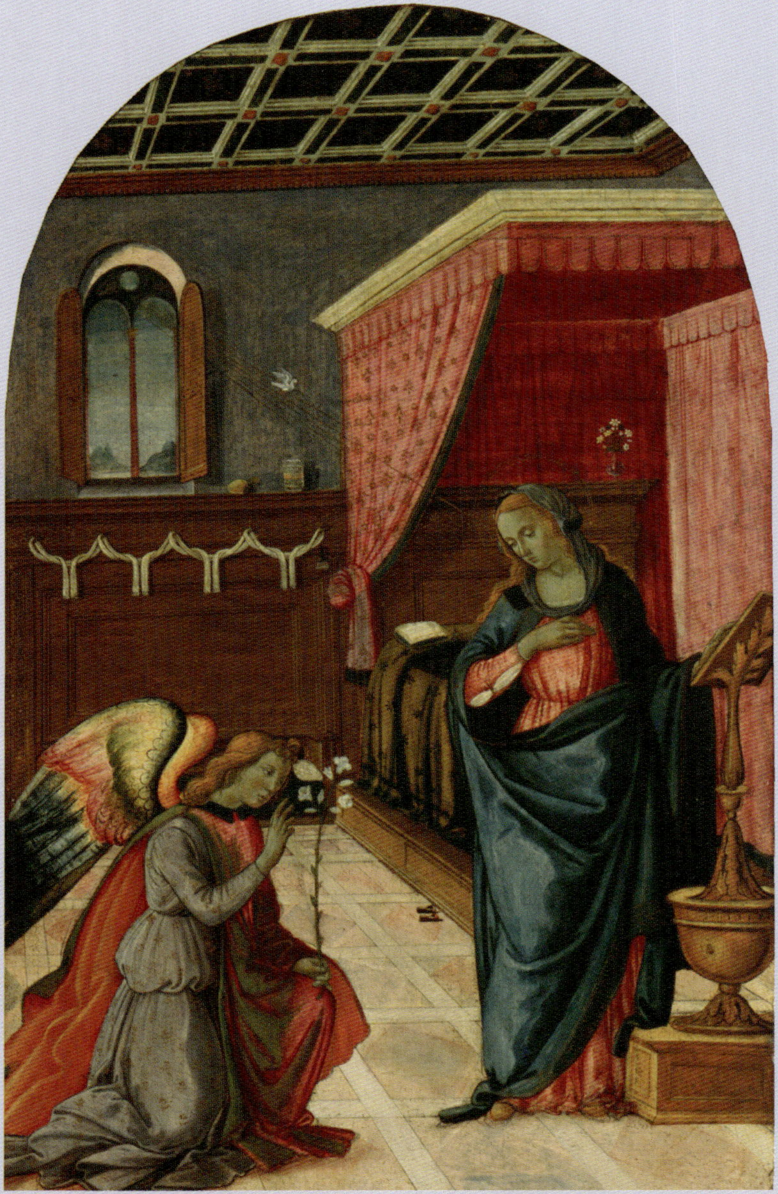

Figure 1. Master of Apollo and Daphne (active 16th century), *The Annunciation*, early 16th century, oil on panel, 35 3/8 x 22 1/4 inches. Gift of Mr. Val A. Browning, from the Permanent Collection of the Utah Museum of Fine Arts.

Home, Lecterns, and Lilies: Symbols of the Annunciation

The Angel Gabriel's announcement to Mary, proclaiming that she had been chosen as the mother of the Messiah, heralds the genesis of the Christian drama. The Annunciation is most often portrayed in a domestic or ecclesiastical interior, which figuratively separates the sacred event from the secular world. Such a setting signals to viewers that hallowed experiences can take place in an intimate space such as the home, transforming it into a holy place. In *The Annunciation* by the artist known as the Master of Apollo and Daphne (Figure 1), Mary has removed the shoes from her feet, further signifying that this quiet bedchamber has become hallowed ground as a result of the angelic visitation. It is in this sacred space that Mary humbly accepts the will of God: "Behold the handmaid of the Lord; be it unto me according to thy word" (Luke 1:38).

According to the tradition popularized by St. Bernard, Abbott of Clairvaux (1090–1153), Mary is often posed at her lectern reading Isaiah's Messianic prophecy declaring that Christ would be born of a virgin (see Isaiah 7:14). White lilies, either held by Gabriel or placed in a vase, represent Mary's purity. Other symbols of her chastity and domesticity include towels, a candle, an enclosed garden, sinks, fire screens, and even polished pots. Frequently accompanying the angelic visitor, a dove descends on a ray of light that emanates from God the Father and touches Mary. This suggests the moment when Gabriel announced to Mary: "The Holy Ghost shall come upon thee, and the power of the Highest shall overshadow thee" (Luke 1:35). The ray of light, as St. Bernard taught, depicts the early Christian dogma that Mary could conceive the Christ Child and still remain a virgin: just as a shaft of light passes through a window without breaking it, so could Mary be with child without losing her virginity.[1]

Artists broadened traditional Annunciation iconography to convey additional meaning. For instance, in Albrecht Dürer's *Annunciation* (Figure 2), the topmost roundel contains a relief of Judith, the Jewish heroine of the Apocrypha who enticed the Assyrian general Holofernes with her beauty, made him drunk, and then severed his head, which she holds in her left hand. The story of Judith and Holofernes in sixteenth-century Nuremburg, Dürer's hometown, symbolized the Virgin's victory over the devil, who is represented in the form of a badger chained beneath the stairs.[2]

1. Margaret B. Freeman, "The Iconography of the Merode Altarpiece," *The Metropolitan Museum of Art Bulletin* 16, no. 4 (December 1957):133.
2. Museum of Fine Arts, Boston, *Albrecht Dürer: Master Printmaker* (New York: Hacker Art Books, 1988), 96.

On the other hand, the thrilling part of the angel's message concerned the Child who would "be called the Son of the Highest" and was to "reign over the house of Jacob for ever" (Luke 1:32–33). Mary's people, the Israelites, had been waiting for this Child for a very long time. The moment had come at last! And she was to be His mother. We can imagine that these thoughts captured her mind for the next few days, and that only gradually was her euphoria tempered by a growing anticipation of what this all meant for her both as a prospective mother and as a person of sterling reputation.

Mary, and Joseph also, grew up in Nazareth, then a small village with a few homes and gardens and orchards. The main east-west road through Galilee ran three miles to the north, through Sepphoris, the main city of the region. There must have been a small synagogue in Nazareth during Mary's youth, as the later story of Jesus' preaching suggests (see Luke 4:16–30). Such a building would have been the center of religious devotion both for Mary and for her parents. But why was Mary's family, descendants of David, living in the north of the country and not in the south near Bethlehem? Their residency in Nazareth may have come about because of an ancestor who became a government functionary in Galilee after Jerusalem's priest-king Aristobulus conquered the northern regions in 104 B.C. Her forebears, and those of Joseph who was also a descendant of David, may have relocated to Galilee because of a perceived or real threat against them by the then ruling Hasmonean family, who were not of the royal lineage of David. Whatever the case, their close family ties to Bethlehem become visible in the story of their journey there to be taxed (see Luke 2:1–5).

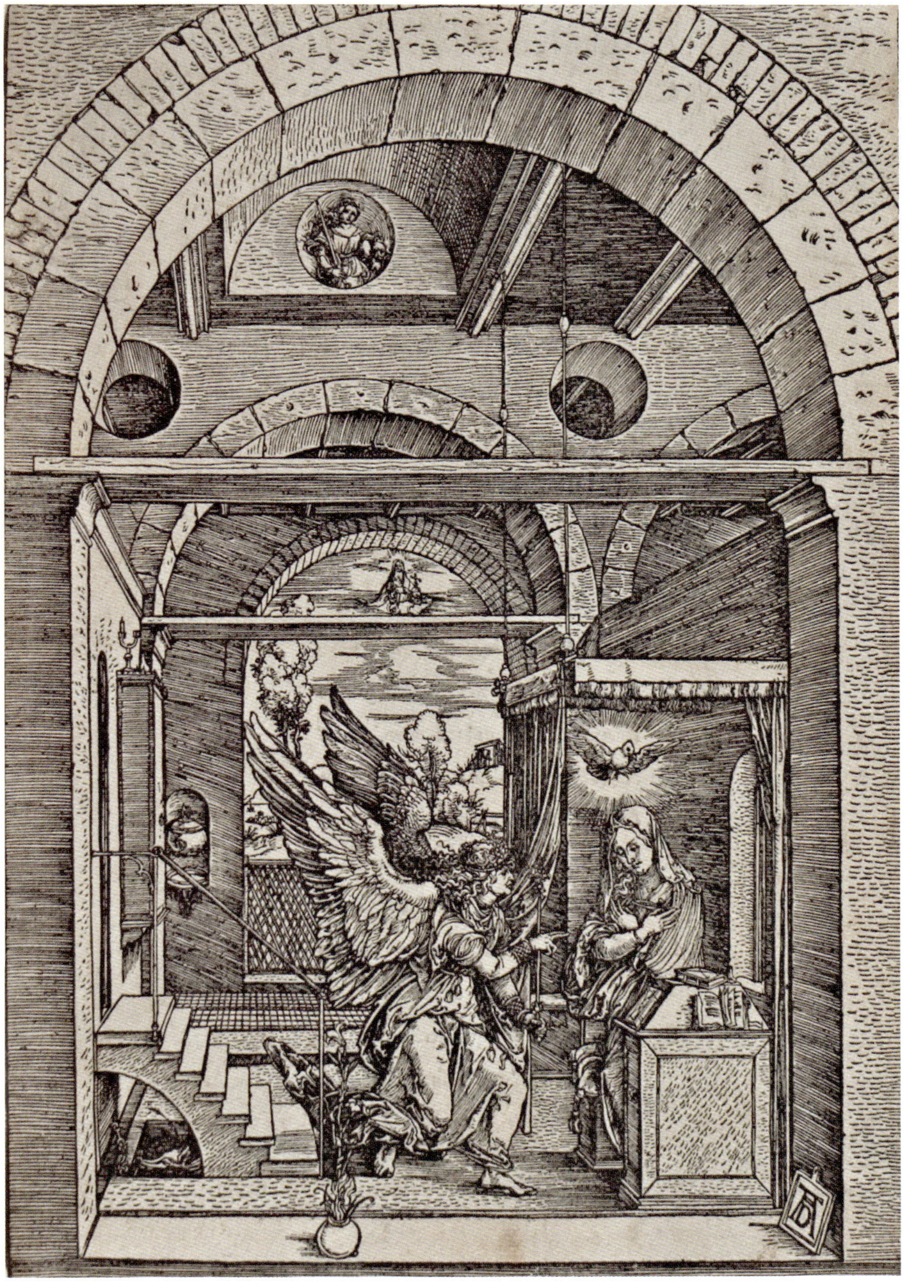

Figure 2. Albrecht Dürer (1471–1528), *The Annunciation*, from the *Life of the Virgin*, ca. 1503, woodcut, 11 5/8 x 8 3/16 inches. Brigham Young University Museum of Art, purchase/gift from Mahonri M. Young Estate.

The angel's announcement to Mary, that her cousin Elisabeth had miraculously "conceived a son in her old age," stood as a virtual command to the young woman to go to visit (Luke 1:36). How Mary finessed with her parents her desire to visit Elisabeth we are not told. The distance was long—almost one hundred miles—and the weather would have been hot in the Jordan Valley where she would likely have traveled. For if Jesus was born in the spring, as the evident birth of the lambs establishes (see Luke 2:8), Mary's journey would have taken place in July, the hottest time of year. Because of potential dangers, she doubtless went in the company of other travelers on their way to Jerusalem or its environs, the probable area where Elisabeth and Zacharias resided.

Mary appears to have known exactly where Elisabeth lived, though there were no street addresses. This observation tells us that she had visited the place, probably in the company of her parents. It was when she came to Elisabeth's home this time that God's Spirit manifested itself in visible, tangible ways. And there is good reason for spiritual manifestations. The eye of God, as we might expect, was tracking Mary, who was by now pregnant with His Son. Elisabeth, for her part, ever since the day that Zacharias, her husband, brought home the news that they were to become parents of a special child, had redoubled her efforts to live worthily before God, as implied in Luke's words, she "hid herself" (Luke 1:24). Hence, when Mary came to Elisabeth's door, the two women together attracted God's Spirit to themselves.

Remarkably, Elisabeth may well have been the one person who, despite age differences, could offer comfort and companionship to her young cousin who, because of her unexpected pregnancy, was now facing squarely the prospect that she would be seen as unfaithful to Joseph and to her parents' teachings. Elisabeth had grown up a daughter in a priest's home, with all of its attendant concern for sacred living (see Luke 1:5). When she married, she and Zacharias stood on a threshold where they could see before them a life together of service to God and of raising children who themselves would serve in the temple. But year after year passed without children, drying up their lives so that they felt a "reproach among men," who regarded them, especially Elisabeth, as somehow out of harmony with God (Luke 1:25). Thus, by the time the angel appeared to her husband, Elisabeth had endured for years the oppressive burdens of being without child and of worrying endlessly whether she was acceptable to God. Her experience, therefore, of feeling herself to be a social outcast and a spiritual failure had effectively prepared her to be a support to Mary who by now was herself feeling alienated from her society and its ennobling norms.

The meeting of Mary and Elisabeth frames one of those special moments when God's love grows thick and rich and sweet, pouring itself so fully into these two women that it comes out of them in a rush of prophecy and divine singing. Mary was the singer, and her song is known as the Magnificat from the first word in its Latin translation (see Luke 1:46–55). Her words enfold both praise for God's kind acts in the past: "He hath filled the hungry"; and for His graciousness in the future: "from henceforth all generations shall call me blessed" (Luke 1:53, 48). To Elisabeth came the Holy Ghost with such invigorating force that her babe "leaped in her womb" (Luke 1:44). Acting for the moment as the herald that her son would become for the Messiah, John's mother announced the Savior's approach through Mary: "Blessed art thou among women, and blessed is the fruit of thy womb." She went on, "Whence is this to me, that the mother of my Lord should come to me?" (Luke 1:42–43). Now Elisabeth knew what Mary knew. To these two women God had entrusted the secret of the ages, the identity of the woman who would bear the Messiah.

Significantly, Elisabeth stood as a first-rank witness of the virgin birth. Within her inspired words we come upon the following: "Blessed is she that believed: for there shall be a performance of those things which were told her from the Lord" (Luke 1:45). What do "those things which were told her" include? Our minds go back immediately to the angel's response to Mary's question about giving birth, "How shall this be, seeing I know not a man?" His reassuring words flowed effortlessly, reassuringly: "The Holy Ghost shall come upon thee, and the power of the Highest shall overshadow thee" (Luke 1:34–35). Here was the sunny prophecy of the approaching virgin birth. Remarkably, Elisabeth senses all of this through the spirit of prophecy that has enveloped her.

Where was Joseph all this time? Luke does not inform readers about any conversation between himself and Mary before she departed for her three-month stay with Elisabeth. It seems that he was in the dark about her condition until after she arrived home. It was then, apparently, that he and others learned of her situation: "She was found with child of the Holy Ghost" (Matthew 1:18). It is evident that Joseph did not initially believe the part of her story about the Holy Ghost, for he moved to put an end to their betrothal, "to put her away privily," not being willing "to make her a publick example," thereby showing his compassionate nature not to draw the meddling attention of others to her embarrassing difficulty. But he was turned by an angel who commanded "in a dream, saying, Joseph, thou son of David, fear not to take unto thee Mary thy wife: for that which is conceived in her is of the Holy Ghost" (Matthew 1:19–20). By intervening, God had set in place a second support for Mary. The first had been Elisabeth. Now Joseph also understood.

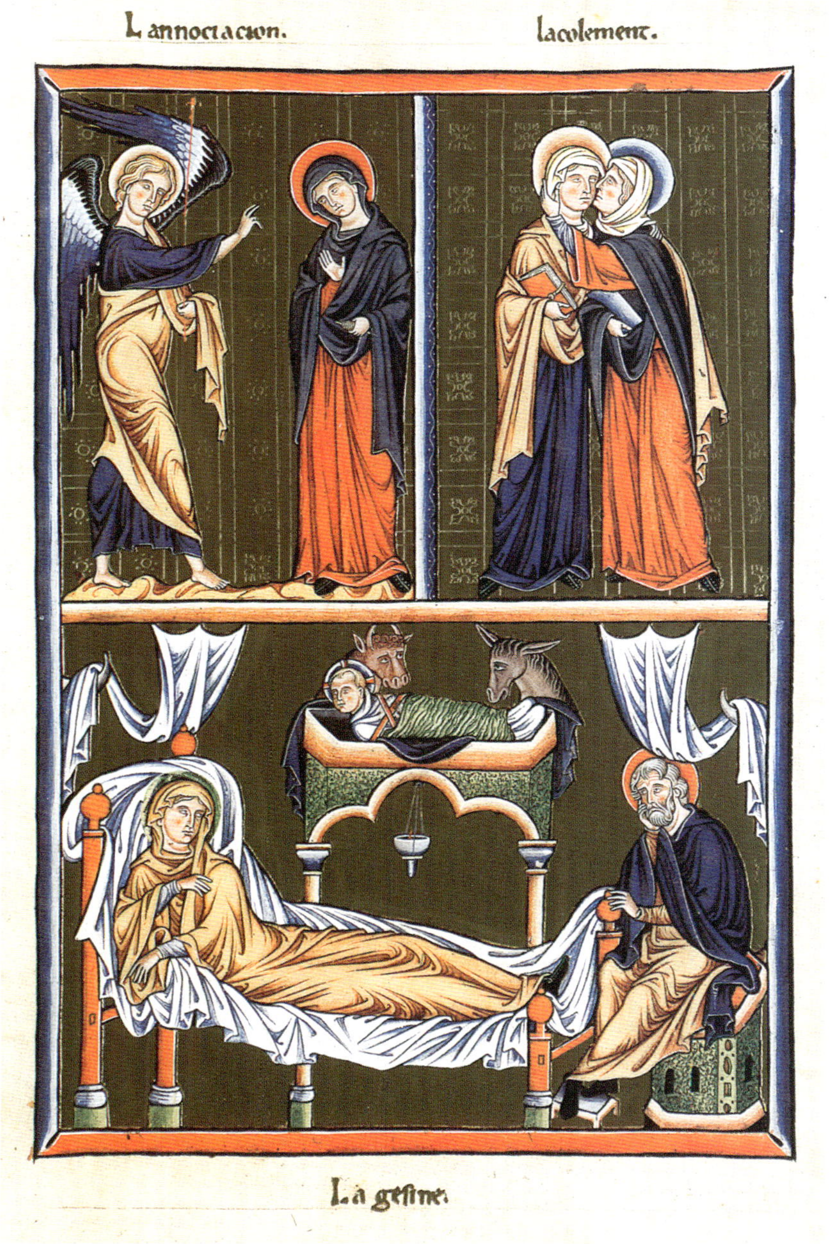

Figure 3. *Annunciation, Visitation, and Nativity*, from *Der Ingeborg Psalter de Danemark* (f. 15r), ca. 1195, illuminated manuscript facsimile (1985), 11 3/4 x 7 1/2 inches. L. Tom Perry Special Collections, Harold B. Lee Library, Brigham Young University, Provo, Utah; ADEVA, Akademische Drück- u. Verlagsanstalt, Austria.

In art, Joseph is often pictured as an older man. In Christian texts that come from the second and fourth centuries (*The Protevangelium of James* and *The History of Joseph the Carpenter*), he appears as old and once-married, thus influencing how Christians thought of him and thereafter portrayed him. But the dates of the composition of these texts raise serious questions about the reliability of the information concerning Joseph. Instead, we should think of him as a younger man, perhaps in his late teens, the typical age for men to marry in his world. His betrothal to Mary would have been initiated by his father's contact with her father. He could not have anticipated that an angel would intervene and bring him to understand that something grand and divine was happening.

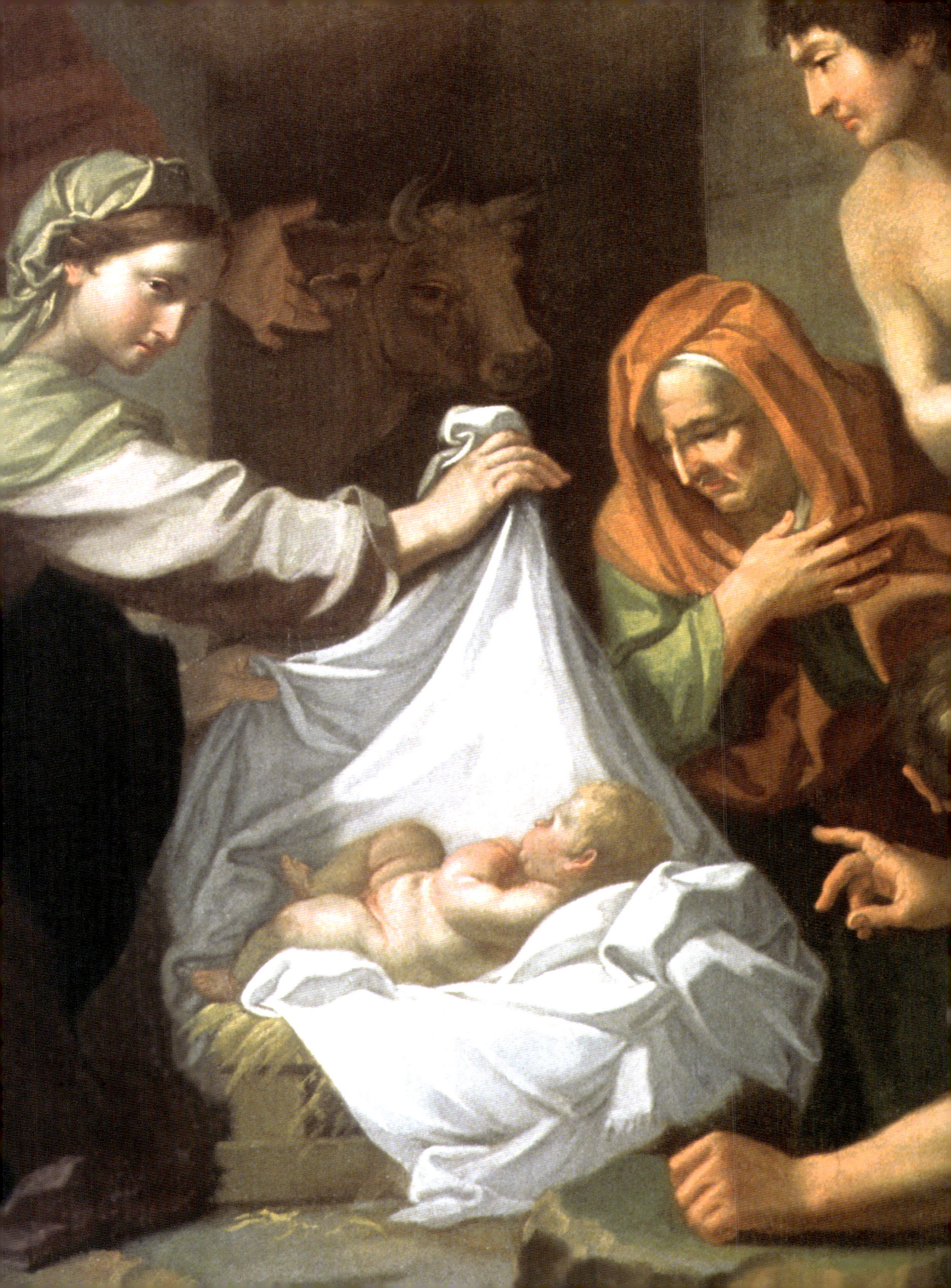

Chapter 2

Birth

The New Testament Gospels intentionally guide readers to Jesus of Nazareth, rehearsing events and teachings of His ministry in such a way "that ye might believe that Jesus is the Christ, the Son of God" (John 20:31). Though their focus rests on Him, He does not stand isolated from others. That is why much of art portrays Jesus in the company of others, for He has come to lead them to Himself and thereby to save them.

In their early verses, the Gospels draw attention to three important themes. And the art that springs from these texts portrays these same themes in visual form. They are birth, home, and sacred moments. The birth, of course, is that of Jesus Himself. Ever close by Him in text and art is His mother Mary. Home becomes important as the place both of Mary's reception of the Angel Gabriel and of the spiritual manifestations that accompanied and followed Mary's visit to the home of Elisabeth and Zacharias. Sacred moments appear in the story of Zacharias's meeting with the angel in the sanctuary of the temple and continue in the stories of the shepherds and wise men.

Births

Except for the Gospel of Mark, which opens as Jesus' ministry begins rather than at an earlier point in His life, the Gospels hold up to view events that preceded Jesus' birth and youth, finally presenting Him as an infant born of a mother into this world. In a word, these reports frame a story about beginnings—human beginnings. Of course, the story of the Savior's birth does not occur in solitude. Woven into these reports are accounts of other beginnings, other births, which take place within families and involve real people with real hopes and fears, particularly Zacharias and Elisabeth. On yet another plane, the records introduce readers to the birth of the Christian movement as it grows from an obscure sect in a remote corner of Palestine to a religion that penetrates the heart of the Roman Empire, a path illumined especially by Luke's book of Acts.

The motif of birth or new beginnings continues in the births of lambs that are born in the spring with the aid of the adult shepherds (see Luke 2:8). Except during the lambing season, one of the children in a family typically kept the sheep through the night (see 1 Samuel 16:11; also 17:15). On a metaphorical level, the birth of lambs may point to the birth of the Lamb of God. In addition, the stories about Simeon and Anna who fuss over the infant Jesus, and the accompanying references to the dawning day of salvation, hold our attention on birth and new beginnings (see Luke 2:25–32, 36–38; also 1:78–79).

Birth is also set off by its opposite, death. One thinks of the birds sacrificed for Mary's ritual cleansing (see Luke 2:24). Moreover, some of the lambs of the Bethlehem shepherds may have been destined for sacrifice for the Passover celebration of that spring. And Simeon's reference to his own nearing death contrasts with birth, continuing the pattern of opposites (see Luke 2:26, 29). In all, death may point to Jesus' own, both as a sacrifice and as a reversal of mortality.

Attributed to Eustache Le Sueur (1616–1655), detail of *Adoration of the Shepherds*, ca. mid 17th century, oil on canvas, 38½ x 53¼ inches. Brigham Young University Museum of Art, purchase/gift from Gloria Teichert, funds provided by Jack R. and Mary Lois Wheatley.

Luke carries his story through other contrasts, not only those that one sees, say, between the doubting Zacharias and the believing Mary but also those visible between the older Elisabeth and the youthful Mary, between the newly born children John and Jesus and the aging Simeon and Anna. Some of the contrasts are almost hidden, such as those associated with the Angel Gabriel, who was Noah in mortality and who announces universal life, but who had witnessed universal death during his own mortal life. With a dramatic touch, Gabriel announces the birth of the Savior who would offer life to those who had died in the flood.

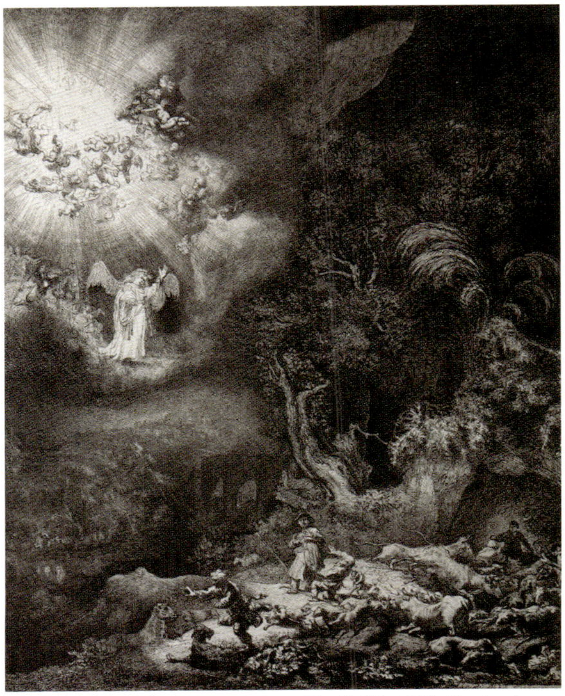

Figure 4. Rembrandt Harmenszoon van Rijn (1606–1669), *The Angel Appearing to the Shepherds*, 1634, burin and drypoint, 10½ x 8¾ inches. Private collection of Shawn and Andrea Merriman.

Home

In blending the theme of birth or new beginnings with that of home, a person has to look only as far as the appearances of the angel first to Zacharias in the house of God and then to Mary in her own home, an observation that becomes apparent when we read that "the angel came in unto her" (Luke 1:28).

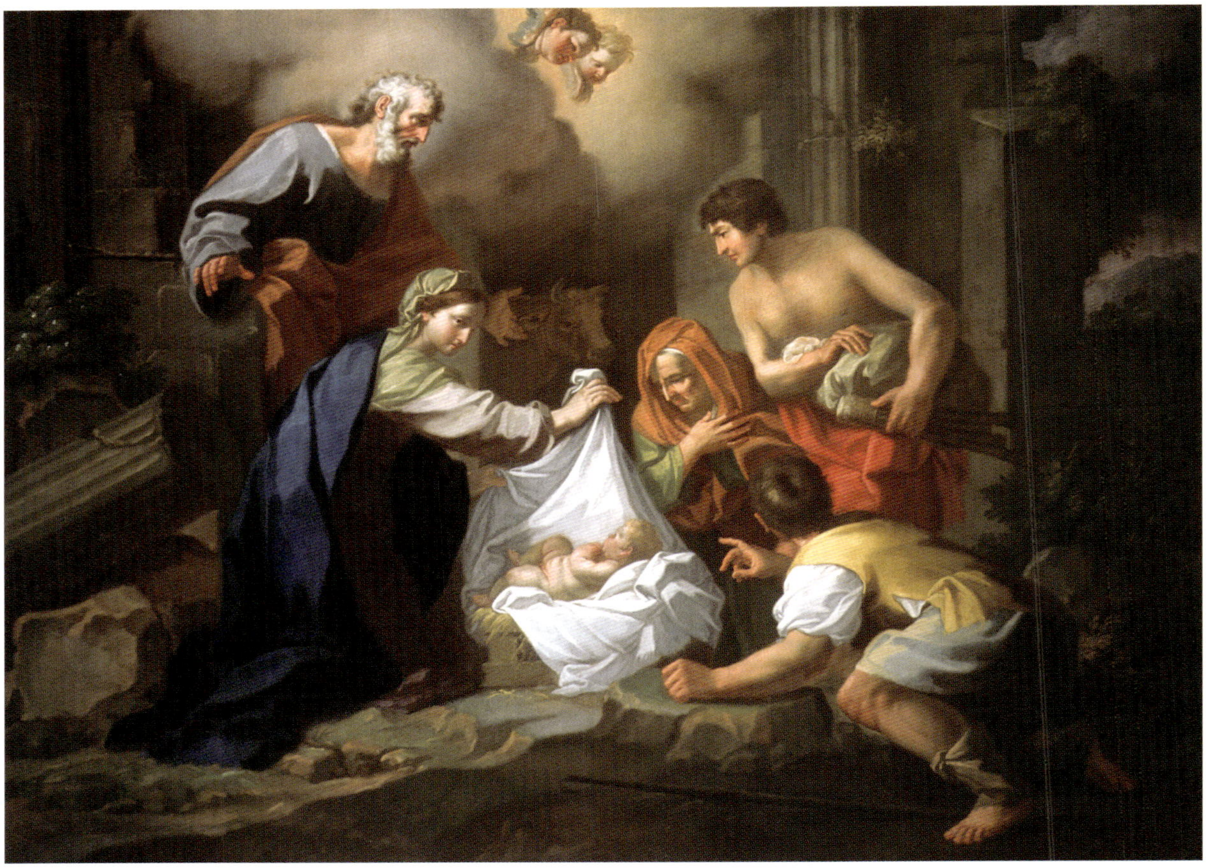

Figure 5. Attributed to Eustache Le Sueur (1616–1655), *Adoration of the Shepherds*, ca. mid-17th century, oil on canvas, 38½ x 53¼ inches. Brigham Young University Museum of Art, purchase/gift from Gloria Teichert, funds provided by Jack R. and Mary Lois Wheatley.

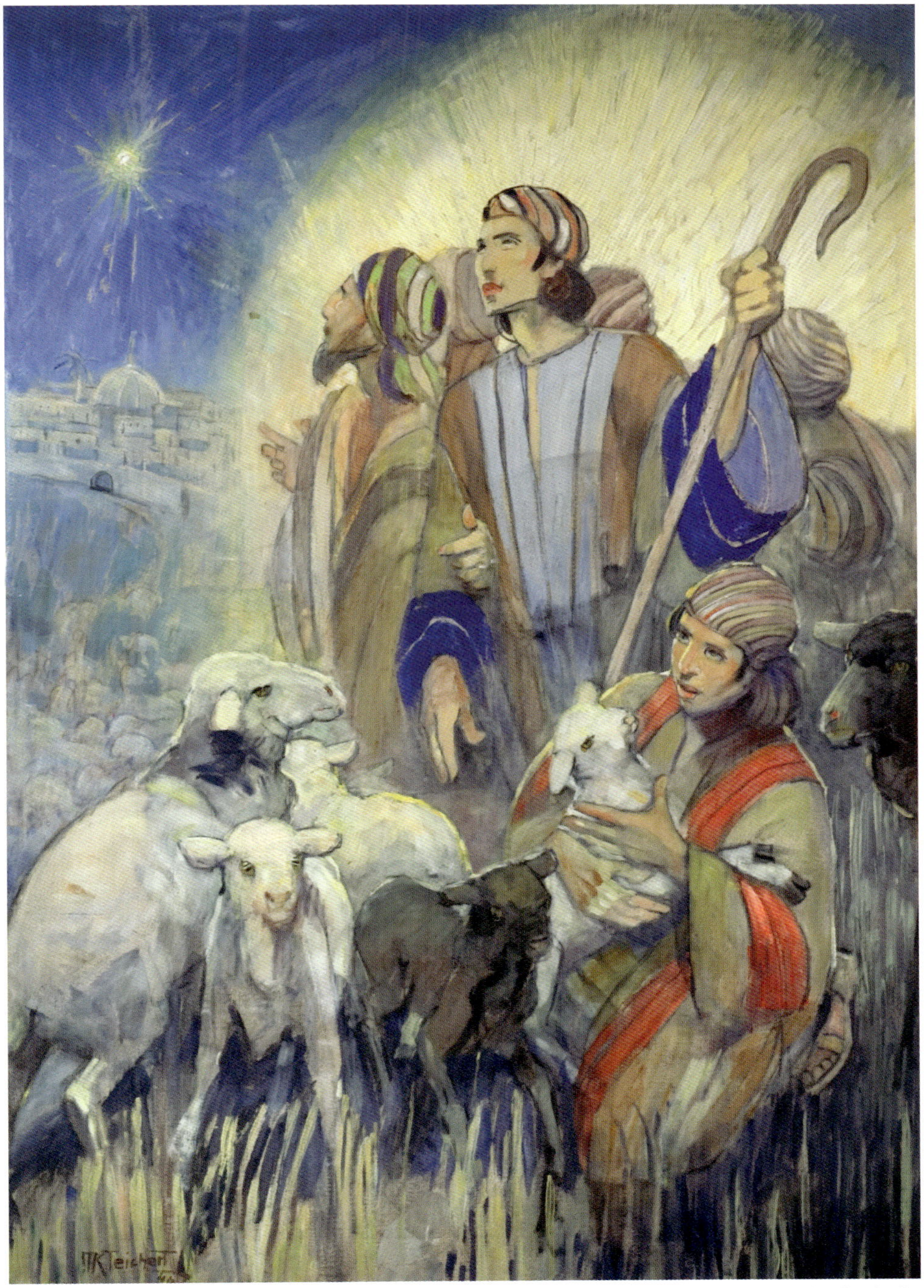

Figure 6. Minerva K. Teichert (1888–1976), *Annunciation to the Shepherds*, 1946, oil on canvas, 69 x 50 inches. The Church of Jesus Christ of Latter-day Saints, Salt Lake Bonneville Stake.

Other important elements in the Gospel stories consist of God's preparation of a family—in a home—to receive spiritual blessings and then to serve. Such divine action meant healing. How so? The appearance of the angel to Zacharias certainly taught him that his own family was not complete. Elisabeth's miraculous pregnancy and her preparation to nurture the promised child would have brought her to a renewed spiritual awareness. And the child John, of course, carried the Holy Ghost from his birth, an observation that carries worlds of meaning for his mother's spiritual state (see Luke 1:15; Doctrine and Covenants 84:27). Thus, a ringing emphasis rests on the spiritual and physical healing of a couple—Zacharias and Elisabeth—so that they became a full family, complete with a

The Nativity

Nativity scenes abound in Christian iconography because they testify of Jesus as the Messiah. Often the scenes take place in ruined buildings or include broken columns (Figures 5, 8, and 9), symbolizing the demise of the Mosaic Law. The motif of angels repairing the holes in the stable roof refers to the Messianic prophecy that "the tabernacle of David that is fallen" would be raised up and Christ Himself would "close up the breaches thereof" (Amos 9:11) (Figure 9).[1] Amid the many symbols of the passing of the Old Law, the advent of the Holy Infant in the humble shelter signals the birth and establishment of the New Law. The presence of the ox and the ass in these scenes was first introduced by the *Gospel of Pseudo-Matthew*[2] (Figures 7, 8, and 9). Their inclusion refers to the scripture in Isaiah 1:3, "The ox knoweth his owner, and the ass his master's crib: but Israel doth not know [its Lord]."

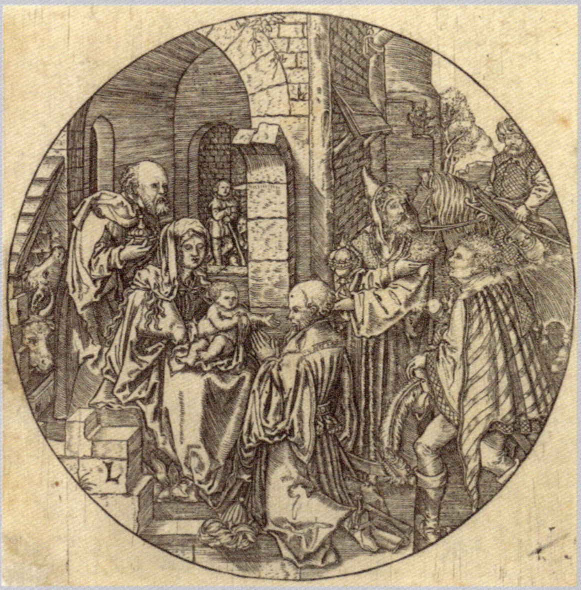

Figure 7. Monogrammist L. (16th century), *The Nativity*, ca. 1550, engraving, 2 13/16 x 2 13/16 inches. Brigham Young University Museum of Art, purchase/gift from Mahonri M. Young Estate.

In addition to testifying of Christ's divinity, nativity scenes often contain subtle yet profound parallels to the Crucifixion. In Marcantonio Raimondi's *The Adoration of the Shepherds* (Figure 9), the Christ Child lies on an altar-like manger alluding to the table of the Lord's sacrament (Eucharist) and suggesting His future sacrifice. The white sheet, as seen in Eustache Le Sueur's *Adoration of the Shepherds* (Figure 5), foreshadows the burial shroud in which the Savior would be wrapped after His crucifixion. In this painting, Mary's gaze captures the attention of the viewer as she displays the Christ Child against the backdrop of

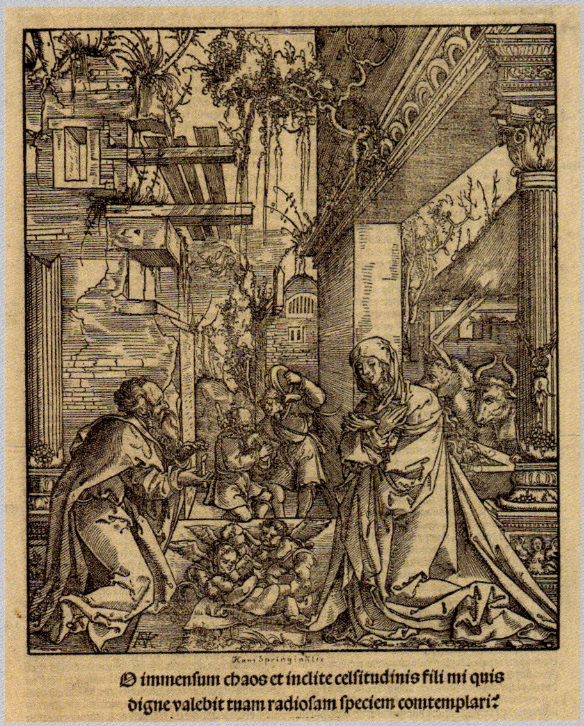

Figure 8. Hans Springinklee (ca. 1490–1540), *Nativity*, ca. 1524, woodcut, 9 x 7½ inches. Brigham Young University Museum of Art, purchase/gift from Mahonri M. Young Estate.

the cloth, recalling Lamentation scenes in which the dead Christ is presented to the viewer for solemn devotion (Figure 79).

Representing the adoration of the Jews and Gentiles respectively, the visit of the shepherds and the wise men to the Christ Child is a familiar Christmas theme. From the second century, the "wise men from the east" (Matthew 2:1) were designated as kings and their agreed number was three, starting the artistic tradition of three men lavishly dressed in royal attire (Figures 7, 17, and 18).[3] However, it was to the unadorned and lowly shepherds that the angel appeared to announce the birth of the Infant Jesus (Figures 4 and 6). Manifesting their humility, the shepherds are often shown removing their hats and kneeling in reverence before the small Babe. They offer a simple lamb, not only as a symbol of their livelihood, but also as an emblematic gift for the Lamb of God (Figure 8).

1. Gertrud Schiller, *Iconography of Christian Art*, trans. Janet Seligman, vol. 1 (London: Lund Humphries, 1971), 81–82.
2. This apocryphal gospel was supposedly written by Matthew but was probably written much later, in the eighth or ninth century. Peter and Linda Murray, *The Oxford Companion to Christian Art and Architecture* (Oxford, UK: Oxford University Press, 1996), 344, 410.
3. Tertullian (ca. 160–230) was the first to suggest that the magi were kings, and it was Origen (185–224) who proposed that the number of wise men was three. Gaston Duchet-Suchaux and Michel Pastoureau, *The Bible and the Saints* (Paris: Flammarion, 1994), 223.

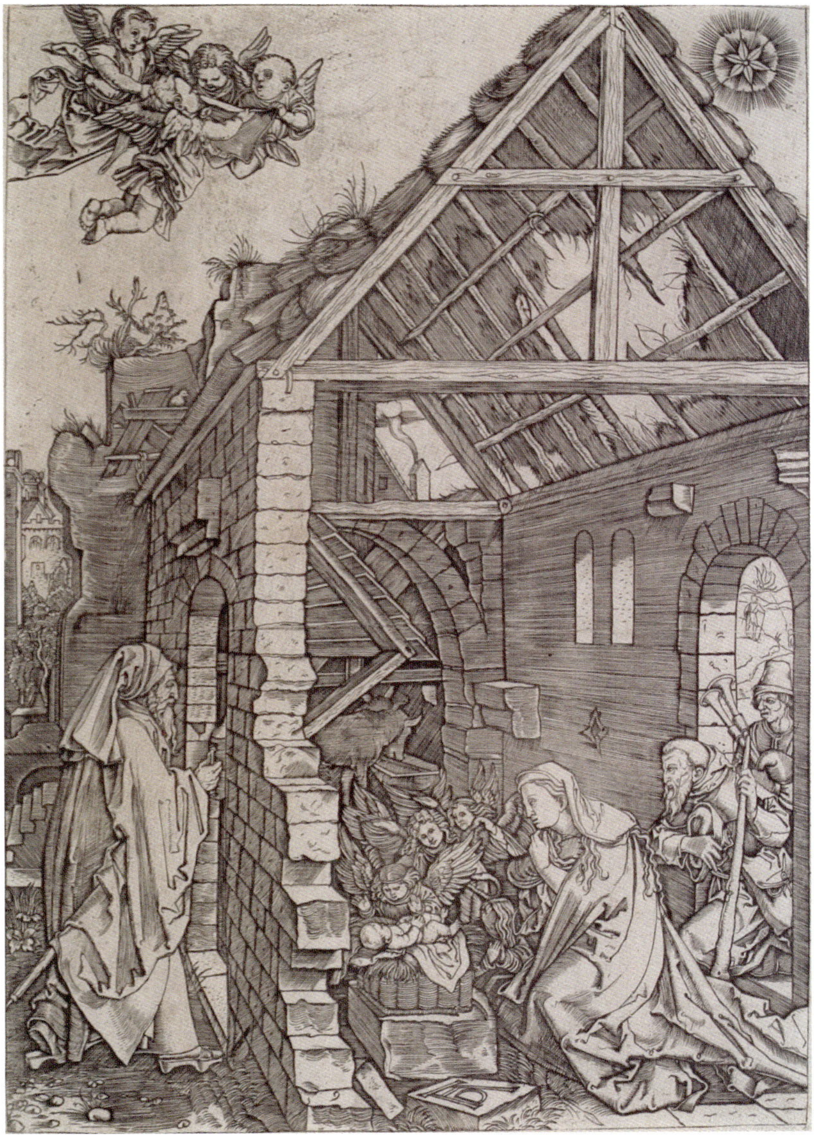

Figure 9. Marcantonio Raimondi (1470–1527), *The Adoration of the Shepherds* (after Albrecht Dürer), ca. 16th century, engraving, 11 5/16 x 8 1/8 inches. Brigham Young University Museum of Art, purchase/gift from Mahonri M. Young Estate.

child who takes away their "reproach among men" and, notably, would "go before the face of the Lord to prepare his ways" (Luke 1:25, 76).

The angel's announcement to Zacharias set in motion a series of spiritual events that would all happen in the home that he shared with Elisabeth. In fact, the number and intensity of spiritual manifestations that occurred in their home within a period of months are astonishing. The first, of course, was Elisabeth's conception of the child (see Luke 1:24). This is followed in the narrative by the warm yet illuminating exchange between Elisabeth and Mary upon Mary's arrival at Elisabeth's home, an exchange that drew in the Spirit of God (see Luke 1:40–55). Moreover, at the circumcision of the infant John, Zacharias' "mouth was opened immediately, and his tongue loosed, and he spake" (Luke 1:64). His healing was miraculous, and those who witnessed it carried deep impressions of God's power ever after (see Luke 1:65–66). In addition, he received the Spirit of God and prophesied about his infant son, all within the home that he and Elisabeth resided in. Hence, the home of Elisabeth and Zacharias had become a spiritual powerhouse equaled only by the temple.

Sacred Moments

One of the earliest indicators of sacred moments occurs in "the temple" or, more accurately, the sanctuary (Luke 1:9). Luke opens his story at one of the most sacred spots on the earth, in God's sanctuary, thus conferring a sense of holiness on Zacharias' experience, as well as on the rest of the story of Jesus. What shall we make of all this? We answer, sacred moments and holy places tie together. For example, the story of redemption opens in Jerusalem at its most sacred spot and ends not only with Jesus' predictions of the destruction of the same temple (see Matthew 24:2; Luke 21:6, 20, 24) but also with Jesus' death at nearby Calvary, an event that itself bestows on Calvary a deep sacral character. In a similar vein, Luke's story begins with an occurrence in the temple that shows God's respect for the Mosaic order, of which the temple is the apex, and ends with a decisive withdrawal of divine pleasure for the current Mosaic order as Jesus dies at the hands of those who hold custodianship of the sanctuary and the Mosaic law.

Another sacred moment involved the shepherds who were in their fields (see Luke 2:8). After seeing the angel and the infant Jesus, the shepherds became witnesses of the first rank, making "known abroad the saying which was told them concerning this child," leading hearers to wonder "at those things which were told them by the shepherds" (Luke 2:17–18). The angel's appearance and announcement to the shepherds, who came from one of the lowest rungs of society, illustrate that God's message is for all. Moreover, the fact that they "found Mary, and Joseph, and the babe" shows their diligence (Luke 2:16) because finding the Savior takes effort. The angel, when giving directions, gave them only what they would find after sustained effort: "the babe wrapped in swaddling clothes, lying in a manger" (Luke 2:12).

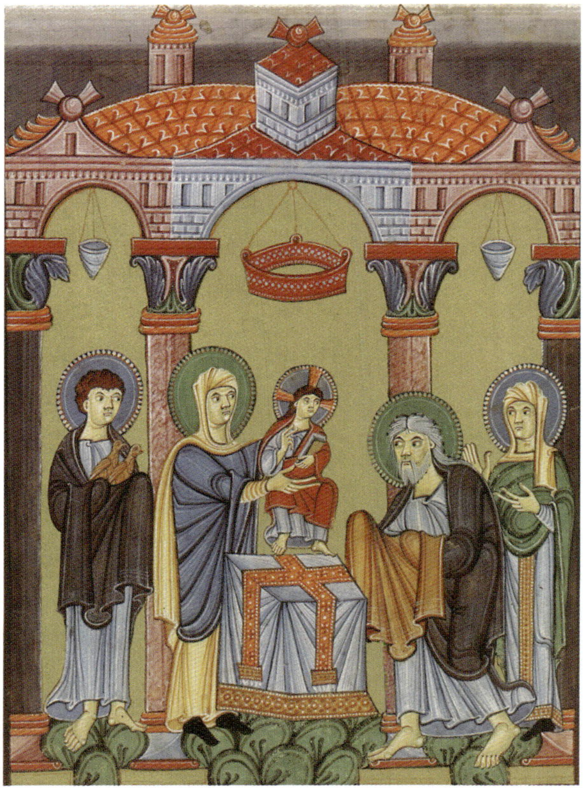

Figure 11. *Presentation*, from the *Gospel Harmony of Eusebius* (f. 28), ca. 1050, illuminated manuscript facsimile (1991–92), 13 7/16 x 9 7/16 inches. Collection of the J. Willard Marriott Library, University of Utah; ADEVA, Akademische Drück- u. Verlagsanstalt, Austria.

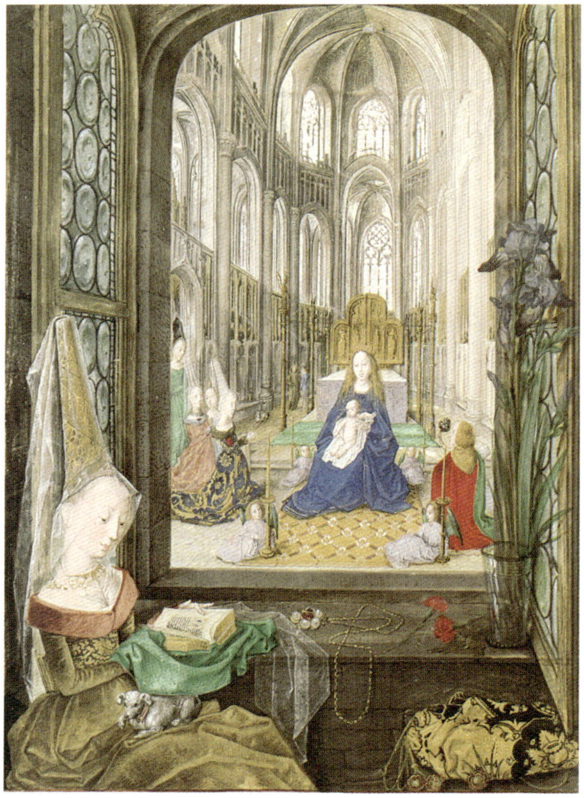

Figure 10. *Maria von Burgund Reading the Book of Hours with Mary in the Background*, from the *Stundenbuch der Maria von Burgund* (f. 14v), ca. 1475, illuminated manuscript facsimile (1995), 7 15/16 x 5 9/16 inches. L. Tom Perry Special Collections, Harold B. Lee Library, Brigham Young University, Provo, Utah; ADEVA, Akademische Druck- u. Verlagsanstalt, Austria.

Simeon and Anna were special witnesses. Simply locating Mary and Joseph within the temple grounds was a miracle because of the immense area, underlining the significance of this moment. Luke underscores this notion, writing that Simeon "came by the Spirit into the temple" (Luke 2:27) and implying the same for Anna. Luke has preserved words from Simeon, who discloses that he had received a promise that he would not die before seeing the Messiah (see Luke 2:26, 29–30). In addition, he prophesied that the child Jesus would become a "light to lighten the Gentiles" as well as to stand as "the glory of [God's] people Israel" (Luke 2:32). His words then took on an ominous tone, declaring that "a sword shall pierce through [Mary's] own soul," an apparent hint that Jesus would die before His mother did (Luke 2:35).

Another sacred moment occurred months later, it seems, with the coming of strangers from afar who sought to see the infant Jesus. The wise men,

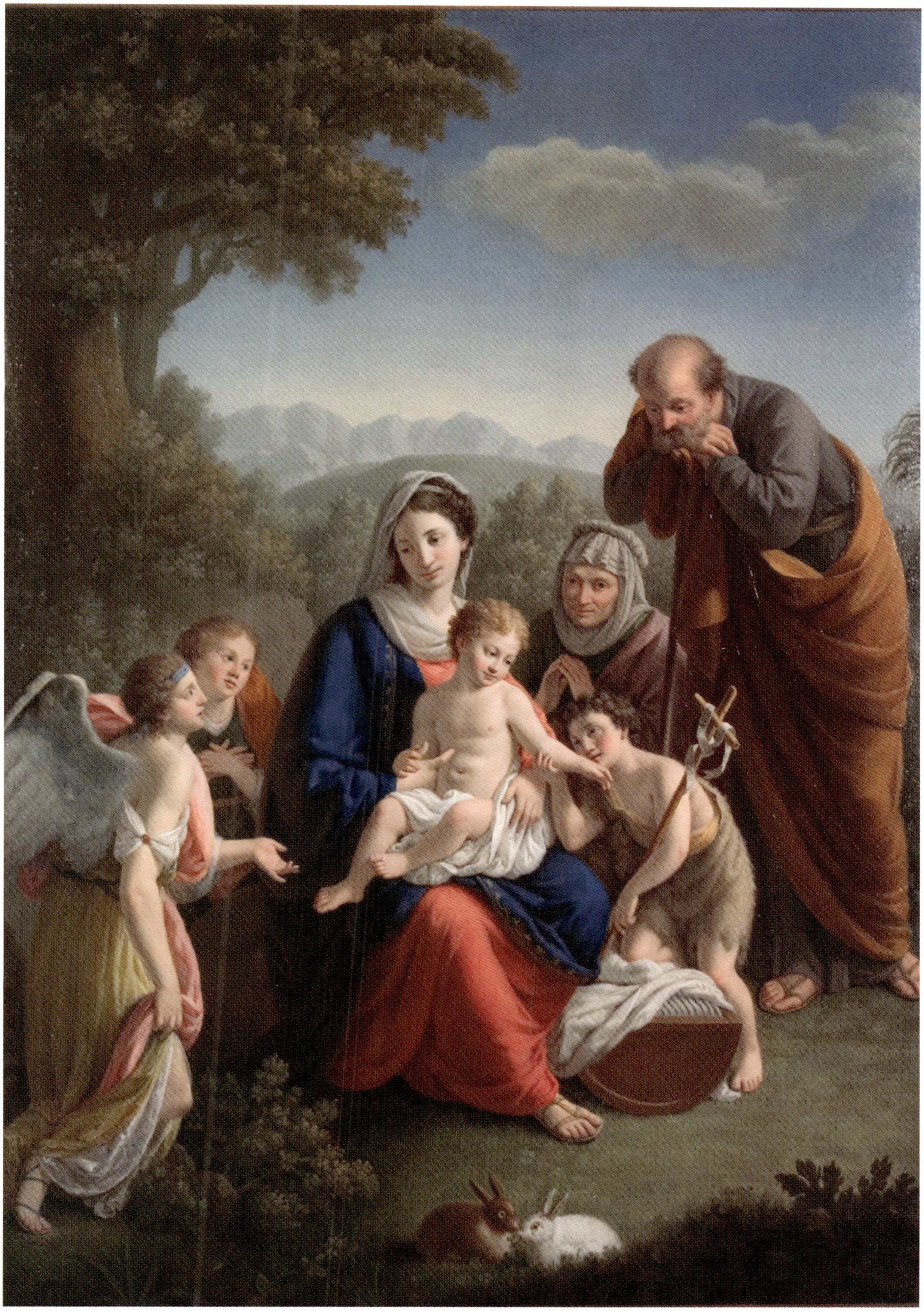

Figure 12. Giuseppe Mazzola (1748–1838), *Holy Family*, ca. 1829, oil on panel, 31 9/16 x 22 13/16 inches. Brigham Young University Museum of Art, gift of Stanford C. Stoddard in memory of his late wife, Ann Dietrich Stoddard.

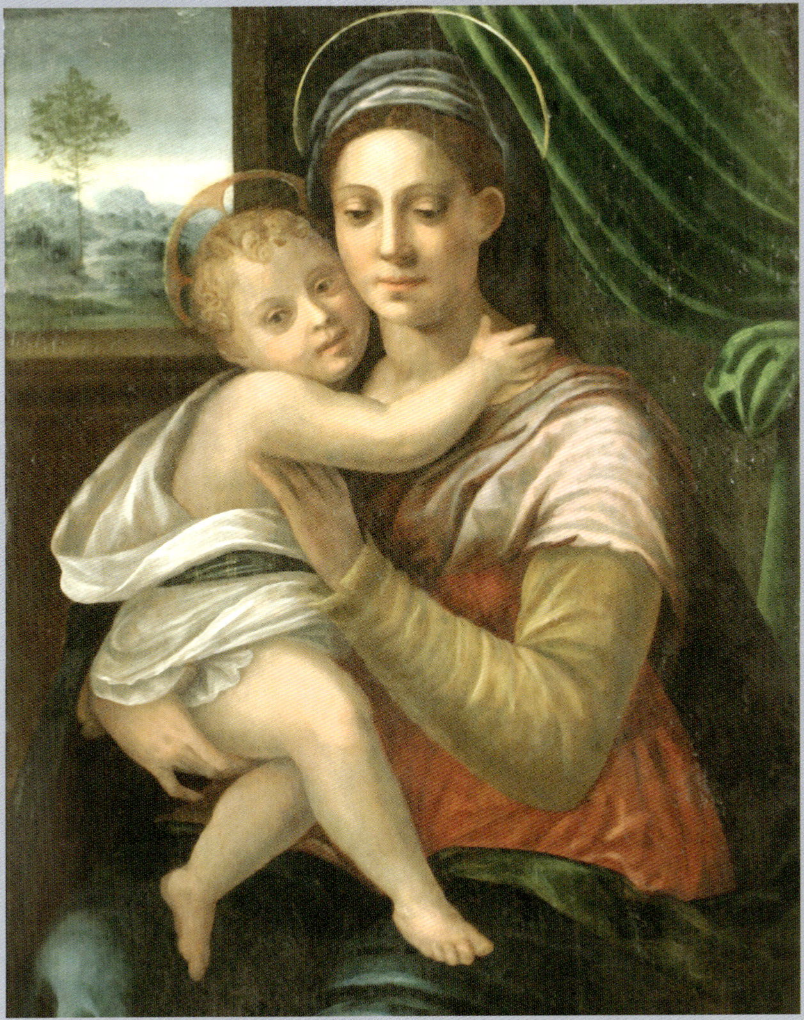

Figure 13. Ridolfo Ghirlandaio (1483–1561), *Madonna and Child*, ca. 1520–35, oil on panel, 33 x 24½ inches. Brigham Young University Museum of Art, gift of Mrs. Hazel Anna Smith.

The Virgin Mary

Second only to the image of Christ, Mary's likeness dominates pre-Reformation Christian art. Her pervasive image testified to the doctrine of incarnation, which declared that the divine Christ took upon Himself the physical nature and form of a mortal man. As evidence of Christ's humanity, the presence of Mary assumed vital significance in Christian art, whether in a Madonna and Child composition, in a narrative cycle of her life, or as part of a Holy Family portrait. These portrayals were devised to undeniably establish Mary as the chosen vessel through which "the Word was made flesh" (John 1:14).

As the mother of Christ, Mary was venerated for her role in the triumph over evil, as referenced in Rembrandt's *The Virgin and Child with the Cat and Snake* (Figure 14). She steps on the head of the snake, thus signifying the victory over Satan. Not only was Mary revered as the mother of God, she was also seen as the most powerful of all intercessors with Christ. Amplified by tradition and apocryphal texts, she acquired numerous other titles such as the Queen of Heaven, symbolized by a crown and a blue mantle over a red gown (Figures 10 and 12). Mary also became a metaphor for the Christian Church. In *Mater Amabilis* (Mother of Maternal Love) images, the tender affection between the infant Jesus and His mother alludes to the loving relationship between Christ and the Church (Figures 10 and 13). Another type of Marian image, the *Virgo Lactans*, depicts Mary suckling the baby Jesus, emphasizing His human nature through the dependence on His mother for sustenance (Figure 16).

Because of Mary's pivotal role in early Christian theology, artists supplemented devotional images with exemplary narrative cycles of her life. Legends surrounding her devout parents, her own miraculous birth, her childhood in the temple at Jerusalem, and her perpetual virginity appeared from the late second century in the apocryphal

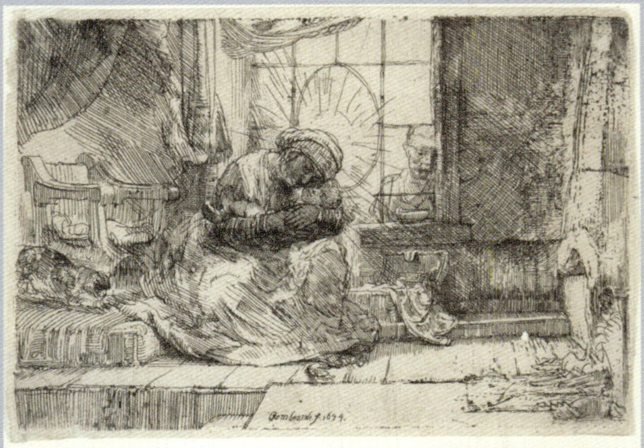

Figure 14. Rembrandt Harmenszoon van Rijn (1606–1669), *The Virgin and Child with the Cat and Snake*, 1654, etching and burin, 3 13/16 x 5 13/16 inches. Brigham Young University Museum of Art, purchase/gift from Mahonri M. Young Estate.

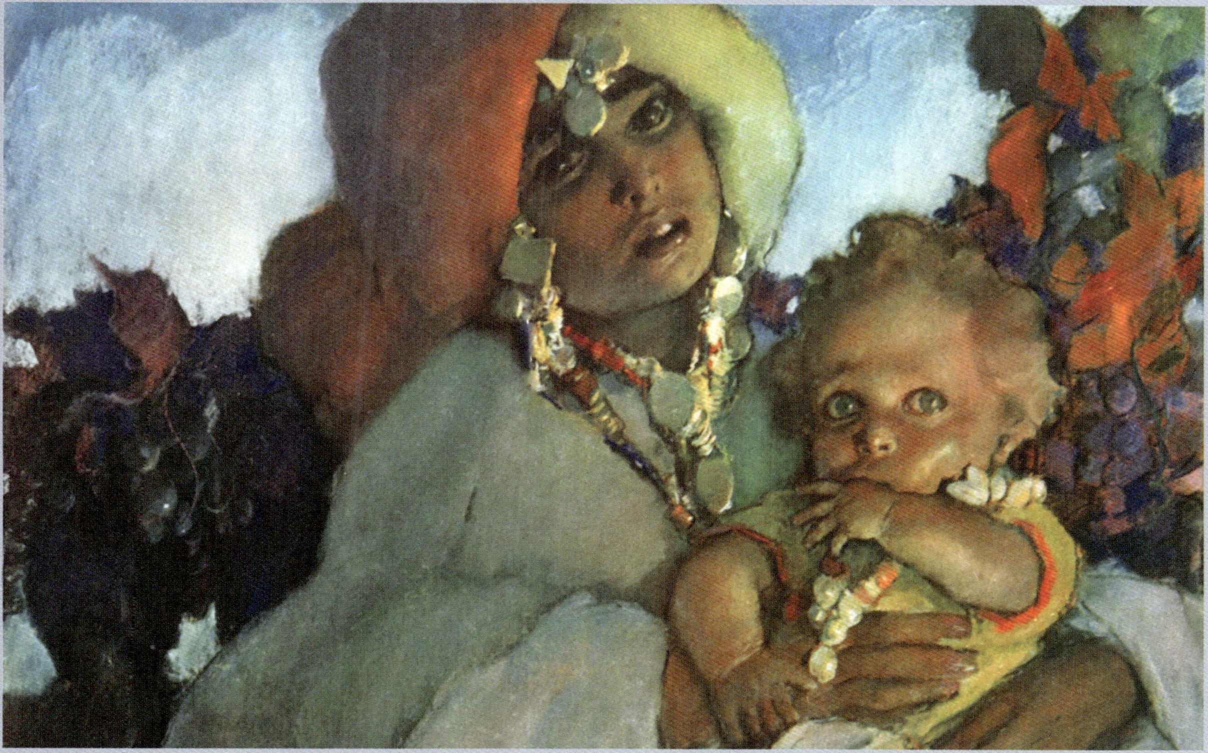

Figure 15. Abel Pann (1883–1963), *Mary with the Child Jesus*, 20th century, serigraph, 24 x 30 inches. Courtesy of Itiel Pann.

Protevangelium of James.[1] Although rejected by the clergy of the Western Church, these legends were perpetuated by theologians of the twelfth and thirteenth centuries, and artists continued to use remnants of these narrative motifs through the nineteenth century.

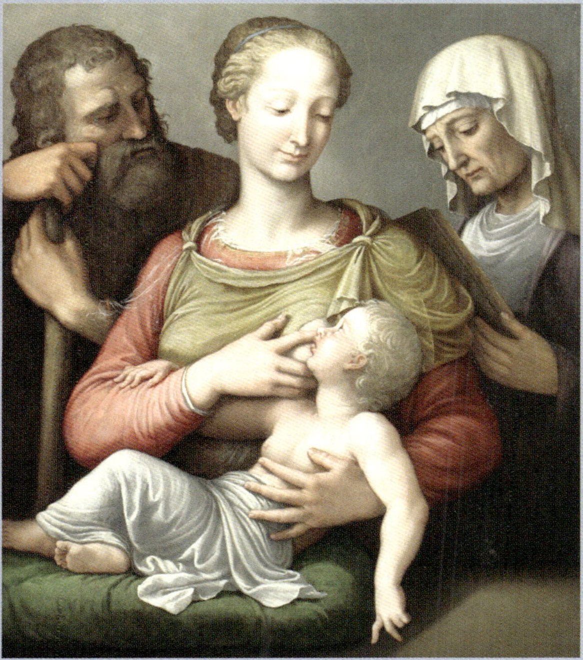

Figure 16. Attributed to Francesco Primaticcio (1504–1570), *Holy Family*, after 1540, oil on canvas, 37 15/16 x 33 11/16 inches. Brigham Young University Museum of Art, gift of Mr. and Mrs. Robert E. Walters.

Mary is also presented prominently in depictions of the Holy Family. In numerous images Mary overshadows Joseph, who is unfavorably rendered as an elderly bearded man. In response to descriptions in apocryphal literature,[2] the Virgin was often placed in the forefront of the composition or portrayed larger in scale than Joseph. At other times, Joseph was positioned outside the walls that enclosed Mary and Jesus, excluding him from the familial scene and further diminishing Joseph's importance (Figures 9 and 14). These artistic conventions underscored the doctrine that Joseph was not the mortal father of Jesus, whereas Mary was the *Theotokos*, or "Mother of God."[3]

1. Murray, *Oxford Companion to Christian Art and Architecture*, 23, 312–13.
2. Legends surrounding the lives of Joseph and Mary were found in such apocryphal books as the *Protevangelium of James* (ca. mid-second century account of Mary's life prior to the Annunciation), the *History of Joseph* (fifth or sixth century), and the *Golden Legend* (thirteenth century compilation of the legends of the saints). From the account in the *Golden Legend* it was surmised that Joseph was a widower with children who became Jesus' brothers and sisters, thus maintaining the doctrine that Mary was a perpetual virgin. Murray, *Oxford Companion to Christian Art and Architecture*, 259.
3. It was not until the early fifteenth century that Joseph's status as the guardian of Jesus was appreciated and his image was elevated to a more vigorous and involved husband and father. Melissa R. Katz and Robert A. Orsi, *Divine Mirrors: The Virgin Mary in the Visual Arts* (New York: Oxford University Press, 2001), 66.

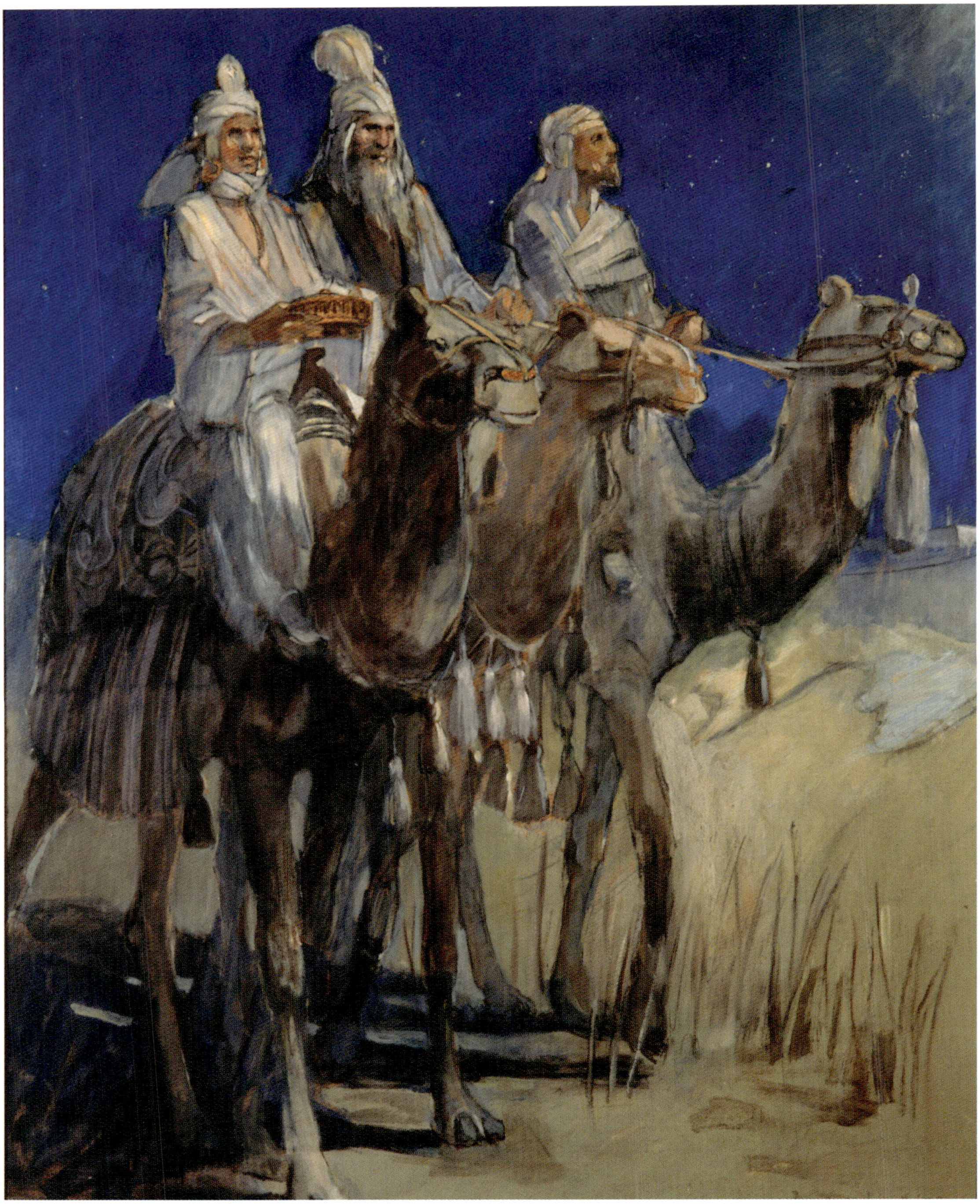

Figure 17. Minerva K. Teichert (1888–1976), *The Three Wise Men*, 1939, oil on canvas, 60 x 45 inches. Brigham Young University Museum of Art.

whose arrival Matthew narrates, remain rather mysterious. Their origins are unclear, though the word that identifies them (Greek *magoi*) suggests they came from Persia. They were very possibly foreign Jews, and they carried gifts that come from south Arabia—frankincense and myrrh. Their appearance in Jerusalem, as persons of some importance, caught the eyes and ears of King Herod, who treated their news about one "born King of the Jews" as carrying a threat to himself (Matthew 2:2). After visiting "the young child with Mary his mother," the wise men disappear as suddenly as they came, departing "into their own country another way," taking with them their impressions at meeting the Holy Child (Matthew 2:11–12).

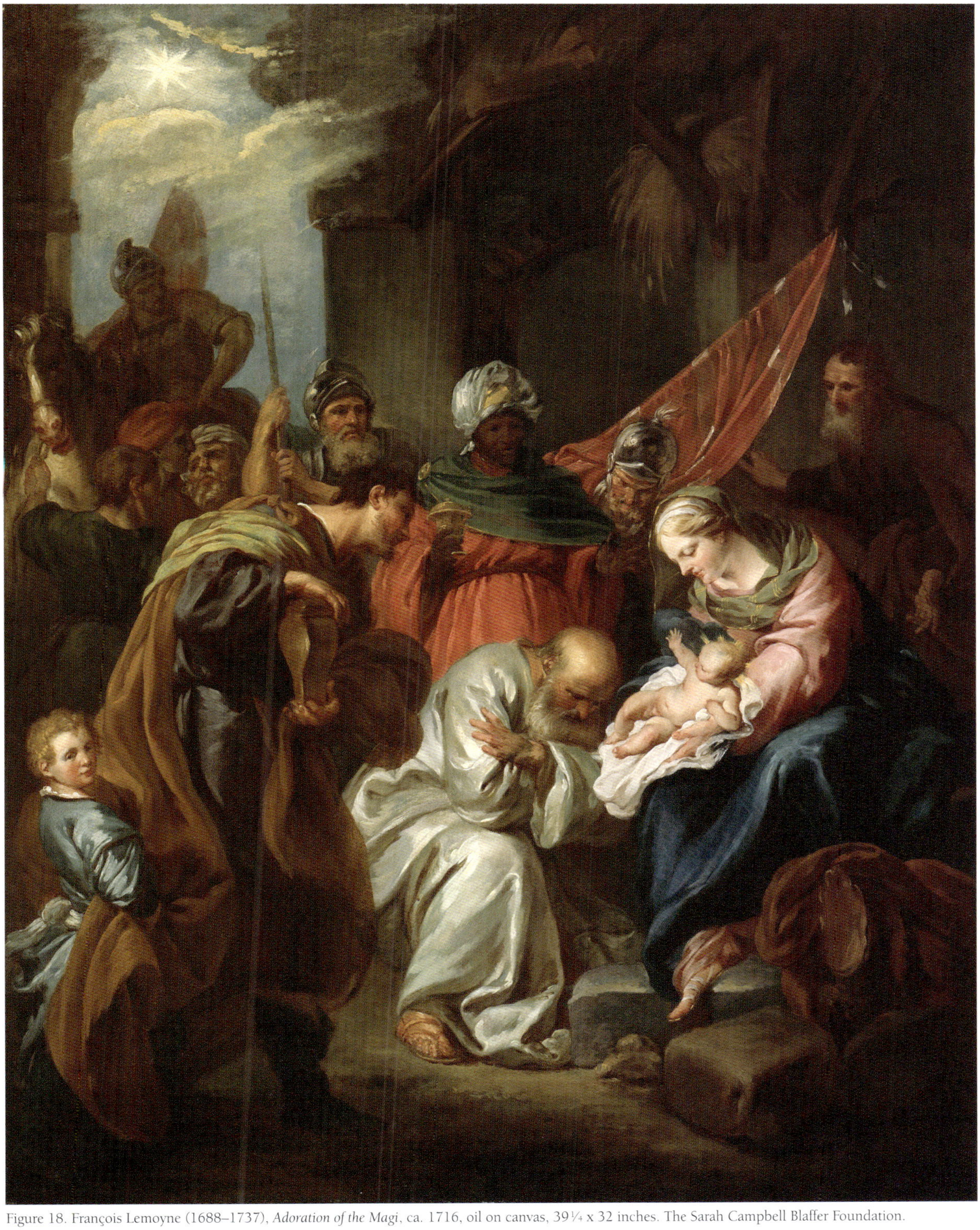

Figure 18. François Lemoyne (1688–1737), *Adoration of the Magi*, ca. 1716, oil on canvas, 39¼ x 32 inches. The Sarah Campbell Blaffer Foundation.

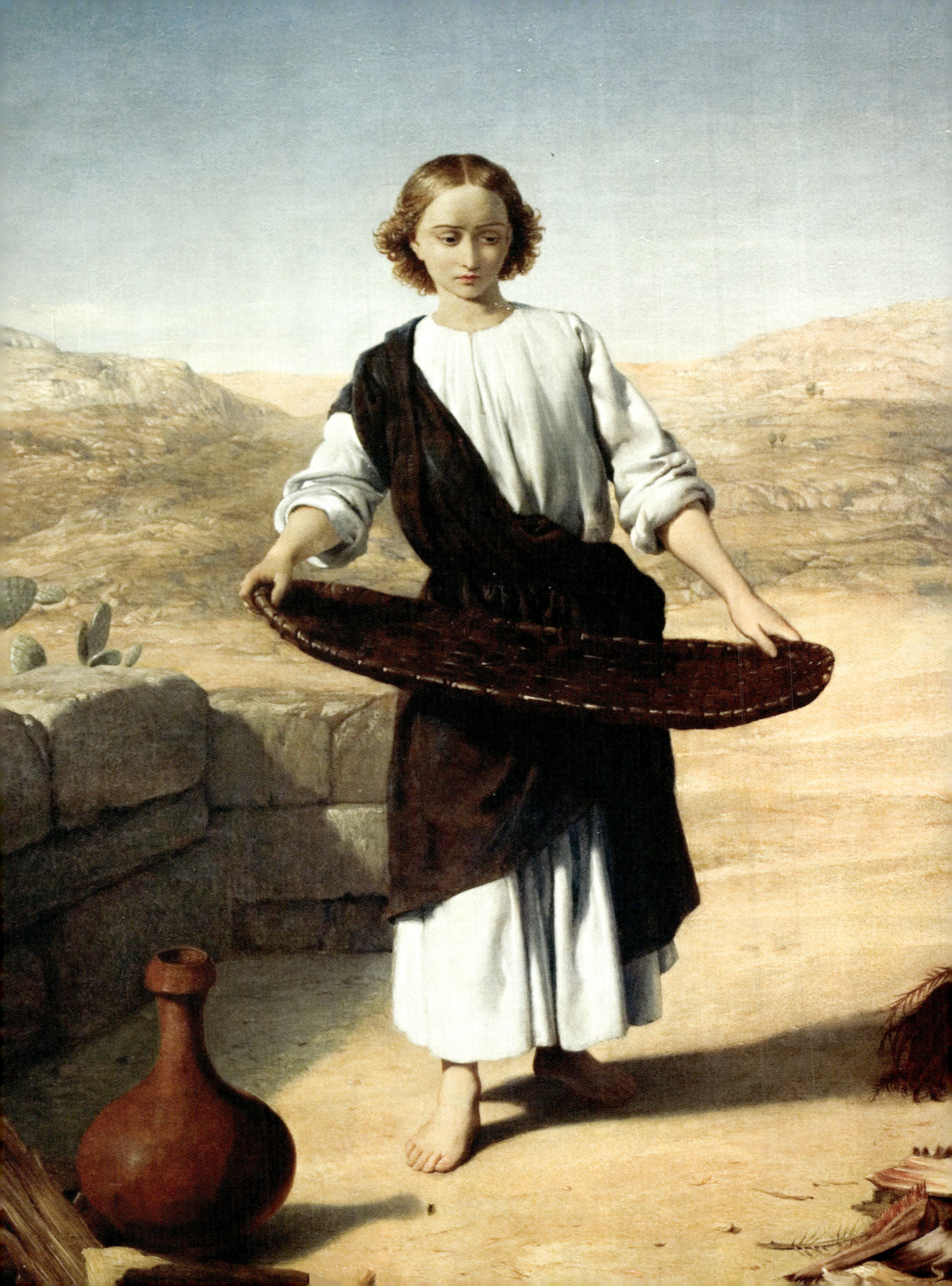

Chapter 3

Youth

Mary and her infant son, Jesus, have captured the attention and imagination of artists, authors, and poets for generations. For there is nothing more tender than a story about a young mother and her first baby, particularly when the babe is a holy child. Only two Gospels, Matthew and Luke, provide word-pictures of events associated with Jesus' early years, but even they do not record much detail about His infancy and youth. Rather, the focus in each Gospel is the detailed retelling of the story of Jesus' suffering, death, and resurrection. Yet, in Matthew and Luke, we do learn something about those first years of the Savior's mortal life.

Earliest Years

Matthew informs us that Mary, Joseph, and Jesus remained in Bethlehem for a much longer time than is usually imagined by believers, including artists, who have sought to depict important events following Jesus' birth.

As many as twenty-four months may have passed after Jesus' birth before the wise men came seeking Him (see Matthew 2:1–13). We note Matthew's use of *young child* rather than *infant* in this part of the narrative (Matthew 2:9, 11, 13, 14, 20). Additionally, Matthew refers to the family living in a *house* at the time of the visit of the wise men rather than in the temporary shelter noted earlier by Luke (see Matthew 2:11), thus hinting that Mary and Joseph had by then moved into more permanent quarters.

The wise men, being warned of God, disappear from the story as suddenly as they appeared (see Matthew 2:11–12). Immediately, the apparently tranquil life of the young family, possibly living among family members in Joseph and Mary's ancestral home, is interrupted as prophesied in Psalms, "The kings of the earth set themselves, and the rulers take counsel together, against the Lord, and against his anointed" (Psalm 2:2). In this case, the "rulers" are specifically identified as Herod and "the chief priests and scribes of the people," who gathered to identify the location of the promised messianic king's birth and later laid plans to kill Him (see Matthew 2:4, 16).

In a few emotionally powerful statements, Matthew relates one of the most infamous incidents recorded in the New Testament, a story depicted in dark hues by artists over the years—the killing of the innocents. "Then Herod . . . slew all the children that were in Bethlehem, and in all the coasts thereof" (Matthew 2:16). Matthew saw the heinous act as the fulfillment of a prophecy of Jeremiah: "In Rama there was a voice heard, lamentation, and weeping, and great mourning, Rachel weeping for her children, and would not be comforted, because they are not" (Matthew 2:17–18; cf. Jeremiah 31:15).

Flight into Egypt

Knowing the evil intent of Herod, "The angel of the Lord appeareth to Joseph in a dream, saying, Arise, and take the young child and his mother, and flee into Egypt" (Matthew 2:13). The gifts received from the wise men, especially the gold, may have provided sustenance for the young family.

John Rogers Herbert, R.A. (1810–1890), detail of *Our Savior Subject to His Parents at Nazareth*, 1860, oil on canvas, 40¼ x 62¼ inches. Brigham Young University Museum of Art, purchased with funds provided by Jack R. and Mary Lois Wheatley.

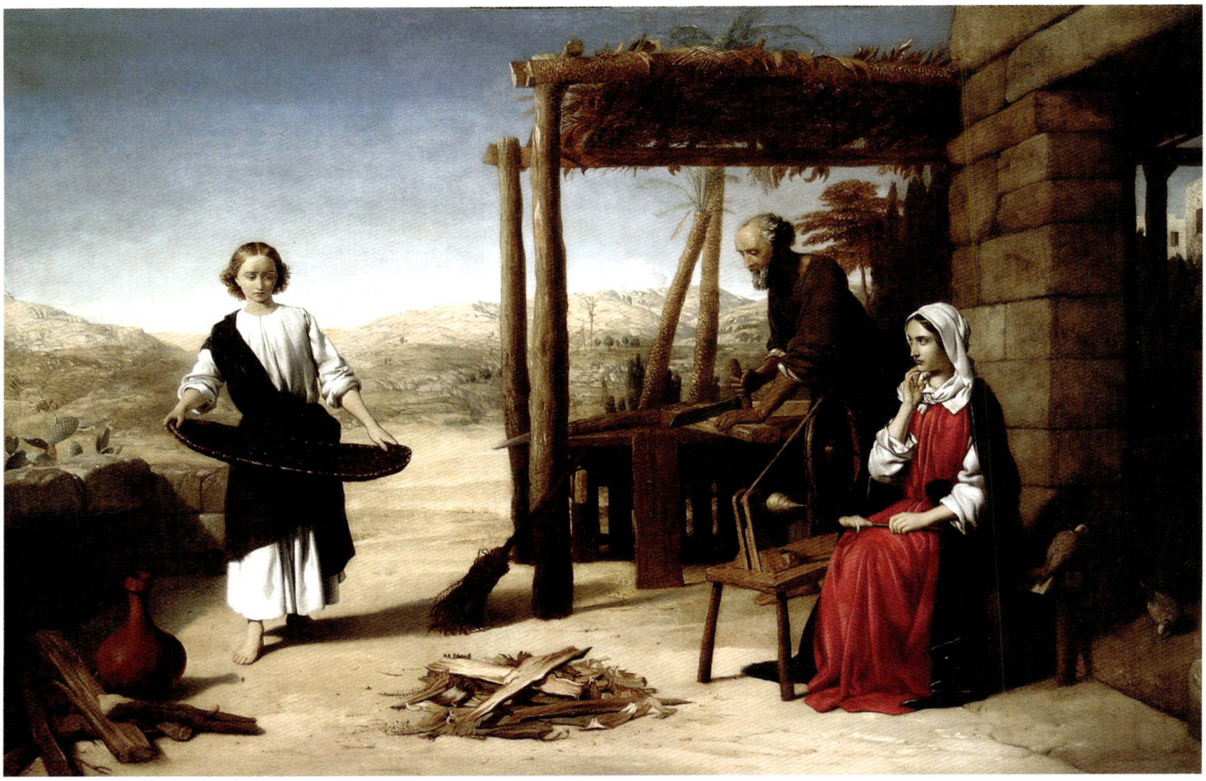

Figure 19. John Rogers Herbert, R.A. (1810–1890), *Our Savior Subject to His Parents at Nazareth*, 1860, oil on canvas, 40 1/4 x 62 1/4 inches. Brigham Young University Museum of Art, purchased with funds provided by Jack R. and Mary Lois Wheatley.

Matthew provides no additional details. What route they followed and their ultimate destination remain unknown, except in later tradition, allowing artists and writers to fill in details not mentioned in the text.

The plot to kill the Christ Child failed when in 4 B.C., King Herod died, along with at least some of his conspirators, and an angel directed Joseph: "Arise, and take the young child and his mother, and go into the land of Israel: for *they* are dead which sought the young child's life" (Matthew 2:20; emphasis added).

Although Matthew is the only one to record this particular event, its basic elements fit well with what we know—from sources outside the New Testament—about Herod the Great during his last desperate and paranoid years. In an odd twist, these sources inform us that Herod had himself escaped to Egypt when he was threatened once in his own life. Matthew testifies that Jesus' stay in the land of the ancient pharaohs was foreseen by God (see Matthew 2:15).

Following Herod's death, his kingdom was divided among his sons, Archelaus, Herod Antipas, and Herod Philip. When Joseph "heard that Archelaus did reign in Judea in the room of his father Herod," Joseph decided not to return to Bethlehem. Being once again warned, he traveled to Galilee, his childhood home, where Herod Antipas reigned (see Matthew 2:22).

Matthew ends his abbreviated account of the flight into Egypt and the family's return by saying, "And he came and dwelt in a city called Nazareth: that it might be fulfilled which was spoken by the prophets, He shall be called a Nazarene" (Matthew 2:23).

The Youthful Jesus in the Temple

We turn to Luke for more details about Jesus' early life. It was in the temple that Simeon and Anna declared their witness of Jesus and His divine mission (see Luke 2:25–38). Luke continues his account by relating an episode in the life of the young Jesus that also has to do with the temple. When He was twelve years of age, He came to Jerusalem from Nazareth with His parents on a pilgrimage to the temple. The story is all the more poignant because the city and the temple would ultimately play a significant backdrop to His final days.

Jerusalem was the center of the Jewish world. It was a cosmopolitan city thronged with people from distant places, especially during such an important feast as Passover. Jesus would thus have been exposed to Jews from around the ancient world, speaking foreign tongues and dialects. The temple itself was an awesome and wondrous place, and its sacred altars and sacrifices, along with the temple priests, provided a central point of reference for Jews everywhere.

The celebration of Passover included the ritual slaying of a lamb in the temple area, resulting in a festal meal in a family circle at sundown. Pilgrims generally stayed in Jerusalem for the seven to eight days of Passover and Unleavened Bread (see Leviticus 23:5–6). Luke tells us that when Mary and Joseph "had fulfilled the days, as they returned, the child Jesus tarried behind in Jerusalem; and Joseph and his mother knew not of it" (Luke 2:43). During the three-day journey back to Nazareth, the group of family and friends generally traveled a short distance on the first day. During the first evening's camp, most likely near Jericho, they discovered that Jesus was not "among their kinsfolk and acquaintances" (Luke 2:44).

Luke then reminds us of an important theme for his entire book—the message and the messenger of God are found in the temple. We notice the wording: "They turned back again to Jerusalem, *seeking him*" (Luke 2:45; emphasis added). Luke's account continues:

> And it came to pass, that after three days they found him in the temple, sitting in the midst of the doctors, both hearing them, and asking them questions.
>
> And all that heard him were astonished at his understanding and answers.
>
> And when they saw him, they were amazed: and his mother said unto him, Son, why hast thou thus dealt with us? behold, thy father and I have sought thee sorrowing.
>
> And he said unto them, How is it that ye sought me? wist ye not that I must be about my Father's business? (Luke 2:46–49).

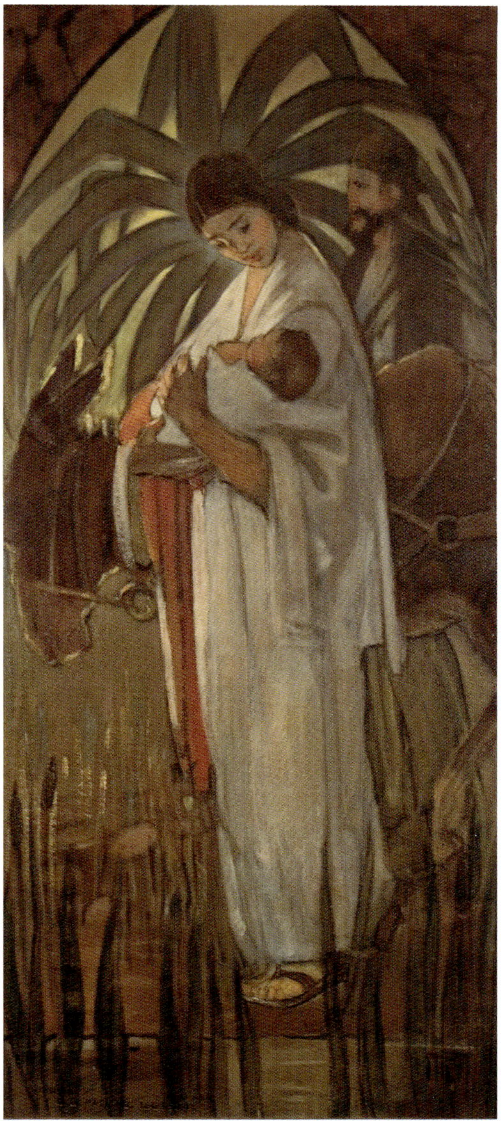

Figure 20. Minerva K. Teichert (1888–1976), *Flight into Egypt*, 1944, oil on canvas, 48 x 21 3/4 inches. Collection of Salt Lake City School District.

An alternative translation renders Jesus' first spoken words in Luke's Gospel: "Why were you searching for me? . . . Didn't you know I had to be in my Father's house?" (New International Version, Luke 2:49). Along with the story of Mary's status as a virgin when Jesus was conceived, the temple story effectively identifies Jesus as the Son of God.

Joseph Instructing Jesus

Jesus' relationship with Joseph has intrigued scholars, theologians, and artists for centuries. The New Testament suggests that Joseph the carpenter (see Matthew 13:55) adopted Jesus as his own son when

Expanding the Narrative

Other than a few brief asides recorded in the Gospel of Luke, not many scriptural references exist that refer to Jesus' infancy and childhood. Matthew notes the young Child's journey to Egypt (Figure 20) and Luke His experience at the temple (Figure 23). Luke abruptly concludes his remarks: "And Jesus increased in wisdom and stature, and in favour with God and man" (Luke 2:52). Because of this lack of descriptive detail, apocryphal legends burgeoned about Christ's boyhood and youth. Brief scriptural passages, such as those describing the flight into Egypt, were embellished to include Herod's pursuit of the Holy Family, the miracle of the cornfield, the destruction of the pagan statues (Figure 21), or the provision of fruit by the bending palm tree.[1]

In addition to depicting these apocryphal narratives, artists concentrated on singular scriptural details for inspiration. References to Jesus as the "carpenter's son" (Matthew 13:55) inspired Krzysztof Krajewski's wood carving and John Rogers Herbert's painting (Figures 22 and 19). Elaborating on this theme, Herbert's work includes symbolic references to other events from Christ's life. The two birds near the doorway likely refer to the "pair of turtledoves, or two young pigeons" offered as a sacrifice when the forty-day-old Jesus was presented at the temple (Luke 2:24). Jesus holds a flat winnowing basket, suggesting the sifting of wheat from the chaff. The red jug in the lower left anticipates the miracle of turning water into wine. Mary holds a spindle, a Byzantine motif inspired by the apocryphal story of the young Virgin spinning thread for the veil of the temple in Jerusalem,[2] the same veil that would rend at the moment of Christ's death on the cross. Mary interrupts her task to gaze pensively at her Son as He looks at the cross formed by the wood scraps that foreshadow His crucifixion.

Like many late-nineteenth-century artists who were prompted by a desire for accuracy, Herbert traveled to the Holy Land to record authentic surroundings in which to portray nonidealized depictions of Christ. Such topographical authenticity, combined with domestic settings, made sacred events more plausible, thus leading the viewer to believe in the reality of Christ's life.

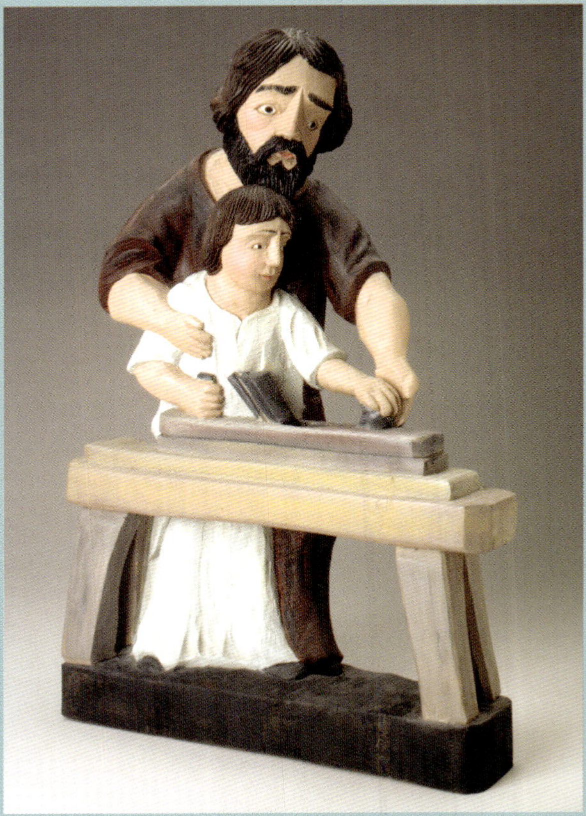

Figure 22. Krzysztof Krajewski (b. 1970), *Saint Joseph with Jesus*, 1992, polychrome wood, 20 inches (height). Private collection of Walter and Mary Whipple.

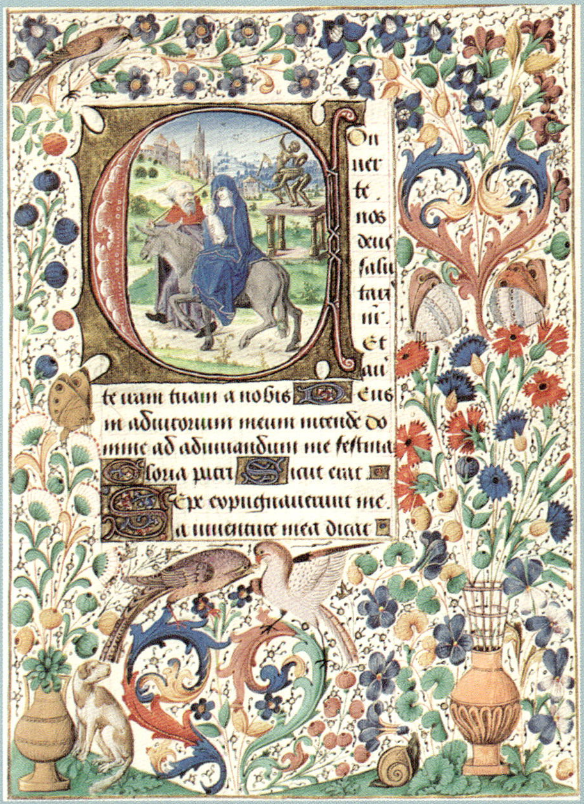

Figure 21. *Flight into Egypt*, from the *Stundenbuch der Maria von Burgund* (f. 112r), ca. 1475, illuminated manuscript facsimile (1995), 7 15/16 x 5 9/16 inches. L. Tom Perry Special Collections, Harold B. Lee Library, Brigham Young University, Provo, Utah; ADEVA, Akademische Drück- u. Verlagsanstalt, Austria.

1. James Hall, *Dictionary of Subjects and Symbols in Art* (New York: Harper & Row, 1979), 124–25.
2. Robert J. Miller, ed., *The Complete Gospels* (Sonoma, CA: Polebridge Press, 1994), 388.

he took pregnant Mary to himself following the command of the angel (see Matthew 1:24; 13:55). That Joseph had become Jesus' legal guardian and was not considered His biological father seems apparent in at least one passage: "Is not this the carpenter, the son of Mary?" (Mark 6:3). Here Jesus is known as the "son of Mary," not of Joseph. The convention of the day would have been to call a person by his father's name, the "son of Joseph," not by his mother's.

Though Joseph is not mentioned even once in Mark's Gospel, he plays a prominent role at the beginning of Matthew's and Luke's accounts. Here the emphasis is on a young family composed of only Joseph, Mary, and Jesus. Yet all four Gospels reveal that by the time Jesus began His public ministry, His immediate family consisted of at least six other individuals beyond His mother—four named brothers and at least two unnamed sisters. The four males are identified as James, Joses, Simon, and Judas (see Matthew 13:55).

We should have no difficulty imagining that Joseph and Mary could have had six children, who all survived to adulthood, between the time of Jesus' birth and near the time of the opening of His public ministry. Any suggestion that Joseph died shortly after the family returned from Jerusalem when Jesus was twelve is an argument from silence. But that Joseph had died before Jesus began His public ministry seems certain.

What did mortal parents, including an adoptive father, teach Jesus along the way? Luke offers some hints. He records, "And [Jesus] went down with them, and came to Nazareth, and was subject [Greek *hypotassomenos,* meaning "obedient"] unto them" (Luke 2:51). He adds, "And Jesus increased in wisdom and stature, and in favour with God and man" (Luke 2:52). Both passages imply parental influences.

That Joseph practiced the Jewish religion is apparent from details provided by Luke in the first two chapters of his Gospel account. As required by the law of Moses (see Exodus 34:23; Numbers 18:15–16), Joseph paid the redemption price for Mary's firstborn and faithfully made the annual pilgrimage to the temple in Jerusalem (see Luke 2:22, 41). Additionally, Matthew describes Joseph as a "just man" (Matthew 1:19). We can safely assume that Jesus followed in the footsteps of His surrogate

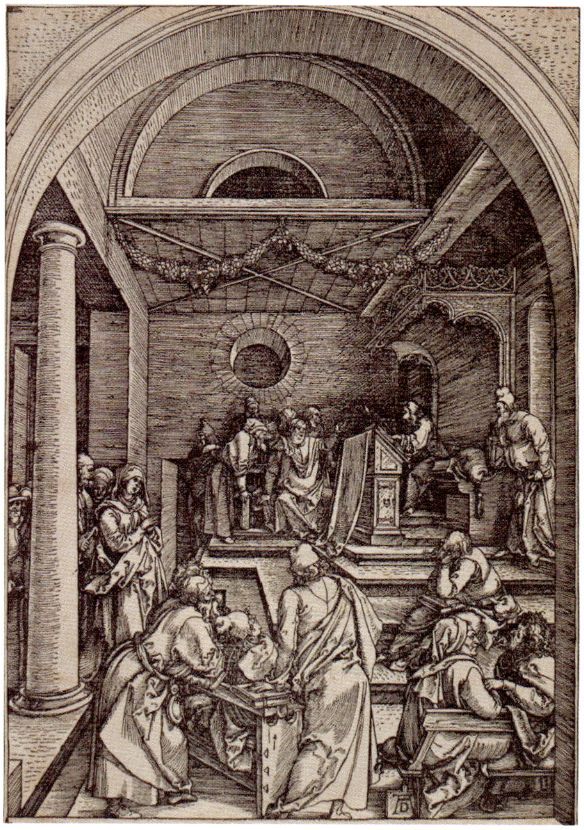

Figure 23. Marcantonio Raimondi (1470–1527), *Young Christ Preaching in the Temple,* after Albrecht Dürer (ca. 16th century), engraving, 11 9/16 x 8 1/8 inches. Brigham Young University Museum of Art, purchase/gift from Mahonri M. Young Estate.

father as He learned what was expected of a young Jewish boy. Loyalty to the Torah, the temple, and the God of Israel formed the main emphasis in the religious education of children at that time. All four Gospels reveal that Jesus, as an adult, lived as a loyal Jew, incorporating into His life the basic commitments and commandments that guided most Jews.

In addition to the religious instruction and example that Joseph was required to provide Jesus as His legal guardian, Joseph would have prepared Jesus to work. Like other fathers in antiquity, he probably taught Jesus his own trade. Joseph is identified as a *tektōn,* often translated as "carpenter" or "builder." Many scholars believe the term may also designate the skills of a stonemason.

For a period of time unknown to us, Joseph provided Jesus a safe and loving environment. The boy grew up as a "tender plant, and as a root out of a dry ground" (Isaiah 53:2). Jesus learned the first lessons of life—how to walk, talk, behave, work, and worship—from a dedicated mother and an exemplary Joseph.

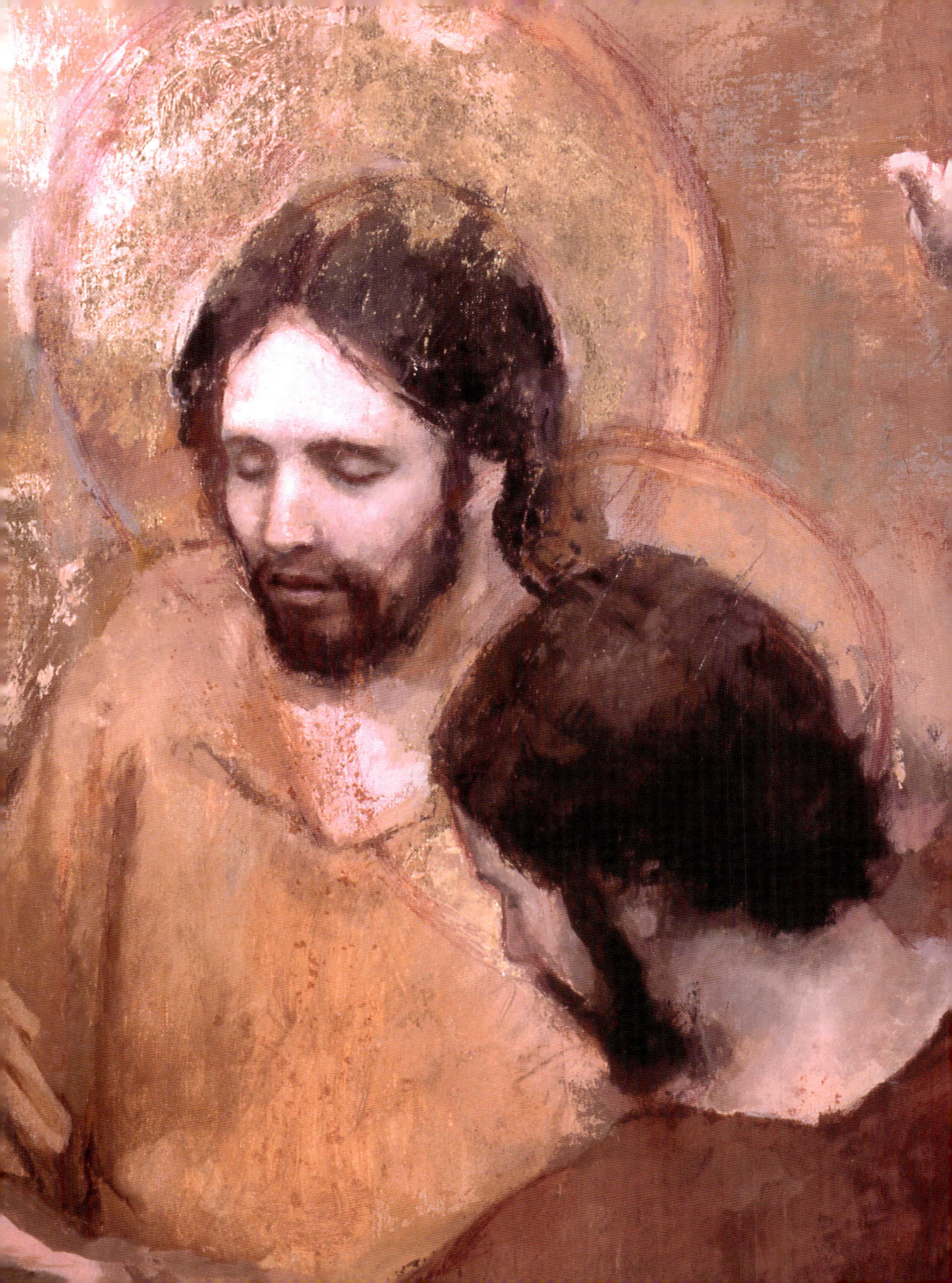

Chapter 4

Baptism and Temptations

Jesus' baptism and temptations, events paired in the Gospels, bring to view an expansive desert, with its attendant lack of food and water and intense heat, broken only by the cool waters of the Jordan River and the ribbon of green vegetation growing along its banks. It was here that John the Baptist performed his healing, saving ordinance; it was here that crowds gathered far from their homes to hear his prophetic words; it was from here that, after His own baptism, Jesus ascended into the desolate hills to face His nemesis, Satan. Notably, this series of incidents bear the marks of auspicious revelation and the humble and resolute character of Jesus' Messiahship.

Baptism

The key personality for this ordinance is John, son of Zacharias and Elisabeth, also known as "the Baptist." Remarkably, he "was ordained by the angel of God at the time he was eight days old . . . to overthrow the kingdom of the Jews, and to make straight the way of the Lord" (Doctrine and Covenants 84:28). On this same remarkable day, when the babe was also circumcised and named, John's father, Zacharias, regained his abilities to speak and hear (see Luke 1:59–64). Extraordinarily, as an infant, John enjoyed the companionship of the Holy Ghost, even "from his mother's womb" (Luke 1:15; Doctrine and Covenants 84:27). John's prophetic calling is hinted at in his declaration that he had been commissioned by one who had "sent me to baptize with water" (John 1:33)—a clear reference to a heavenly authorization before presuming to baptize Jesus.

It seems apparent that John and Jesus, distant cousins, had not met one another in the years before Jesus came to John, for the Baptist declared "I knew him not," as if he did not recognize the Savior's adult features (John 1:33). Whether they had associated together as youths remains unknown, though art often portrays them together as children. What John did know from the heavenly visitor was that he would recognize the Chosen One. How? A celestial person "said unto me, Upon whom thou shalt see the Spirit descending, and remaining on him, the same is he which baptizeth with the Holy Ghost" (John 1:33). Whatever else he had learned about Jesus, John came to understand clearly, and to testify with humble deference, that "one mightier than I cometh, the latchet of whose shoes I am not worthy to unloose" (Luke 3:16).

Those who came to hear John's preaching and to accept baptism had to travel a long distance through the wilderness to reach the spot in the Jordan Valley at "Aenon near to Salim" where "there was much water" (John 3:23). Most of the country's population lived in the high hills above the valley. The long trip would have reminded some of the trek that their forebears undertook with Moses through the wilderness. The connection to the Exodus is not to be missed and links John's renewing acts with the ancient covenant made in Sinai.

The crowds that came to John had probably heard that the baptism he offered resembled the ordinance that Gentiles received when they

J. Kirk Richards (b. 1976), detail of *The Baptism of Christ*, 2006, oil on canvas, 62 x 35 inches. Courtesy of the artist.

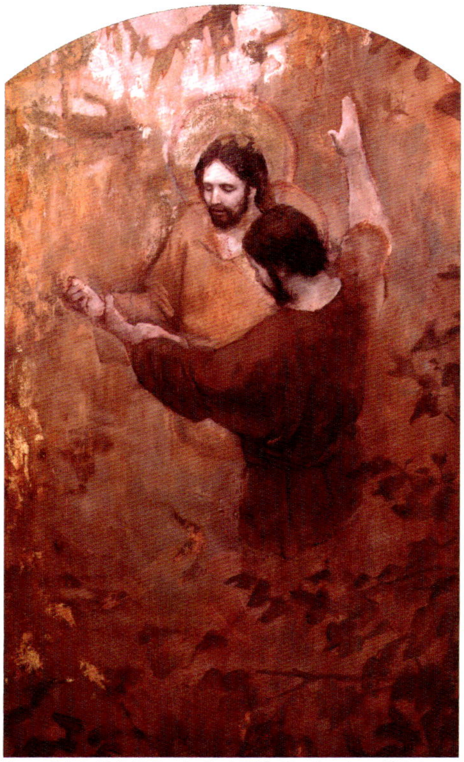

Figure 24. J. Kirk Richards (b. 1976), *The Baptism of Christ*, 2006, oil on canvas, 62 x 35 inches. Courtesy of the artist.

became converts to Judaism. Thus, though those who sought John were for the most part Israelites, they had to decide whether to accept what appeared to be an ordinance specifically for Gentiles. For a Jew, or even a Samaritan, this would have been a major leap of faith and an ultimate act of humility. This aspect seems to underlie John's words about old family lineages: "Think not to say within yourselves, We have Abraham to our father: for I say unto you, that God is able of these stones to raise up children unto Abraham" (Matthew 3:9). Believers demonstrated their humility when they "were baptized of him in Jordan, confessing their sins" (Matthew 3:6).

To those who endured the rigors of the trip to where John was baptizing, the Baptist spoke words of counsel and warning, direct and plain. Warning religious leaders—"many of the Pharisees and Sadducees"—he thundered, "Bring forth . . . fruits meet for repentance" (Matthew 3:7–8). Of tax collectors he demanded, "Exact no more than that which is appointed you" (Luke 3:13). To soldiers, most likely the Samaritans who made up the local

Changed Doctrine, Altered Images

The history of changing baptismal practices is well documented in the artistic representations of Christ's baptism. Early depictions showed Him unclothed and standing in the chest-high water of the Jordan River, indicating His baptism by immersion (Figure 25). Over time immersion was deemed unnecessary and was superseded by affusion (pouring on of water), thereby causing a similar shift in baptismal representations. By the time of the Renaissance and thereafter, Christ was most often portrayed wearing a loincloth and standing ankle-deep in the river, while John the Baptist, in his traditional camel-hair raiment, stands on the bank and pours water over His head with a cup or shell (Figures 26 and 27).

Baptism scenes often include references to the three members of the Godhead. The Holy Ghost descends upon Christ in the form of a dove. Sometimes the dove holds an olive branch or a vial of consecrated oil with which he anoints the head of Christ to represent the bestowal of the Holy Ghost. In early representations, a hand emerging from an opening in the heavens symbolized the presence of God the Father (Figure 25). By the end of the twelfth century, the hand was replaced by the figure of God (Figure 26).[1]

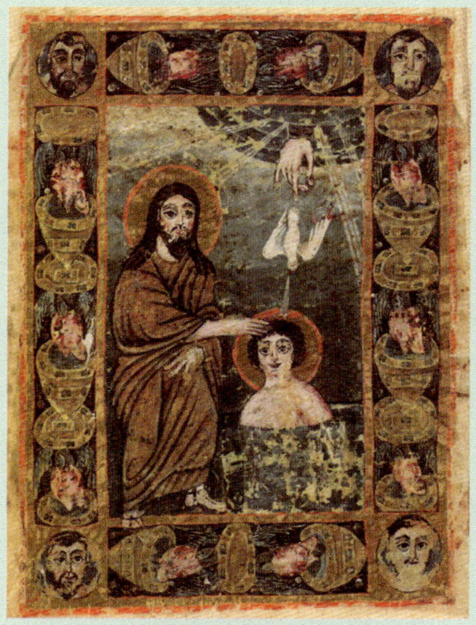

Figure 25. *Baptism of Christ*, from the *Codex Etschmiadzin* (f. 229v), ca. 989, illuminated manuscript facsimile (1999), 13¾ x 10¼ inches. L. Tom Perry Special Collections, Harold B. Lee Library, Brigham Young University, Provo, Utah; ADEVA, Akademische Drück- u. Verlagsanstalt, Austria.

1. Schiller, *Iconography of Christian Art*, 139.

Roman army squadrons, he sternly instructed, "Do violence to no man, neither accuse any falsely; and be content with your wages" (Luke 3:14). To others he declared the need for ennobling charity: "He that hath two coats, let him impart to him that hath none; and he that hath meat, let him do likewise" (Luke 3:11). It becomes apparent that receiving baptism is to be accompanied by a commitment to righteous living.

When John baptized Jesus, the heavens responded by disclosing who Jesus is. Matthew indicates that, at the approach of Jesus, John somehow recognized Him and then momentarily resisted baptizing Him: "I have need to be baptized of thee, and comest thou to me?" John knew that he was to baptize the Savior but, because he knew who Jesus really is, seemed overwhelmed when the moment arrived. It was Jesus who disarmed John's reluctance by saying to him, "Suffer it to be so now: for thus it becometh *us* to fulfil all righteousness" (Matthew 3:14–15; emphasis added). Plainly, John was to be a part of fulfilling "all righteousness" (see 2 Nephi 31:4–9). The baptism that followed, completing the steps of "all righteousness," invited the revelation about Jesus' true identity. For as He rose from the water, "the heavens were opened unto him, and he saw the Spirit of God descending like a dove, and lighting upon him: And lo a voice from heaven, saying, This is my beloved Son" (Matthew 3:16–17). What becomes clear from this account, and is not clear in the other synoptic reports (see Mark 1:10–11; Luke 3:21–22), is that the revelation was for John and perhaps others. By saying of Jesus, "This is my beloved Son," God aims His words to both John and additional witnesses.

That John was to receive this sure testimony by beholding the descent of the Spirit becomes apparent in the fourth Gospel where the Baptist repeats the words of the heavenly messenger: "Upon whom thou shalt see the Spirit descending, and remaining on him, the same is he which baptizeth with the Holy Ghost. And I [John] saw, and bare record that this is the Son of God" (John 1:33–34). This experience was the supreme, confirming moment for John. To this point he had borne witness because of what his parents had doubtless taught him and because of what his heavenly visitor had certainly said to him. But at this moment he personally witnessed

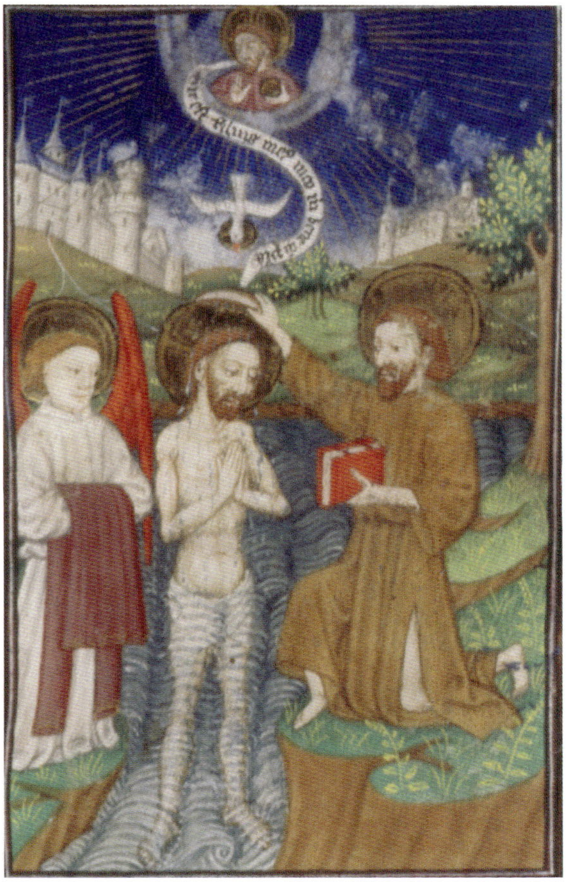

Figure 26. Master of Sir John Fastolf (active ca. 1420–1460), *Baptism of Christ*, from the *Book of Hours* (f. 46r), ca. 1420–30, illuminated manuscript, 8 ½ x 6 ½ inches. The Pierpont Morgan Library, New York. MS M.27, f. 46r. Photograph © The Pierpont Morgan Library, New York.

the signs of the Son of God—the descending Spirit and the heavenly voice.

Temptations

From the waters of the Jordan River, Jesus retreated into the high, dry desert hills that parallel the river course. Here He fasted; here He became weak physically while growing stronger spiritually; here He faced and beat back His ancient nemesis, the devil. When, in an earlier scene, the Father chose Jehovah to implement the Father's plan, the devil and his allies rebelled but were vanquished. Even so, Satan drew a third of the hosts of heaven into his dark kingdom (see Moses 4:1–4; Abraham 3:24–28; Doctrine and Covenants 29:36–38; Revelation 12:1–9). Now, as Jesus was commencing His mortal ministry, the devil ventured out to test the Savior's will.

Tradition locates two of the temptations—to change stones to bread and to rule earthly kingdoms—in the generally bleak hills that lie between Jerusalem and the Jordan Valley. Here, except for wild animals and the occasional shepherd and sheep, a person can be absolutely alone. There is little water and almost nothing to eat but insects and roots. The other temptation, of course, occurred in Jerusalem, where Satan goaded Jesus to throw Himself from "a pinnacle of the temple" (Luke 4:9).

Submitting Himself to the Spirit, which had just descended upon Him at His baptism, Jesus was led "into the wilderness." There, according to Matthew and Luke, He spent forty days fasting. Mark reports that during this ordeal, He spent time "with the wild beasts," perhaps fulfilling the prophecy of Isaiah that the era of the Messiah will see peace in the animal kingdom. Mark also informs us that in this barren and lonely place, "angels ministered unto him" (Mark 1:12–13; see also Isaiah 11:6–9).

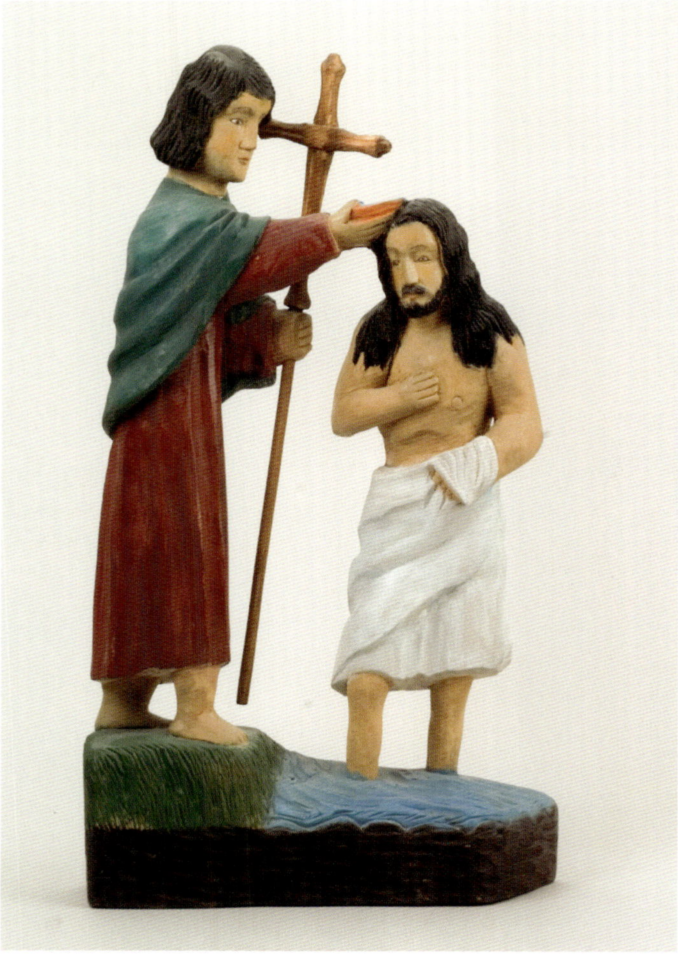

Figure 27. Jan Krajewski (b. 1935), *Baptism*, ca. 1990, polychrome wood, 17 inches (height). Private collection of Walter and Mary Whipple.

According to Matthew and Luke, it was at the end of this spiritually intense six weeks that Satan presumed to approach Jesus. By this point, Jesus was in a physically reduced state, for He had eaten "nothing" and now "hungered" (Luke 4:2). In contentious words that challenged Jesus' recently revealed identity, the devil hissed again and again, "If thou be the son of God. . . ." Embedded deep within this challenge stood a clear reference to the beginning, to the creation of the world, when God had said to His Son, "Let us make man in our image," and then He had "formed man of the dust of the ground" (Genesis 1:26; 2:7). In fact, John had alluded to that moment when he declared that "God is able of these stones to raise up children unto Abraham" (Matthew 3:9; Luke 3:8).

At the Creation, the Savior had been a full participant (see Abraham 5:7–9). Now Satan was challenging Jesus to show His old powers by taking something earthly and making it into something else—anciently, dust into a living being, now, stones into bread. Although, as He had demonstrated eons before and as John had been promising, Jesus possessed power to turn the stones into bread to satisfy His hunger, He refrained. Bodily appetites were not to rule His will.

For the next two temptations, our two sources, Matthew and Luke, preserve a different order. Following Matthew, we read that "the devil taketh [Jesus] up into the holy city, and setteth him on a pinnacle of the temple" (Matthew 4:5). The Joseph Smith Translation adjusts the reading of the latter part of this statement: "*the Spirit* setteth him on the pinnacle of the temple" (JST, Matthew 4:5; emphasis added). Because of the discovery of an inscribed stone next to the southwest corner of the temple grounds, repeating the words "the place of trumpeting . . . ," some believe that the "pinnacle of the temple" refers to this corner, which overlooks, to the west, the Tyropean Valley and the upper city. It was in this prominent and visible place that Satan issued his second challenge: "If thou be the Son of God, cast thyself down"(Matthew 4:6). What would happen? The devil reached

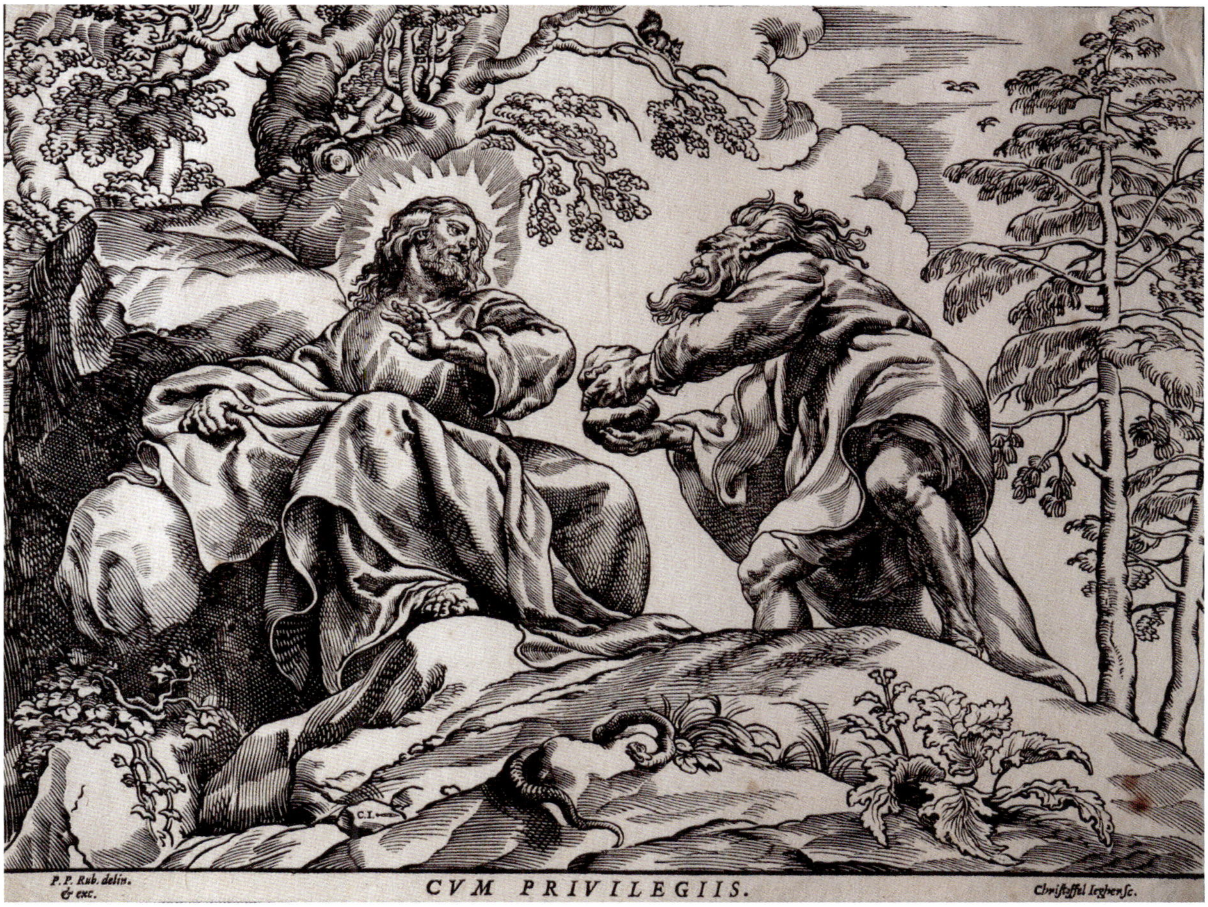

Figure 28. Christoffel Jegher (ca. 1596–1653). *Temptation of Christ* (after Peter Paul Rubens), 1633, woodcut, 12¾ x 17⅛ inches. Private collection of Shawn and Andrea Merriman.

for a passage in Psalm 91:11–12 to describe it: "[God] shall give his angels charge over thee, to keep thee in all thy ways. They shall bear thee up in their hands." What would be a grander sign of Jesus' divine identity than to throw Himself off the wall above the busiest street of the city and float safely to earth with the aid of angels? Once again, Jesus resisted, citing a passage from the Law, "Thou shalt not tempt the Lord thy God" (Matthew 4:7; citing Deuteronomy 6:16). Jesus would not announce Himself in this way.

The third temptation took place on "an exceeding high mountain" where Satan "sheweth him all the kingdoms of the world, and the glory of them" (Matthew 4:8). According to the Joseph Smith Translation, not the devil but "the Spirit . . . taketh [Jesus] up . . . and sheweth him all the kingdoms of the world." Only then did "the devil [come] unto him again" and say, "All these things will I give thee, if thou wilt fall down and worship me" (JST, Matthew 4:8–9). It was a desperate act. Even before this moment, Satan was beaten. The pattern had been clear from the moment Jesus resisted making stones into bread to relieve His grinding hunger. Satan would not be able to crack the Savior's resolve. The offer of worldly honor was hollow, vapid. Again the Savior quoted a passage from the Law, the most venerated part of scripture: "It is written, Thou shalt worship the Lord thy God, and him only shalt thou serve" (Matthew 4:10, citing Deuteronomy 6:13). Jesus' kingdom would not be as earthly realms.

In their own way, and like the story of the baptism, the temptations reveal who Jesus is. In a word, He is the Messiah, and His gospel is the antithesis to Satan's plan. In the competition for influence among the people of the earth, Jesus points to a course of inner discipline rather than force or indulgence; His path is one of inner strength rather than outward display; His approach is to respect the created order rather than try to change or manipulate it for His own ends.

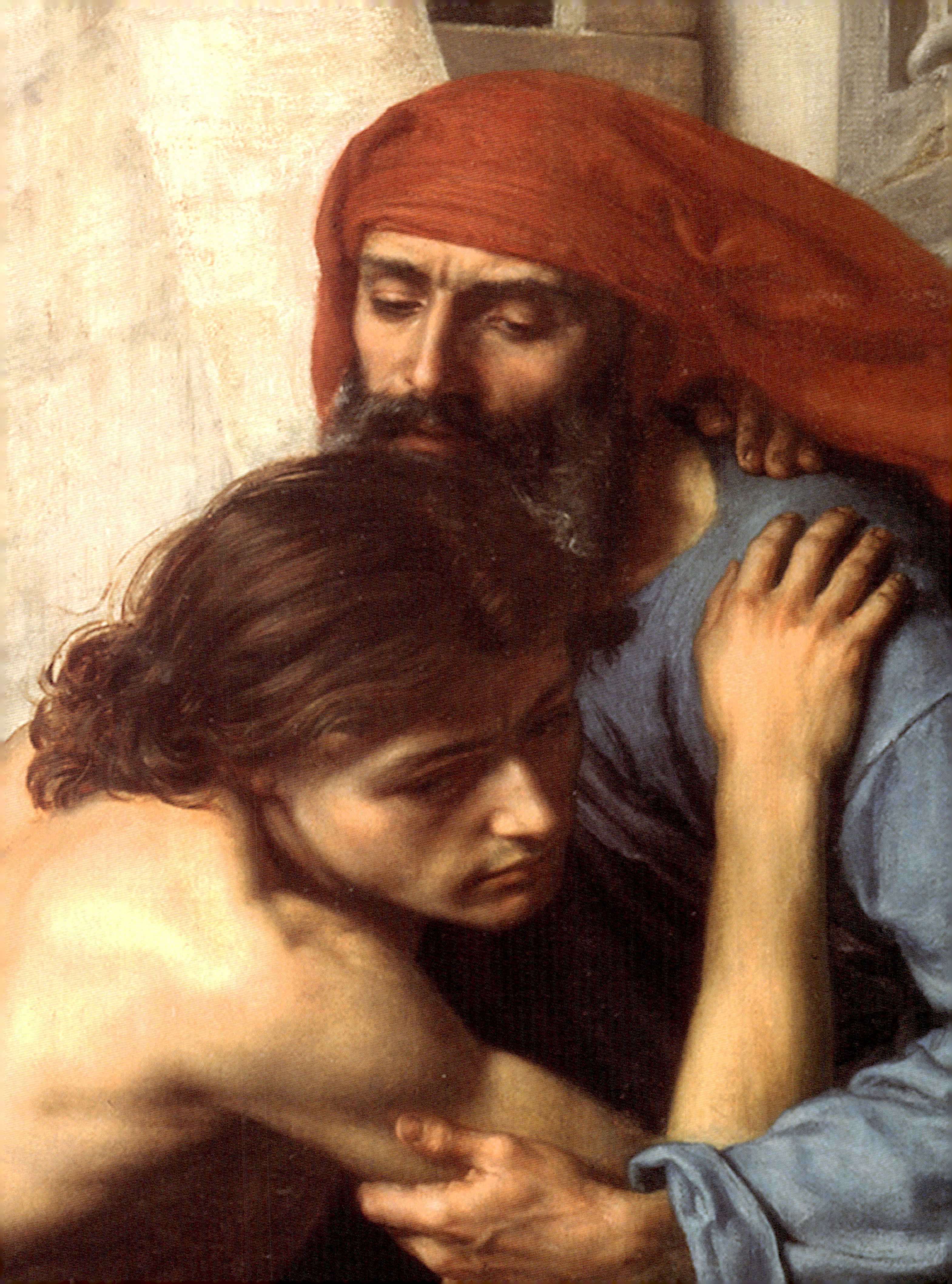

Chapter 5

Sermons and Teachings

For hundreds of years, artists have found inspiration in scriptural portrayals of Jesus as a teacher. With its descriptions of five blocks of teachings, including the Sermon on the Mount (see Matthew 5:1–7:29); the early apostolic mission (see Matthew 10:11–42); the parables (see Matthew 13:1–52); the kingdom of heaven discourse (see Matthew 18:1–35); and the Olivet discourse (see Matthew 24:1–25:46), the Gospel of Matthew has been particularly inspiring.

According to a second portrayal, that of Mark, Jesus began His ministry in the synagogue in Capernaum. On the Sabbath day, the synagogue service featured prayers, scripture reading, and teaching. Any male of sufficient learning could be invited to teach. The people present on this occasion were "astonished at his doctrine: for he taught them as one that had authority, and not as the scribes" (Mark 1:22). What gave further weight to His teaching was His healing of a man with "an unclean spirit," and "immediately [Jesus'] fame spread abroad throughout all the region round about Galilee" (Mark 1:23, 28).

Although Jesus' sermons and sayings were given to specific people at specific times and places, His life-enhancing teachings bear universal meaning and thus have been preserved, read, and heard by countless people over the last two millennia—who are still captivated by His insightful words, parables, and exhortations. Countless artists have attempted to capture visually what the Gospels' word-pictures preserve as a result of Jesus' "preaching the gospel of the kingdom of God" (Mark 1:14).

Parables

The Gospels of Matthew, Mark, and Luke highlight Jesus' parables. The word *parable* derives from the Greek word that means "setting side by side," allowing a comparison of one thing to another. These succinct, memorable stories are key to understanding His mission to the last, least, and lost. Jewish society of this period was, in many respects, a typical ancient society. It consisted mostly of the poor and the very poor. Among the poor were also the vulnerable—notably women, children, and slaves. We should not be at all surprised that a variety of people, not just prominent men, figure in Jesus' profound parables.

In many instances, He told twin parables—one that would resonate with men and one that would speak more directly to women. Typical would be the parables of the lost sheep and lost coin that are linked in Luke 15:3–10.

The parables of Jesus reflect the numerous roles that men played—bridegrooms, doctors, judges, merchants, priests, publicans, poor men, servants, sons, and more. The female characters include bridesmaids (virgins), a woman searching for a lost coin, a widow seeking justice, and a handful of unspecified wives, mothers, and daughters whom Jesus mentions in general terms. Most of these women's experiences describe situations intimately familiar to women as part of the rhythms of their daily life—sewing patches, baking bread, making wine, sending for the doctor, serving meals, sweeping the house, watching children play in the market, and so forth.

Sir Edward John Poynter, P.R.A. (1836–1919), detail of *The Prodigal's Return*, 1869, oil on canvas, 47 1/4 x 36 inches. Brigham Young University Museum of Art, purchased with funds provided by Ira A. and Mary Lou Fulton.

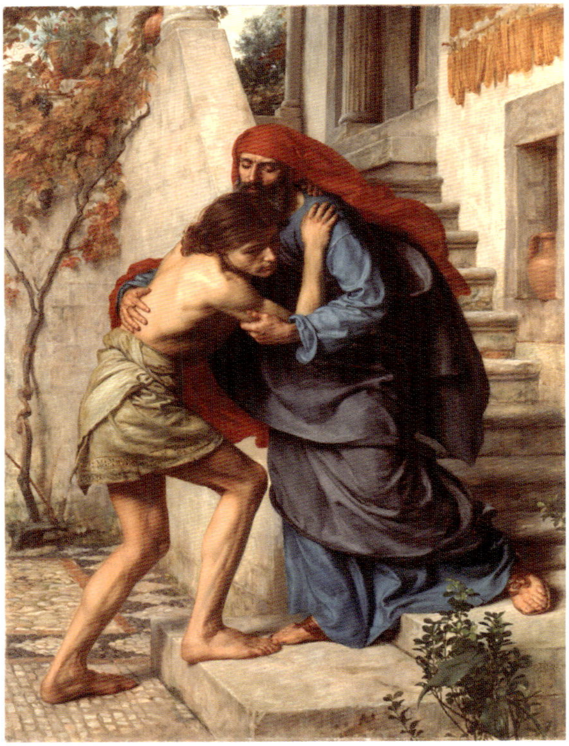

Figure 29. Sir Edward John Poynter, P.R.A. (1836–1919), *The Prodigal's Return*, 1869, oil on canvas, 47 1/4 x 36 inches. Brigham Young University Museum of Art, purchased with funds provided by Ira A. and Mary Lou Fulton.

For a time, so extensively did the Master employ the parable as a teaching device that Mark observes, "without a parable spake he not unto them" (Mark 4:34). These homely examples—a bridegroom and a lamp, a Samaritan traveler on the road to Jericho, a seed and a field—so familiar in the first-century Jewish world, were often made more memorable by an unexpected turn in the stories: the despised Samaritan becomes the hero, the patch tears the cloth, the wine bursts the skins, the lamp is put under the bed, the master serves the meal to his servants, and the friend calls at midnight.

The Sermon on the Mount

Matthew is the disciple who preserves Jesus' most famous and most quoted discourse, the Sermon on the Mount (see Matthew 5–7). Additionally, Luke records a lesser-known version of what may have been the same sermon, identified as the Sermon on the Plain (see Luke 6:17–49).

In Matthew's account, Jesus ascends a mountain to teach (see Matthew 5:1). This event parallels Moses' experience on Mount Sinai when he receives authoritative teachings that will be passed on to Israel. Jesus, like Moses, now hands to Israel new teachings and commandments.

The sermon begins with the Beatitudes—nine blessings. The words continue to echo beyond the beautiful hills overlooking the tranquil Sea of Galilee with as much power and sublimity as they did two thousand years ago:

> Blessed are the poor in the spirit: for theirs is the kingdom of heaven.
> Blessed are they that mourn: for they shall be comforted.
> Blessed are the meek: for they shall inherit the earth.
> Blessed are they which do hunger and thirst after righteousness: for they shall be filled.
> Blessed are the merciful: for they shall obtain mercy.
> Blessed are the pure in heart: for they shall see God.
> Blessed are the peacemakers: for they shall be called the children of God.
> Blessed are they which are persecuted for righteousness' sake: for theirs is the kingdom of heaven.
> Blessed are ye, when men shall revile you, and persecute you, and shall say all manner of evil against you falsely, for my sake. (Matthew 5:3–11)

Such were the spirit and power of His teachings that people were "astonished at his doctrine: For he taught them as one having authority" (Matthew 7:28–29), and when He came "down

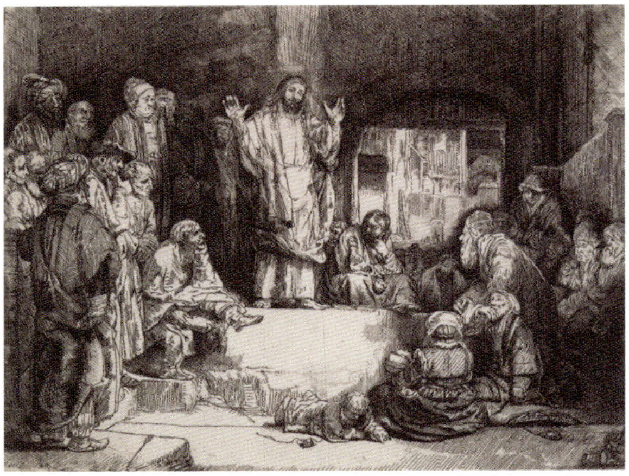

Figure 30. Rembrandt Harmenszoon van Rijn (1606–1669), *Christ Preaching (La Petite Tombe)*, ca. 1652, etching and drypoint, 6 3/8 x 8 3/8 inches. Brigham Young University Museum of Art, purchase/gift from Mahonri M. Young Estate.

Protestant Art

Perhaps the most significant upheaval in the history of Christian art came as a result of the sixteenth-century Protestant Reformation. Whereas the Catholic Church sanctioned imagery as an aid to communicating with Deity, many Protestant leaders believed that images would lead to idolatry. Thus, numerous altarpieces and sculptures were destroyed or removed from Protestant churches, and religious imagery became the prerogative of private devotion.

Certain biblical narratives, however, still had a place in Reformation art. Parables such as the lost sheep (Figure 34) and the prodigal son had particular appeal. Symbolizing the Protestant emphasis on God's grace and mercy for the repentant sinner, *The Prodigal's Return* by Sir Edward John Poynter (Figure 29) captures the tender relationship between a father and his son. The richly embroidered hem of the son's tattered garment speaks of the status he once enjoyed in his father's household.[1] Humbled by his impoverished condition, the penitent son looks away, overcome with shame and remorse, as his father draws him near in a redeeming embrace. The contrite spirit of the son and the compassionate affection of the father combine in a moment of sweet reconciliation wherein the two figures merge into one, focusing on the singular message of repentance and forgiveness.

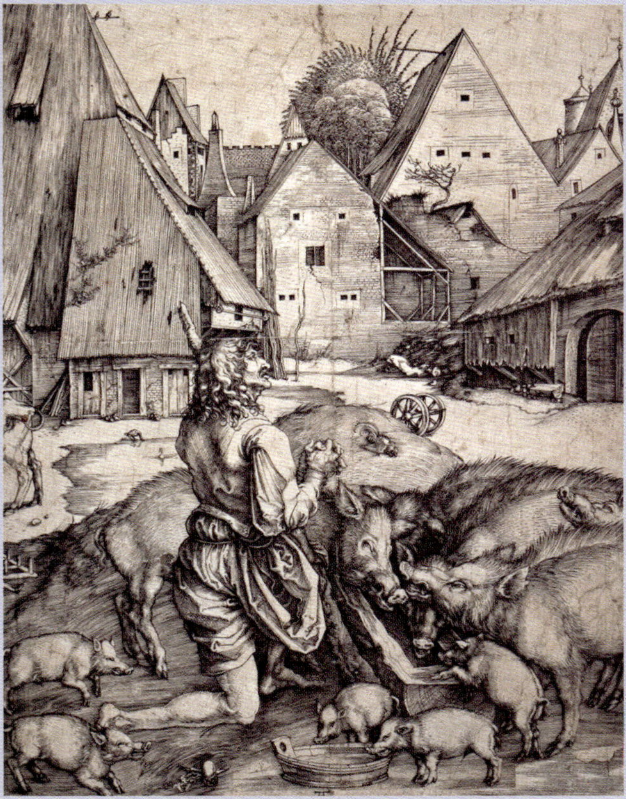

Figure 32. Albrecht Dürer (1471–1528), *Prodigal Son Amid the Swine*, ca. 1496, engraving, 9 3/8 x 7 3/8 inches. Brigham Young University Museum of Art, purchase/gift from Mahonri M. Young Estate.

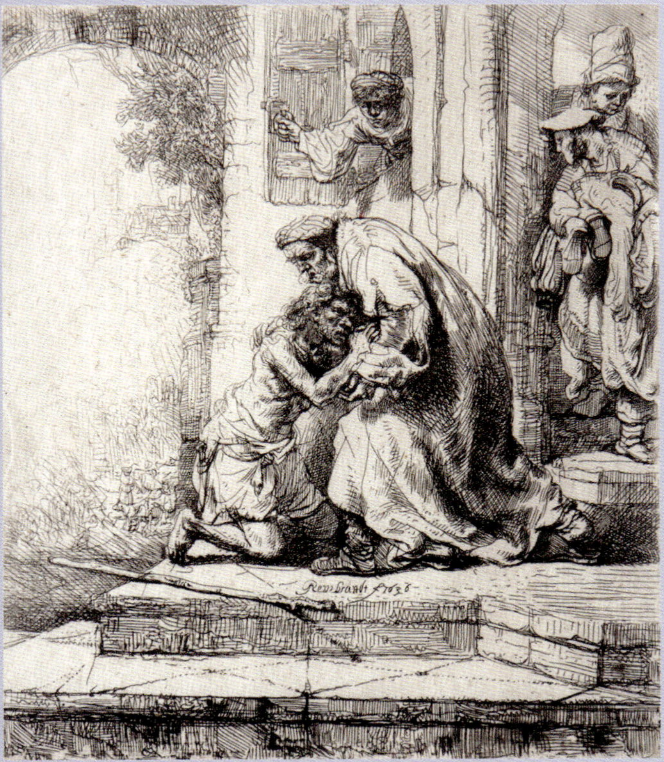

Figure 31. Rembrandt Harmenszoon van Rijn (1606–1669), *The Return of the Prodigal Son*, 1636, etching, 6 1/4 x 5 7/16 inches. Private collection of Shawn and Andrea Merriman.

The theme of the raising of Lazarus gained Protestant popularity as well. It prefigured Christ's resurrection and manifested His love for Lazarus, and thus all mankind. In Rembrandt's 1632 etching of this subject (Figure 36), Christ stands as an imposing and commanding figure embodying the power necessary to call Lazarus forth from the grave. Armaments hang from a cloth suspended from the top of the rock-hewn tomb, referring to an apocryphal legend of Lazarus' military skills and linking his triumph over the grave with Christ's victory over death.[2]

1. Special thanks to Elizabeth Gray Patel for calling attention to the adorned hem on the Prodigal's garment.
2. Martha M. Peacock, ed., *Rembrandt as Printmaker: An Exhibition at Brigham Young University* (Provo, Utah: Brigham Young University Press, 1988), catalogue 7.

from the mountain, great multitudes followed him" (Matthew 8:1).

The Woman at the Well

In Samaria was a well to which the women came daily to draw water—a precious resource in an arid land—water to drink, cook with, wash themselves and their families, and give life to their small gardens of cucumbers, leeks, melons, and onions.

This well was the setting for one of Jesus' most memorable sermons, given in this instance to an individual.

Jesus came to this well at noon, on the second day of a long, dusty journey from Jerusalem more than forty miles away. He and His disciples were weary and doubtless thirsty.

The well was perhaps a hundred feet deep, and the daily task of drawing water was relegated to servants (slaves) or, for poorer families, to the women. On this day, a Samaritan woman came to use a small, unbreakable leather bucket to draw water from the well. She planned to pour the water into a clay water pot, which she would carry on her head to pour its contents at home into a large clay storage jar. She probably made several trips daily, as her ancestors had done for nearly a millennium before.

Evidently, Jewish law or custom at the time prohibited Jews from using any vessels touched by Samaritans because such vessels were considered ritually impure. Jesus openly violated this convention when He said to her, "Give me to drink" (John 4:7). The woman's surprised reaction tells the whole story: "How is it that thou, being a Jew, askest drink of me, which am a woman of Samaria?" (John 4:9).

With His disciples gone away into the city to buy food, Jesus engaged the woman in a conversation in which He said: "If thou knewest the gift of God, and who it is that saith to thee, Give me to drink; thou wouldest have asked of him, and he would have given thee living water" (John 4:10).

Her mind at first stirred on the level of physical wells and buckets, but Jesus intended something greater. She sensed something unusual in Him and began to address Him respectfully as "Sir" (John 4:11). The Greek *kyrie* can be translated "Sir" but also means "Lord"; most likely, there is a progression to more honorific meanings because the

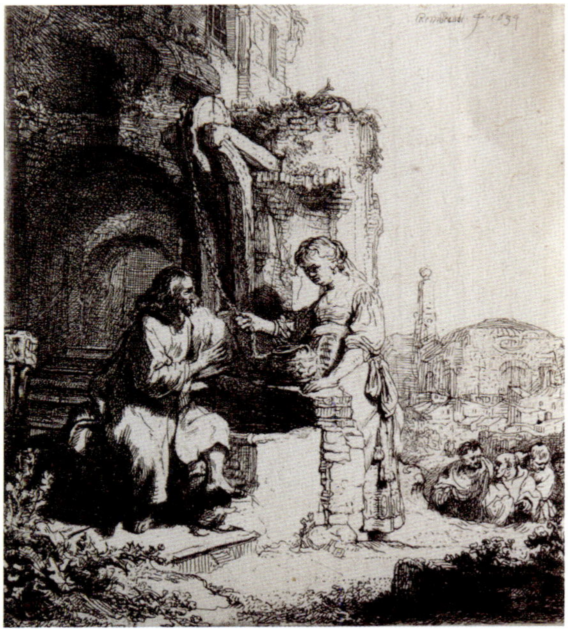

Figure 33. Rembrandt Harmenszoon van Rijn (1606–1669), *Christ and the Samaritan Woman among Ruins*, 1634, etching, 4 15/16 x 4 1/4 inches. Private collection of Shawn and Andrea Merriman.

woman repeats it with increasing respect throughout their conversation (see John 4:15, 19).

Jesus identifies her thirst for something far greater than the water from that well and offers her a spring of living water—an unfailing source of life, even the gift of the Spirit. After this unusual Jew demonstrated that He knew clearly her past and present lifestyles, "the woman saith unto him, Sir, I perceive that thou art a prophet" (John 4:19), and when she specifically questioned Jesus further about the Messiah, "Jesus saith unto her, I that speak unto thee am he" (John 4:26).

This is the first recorded instance in John's Gospel where Jesus openly declared to anyone that He was the expected Jewish Messiah. Marveling at His power and teachings, "The woman then left her waterpot, and went her way into the city, and saith to the men, Come, see a man, which told me all things that ever I did: is not this the Christ?" (John 4:28–29).

The Sermon on the Mount of Olives

If the Sermon on the Mount is considered one of the most majestic and inspiring teachings given to men and women, the sermon on the Mount of Olives, known as the Olivet Discourse, is certainly one of the most prophetic utterances recorded in

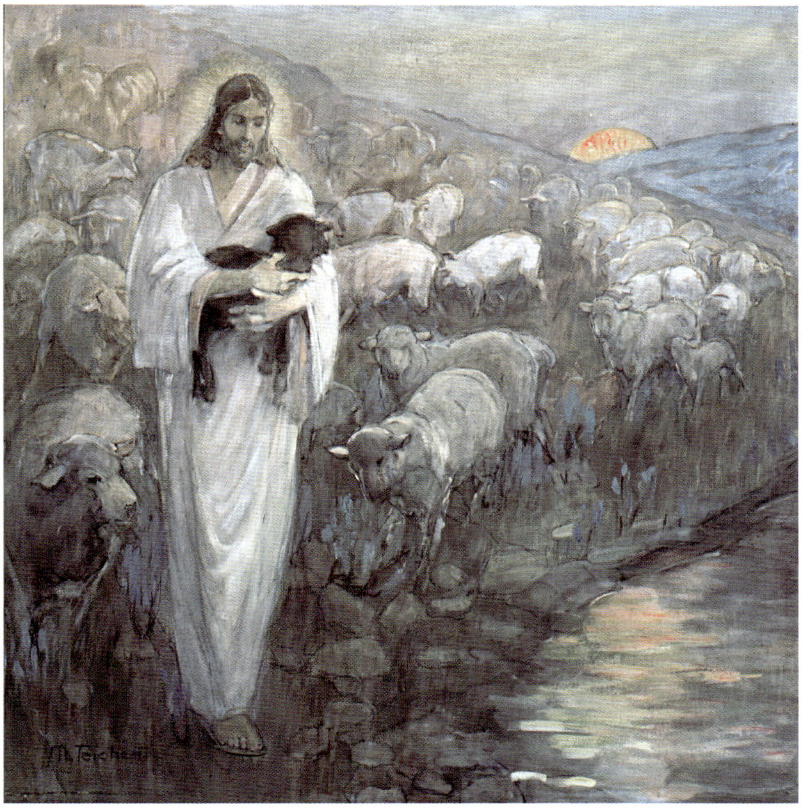

Figure 34. Minerva K. Teichert (1888–1976), *Rescue of the Lost Lamb*, ca. 1939–40, oil on canvas, 48 x 48 inches. The Church of Jesus Christ of Latter-day Saints, Salt Lake Bonneville Stake.

scripture (see Matthew 24:1–51; 25:1–46; cf. Mark 13, Luke 17, 21).

Unlike many of Jesus' other sermons, this one, given during the final days of His mortal ministry, was delivered only to His closest disciples, the Twelve, away from the gaze of the crowds and from His enemies. Jesus and His disciples had left the temple area and gathered on the Mount of Olives, a large, elevated site of some forty acres from which they had a commanding view of the Holy City and the jewel of that city, the temple itself (see Joseph Smith—Matthew 1:4).

From this vantage point, the disciples asked Jesus about the temple, most likely impressed by its walls, courtyards, buildings, and altars. Jesus must have startled them, "See ye not all these things? verily I say unto you, There shall not be left here one stone upon another, that shall not be thrown down" (Matthew 24:2).

Although Matthew's Gospel ends with Jesus' suffering, death, burial, and resurrection, the focus of this important sermon ultimately looks forward to the intervening events, preceding His return in glory (Matthew 24:4–31). The disciples learned that before that promised day, however, Jerusalem would fall to an unnamed enemy and its temple would be destroyed.

The Prophet Joseph Smith's work on this sermon has given clearer context and order to Jesus' words that make the interpretation of difficult concepts fairly straightforward.

Yet we feel that something is very familiar with this sermon, as it includes six parables. Five of the parables are preserved in Matthew's account (see Joseph Smith—Matthew 1:47–48; Matthew 24:45–51; Matthew 25:1–13, 14–30, 31–46); and a final one preserved in Mark (see Mark 13:33–37).

Jesus' final parable in this sermon, sometimes identified as the parable of the sheep and goats (Matthew 25:31–46), begins "When the Son of man shall come in his glory, and all the holy angels with him, then shall he sit upon the throne of his glory." The sermon continues when Jesus describes the scenes of what would be the basis of a favorite hymn of the Prophet Joseph Smith, "A Poor Wayfaring Man of Grief" (*Hymns*, no. 29).

Jesus Following His Death and Resurrection

Jesus' teaching and preaching continued after His death and resurrection (see Luke 24:36–53; 3 Nephi 9–18). How grateful we are that His disciples preserved His teachings and sermons by writing them down. These remarkable, firsthand accounts were treasured and copied, thus making them available for future disciples to read and study that they, too, could stand in amazement, as did those who first heard Him at the synagogue on the northern shore of the Sea of Galilee so many years ago: "And they were astonished at his doctrine: for he taught them as one that had authority, and not as the scribes" (Mark 1:22).

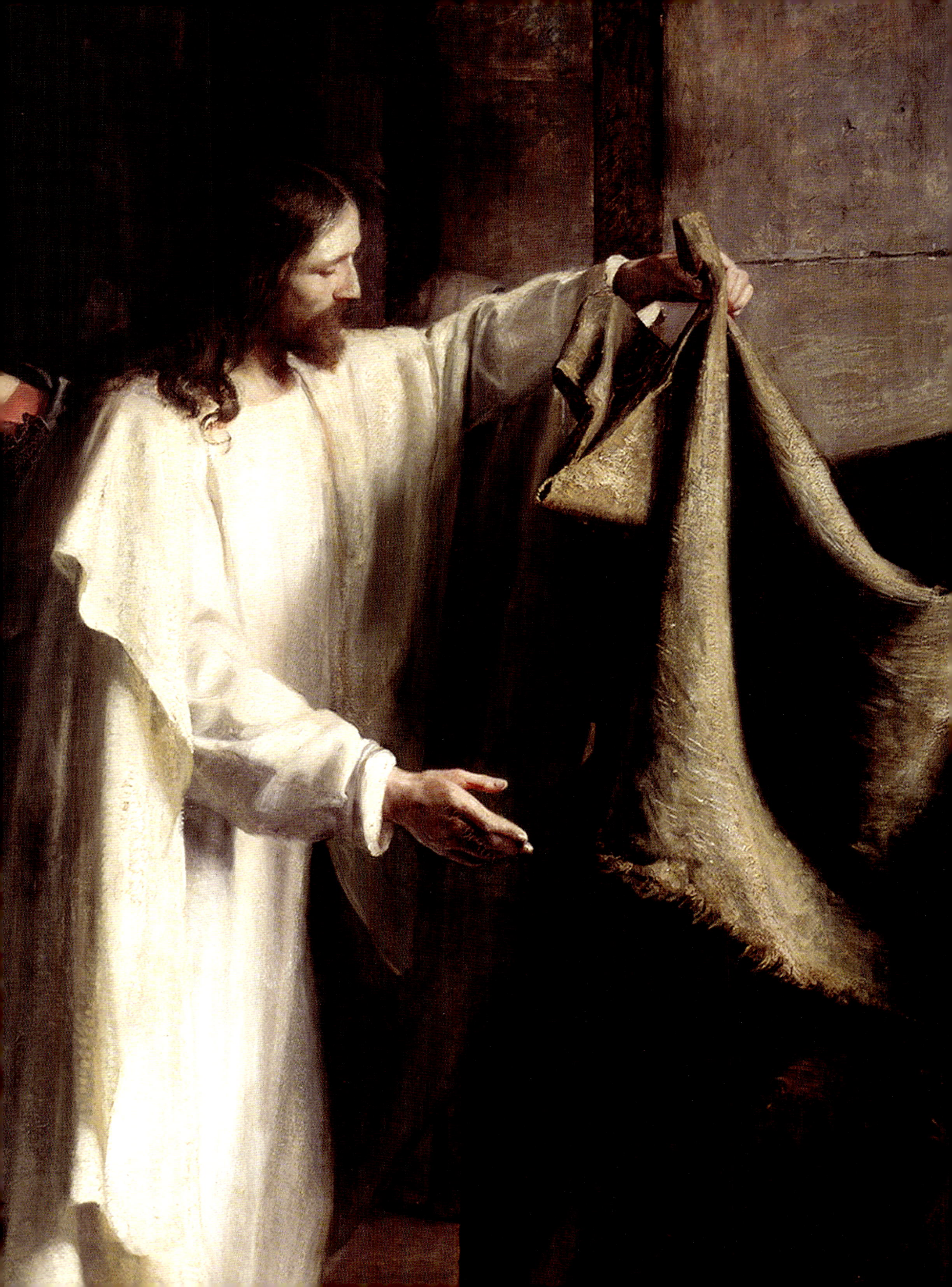

Chapter 6

Miracles

The miracles of Jesus do much to reveal who He is. Memorable in their retelling and stunning in their power, these miraculous acts brought heaven's mercies to earth, making lives whole and opening the doors to eternity for recipients and witnesses alike.

Ancient prophecy anticipated little of the Messiah's miraculous power, instead focusing mainly on His governance and atonement (see Isaiah 9:6–7; 11:1–5; 52:13; 53:12). It was to a New World prophet and a king that angelic voices declared that people "afflicted with all manner of diseases, and with devils and unclean spirits" would be "healed by the power of the Lamb of God," and that the Coming One would work "mighty miracles, such as healing the sick, raising the dead, causing the lame to walk, the blind to receive their sight, and the deaf to hear" (1 Nephi 11:31; Mosiah 3:5).

Reports in the New Testament Gospels chronicle the fulfillment of these prophetic words. And art reverently and deftly captures special miraculous moments from Jesus' ministry. Three types of miracles stand out.

Power over Human Diseases

Jesus' power over human ills was manifest early in His ministry when He healed Peter's mother-in-law who suffered from a fever (see Mark 1:29–31; Luke 4:38–39). Even more dramatic healings followed. For example, in Jerusalem, one of Jesus' earliest miracles occurred next to one of the main sources of water for temple services, the pool of Bethesda, which lay only a hundred yards to the north of the temple grounds. There, during a special feast, Jesus went into a pagan complex of pools and baths dedicated to the healing god Asclepius. He sought and found a man "which had an infirmity thirty and eight years" (John 5:5). Plainly, this Jewish man, spending the feast in a pagan shrine, had given up on the power of his religion to bring healing and comfort.

When Jesus approached him unexpectedly and asked, "Wilt thou be made whole?" the man seemed unable to grasp the high gift that the Savior was offering until "Jesus saith unto him, Rise, take up thy bed, and walk." The result of Jesus' words was dazzling, for "immediately the man was made whole." Moreover, he "took up his bed, and walked" (John 5:5–6, 8–9). The extraordinary power involved in enabling a man who physically had moved little for years—strengthening muscles and tendons and restoring balance—has brought readers through the centuries to marvel at the miracle.

In Galilee, Jesus announced Himself in Capernaum by healing "a man with an unclean spirit" on the Sabbath day in the synagogue. That event was noised through the town so that, at the end of the Sabbath day, "when the sun did set," people "brought unto him all that were diseased" and "he healed many that were sick of divers diseases" (Mark 1:23, 32–34). From this point on, His miracles drew widespread attention. After He had chosen the Twelve, they became the most constant witnesses to displays of His power. The scenes must have been breathtaking. One further example will demonstrate this point.

We do not know how many of the Twelve

Carl Heinrich Bloch (1834–1890), detail of *Christ Healing the Sick at Bethesda*, 1883, oil on canvas, 110 13/16 x 125 13/16 inches. Brigham Young University Museum of Art, purchased with funds provided by Jack R. and Mary Lois Wheatley.

were present in a Capernaum home where Jesus was teaching. But we know that people, intrigued by what they had heard about Him, "were come out of every town of Galilee, and Judea" to hear and see Him. When a group of men who were seeking Jesus' healing help for a friend afflicted with palsy were unable to enter the home "because of the multitude," they "went upon the housetop, and let him down through the tiling" into the room where Jesus sat. Then Jesus surprised everyone. Instead of the expected healing, He said to the afflicted man, "Thy sins are forgiven thee" (Luke 5:17, 19–20).

Some in the crowd who knew the law—"the scribes and the Pharisees"—asked aloud, "Who can forgive sins, but God alone?" (Luke 5:21). It was exactly the right question. And Jesus responded in a most interesting way: He healed the man, but only after making clear that the miracle would establish His authority to forgive sins. Speaking first to those gathered in the house, "that ye may know that the Son of man hath power upon earth to forgive sins," He then said to the sick man, "Arise, and take up thy couch, and go into thine house. And immediately he rose up before them" (Luke 5:24–25).

As He would do in Jerusalem for the man at the pool of Bethesda, so He did for the palsied man in this home: He surmounted the debilitating forces of long-term illness. But in the case of the Galilean man, the healing became the occasion for uncovering His greater power, that of forgiving sins.

Power over Natural Elements

Readers of the Gospels will know that nature would respond to her king. For instance, when Jesus was crossing the Mount of Olives before His triumphal entry into Jerusalem, and some were demanding that He silence the adoring crowd, He answered that "if these [people] should hold their peace, the stones would immediately cry out" (Luke 19:40). Such a response by nature was demonstrated in a series of miracles that show Jesus' control over natural elements.

One of the most famous of such miracles

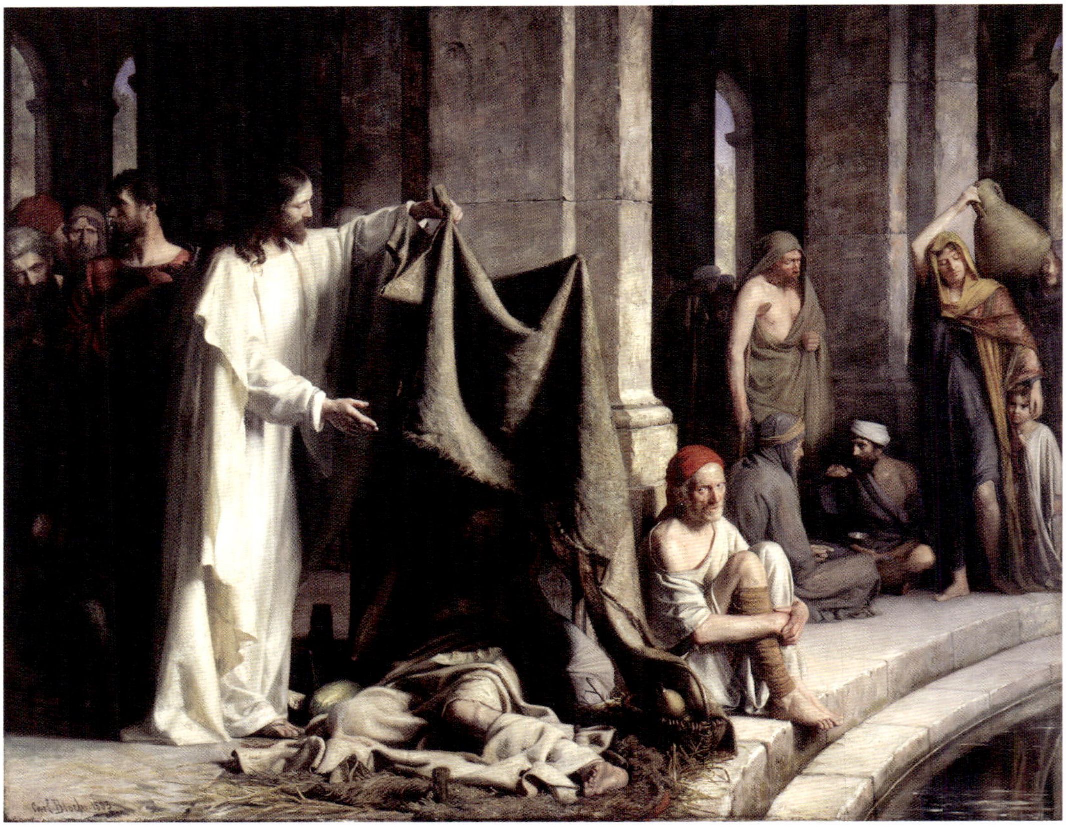

Figure 35. Carl Heinrich Bloch (1834–1890), *Christ Healing the Sick at Bethesda*, 1883, oil on canvas, 110 13/16 x 125 13/16 inches. Brigham Young University Museum of Art, purchased with funds provided by Jack R. and Mary Lois Wheatley.

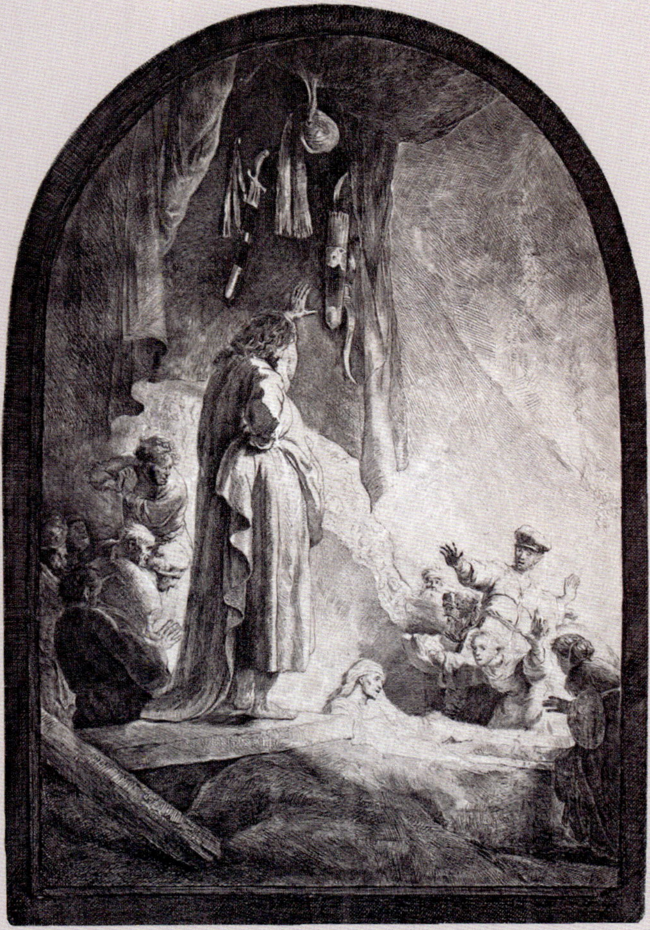

Figure 36. Rembrandt Harmenszoon van Rijn (1606–1669), *The Raising of Lazarus* (Large Plate), ca. 1632, etching and burin, 14 11/16 x 10 3/8 inches. Brigham Young University Museum of Art, purchase/gift from Mahonri M. Young Estate.

Artistic Conventions

In an attempt to make their works more compelling, artists have adopted conventions that seek to involve the viewer. For instance, in Carl Heinrich Bloch's *Christ Healing the Sick at Bethesda* (Figure 35), the curved steps surrounding the pool appear to extend beyond the canvas, including the viewer in the miraculous proceeding. Light and darkness also engage spectators by emphasizing a particular event or figure. The infirm man who receives Christ's healing command is the object of the scriptural account, yet he lies hidden in shadow beneath the coarse canopy. Instead, the light rests upon two other figures—Christ and the red-turbaned man. It is understandable that Christ, the Divine Healer, would be illuminated, but the equal prominence given to the turbaned man raises questions. Why does he stare? What does he symbolize? What is his relationship to the viewer? Perhaps the man's piercing gaze is meant to thwart others who would enter the pool before him, or perhaps he is pleading for assistance. Either unaware or skeptical of Jesus' power to heal, he continues to wait for the waters to move, suggesting man's inclination to trust in superstitions rather than in Christ. Whatever his motives, his confrontational expression solicits an emotional response and acknowledges the onlooker as a participant in the story.

Just as an outward gaze engages the viewer's attention, so does the convention of focusing on a single figure add piquancy to the scene, as in Minerva Teichert's *Miracle of the Loaves and Fishes* (Figure 37). Typical compositions depicting this event often view it from afar, attempting to encompass the entire multitude in order to convey the magnitude of the miracle. Teichert, however, concentrates on a single youth who offers to Christ his five barley loaves and two small fishes. By narrowing the scene, Teichert portrays the intimacy of the miracle—Christ's interaction with the one.

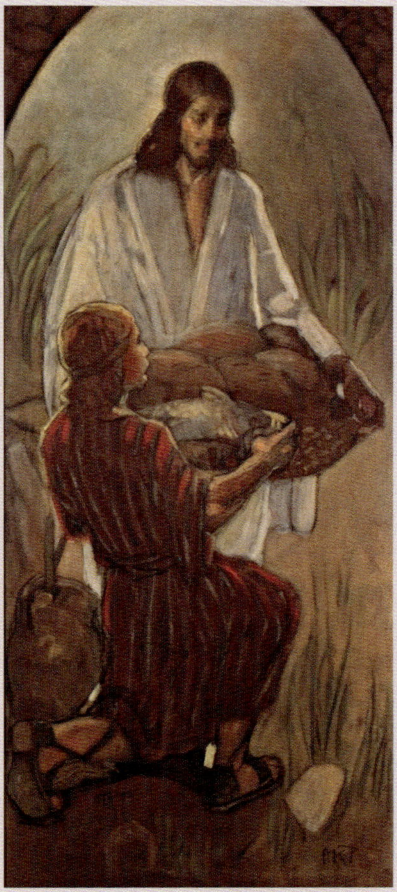

Figure 37. Minerva K. Teichert (1888–1976), *Miracle of the Loaves and Fishes*, 1944, oil on canvas, 48 x 21 3/4 inches. Collection of Salt Lake City School District.

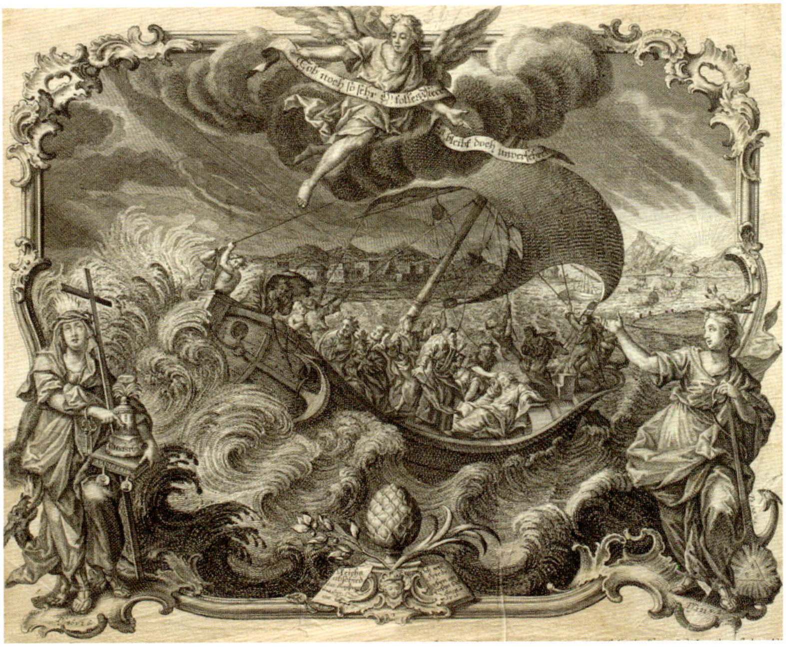

Figure 38. Christoph Friedrich Hörmann von und zu Guttenberg (b. 1715), *Christ and the Tempest*, 18th century, engraving, 9 11/16 x 11 7/8 inches. Brigham Young University Museum of Art, purchase/gift from Mahonri M. Young Estate.

appears in the second chapter of the Gospel of John, in which water is turned to wine. Carrying echoes of the divine power entrusted to Moses (see Exodus 4:9), this miracle was performed in response to a request by Jesus' mother that He solve a social crisis at a wedding in the village of Cana in Galilee. Jesus first bade servants at the wedding feast to fill the six stone jars that were at hand and together held nearly one hundred gallons of liquid. From the water, Jesus created such a superb wine that the host, "the governor of the feast," playfully accused the bridegroom of having held back "the good wine" from the guests. Those who were paying attention, including Jesus' disciples and the servants, witnessed the unveiling of "his glory" through the miracle (John 2:9–11).

A second instance is similar, though it involved many more potential witnesses. All the Gospels recount Jesus miraculously feeding five thousand people. Though the details differ from report to report, all convey the sense of a revealed divine majesty. John ties the miracle to the time of Passover, in the springtime, linking Jesus' act to the Exodus and to celestial deliverance and to manna (see John 6:4). And the miracle's sacramental character cannot be missed.

All the accounts portray Jesus and the Twelve conversing late in the day about how to feed so many who were by now hungry and had been with Him all that day. In each report, Jesus challenges His disciples' grasp of who He is and what He is able to do by asking them how they would help the multitude. It also becomes clear that Jesus is the host, for He takes charge by urging people to sit down, by giving thanks to God, and by breaking the bread, thus making the meal a sacred experience. Though originally there was an insufficient number of fishes and loaves to feed such a throng, at the end, astonishingly, His followers gathered twelve baskets of leftover food, each basket likely carried by one of the Twelve (see Matthew 14:13–21; Mark 6:32–44; Luke 9:10–17; John 6:1–13).

Only the Twelve stood as first-rank witnesses of Jesus' power over the raw fury of nature as seen in His stilling of a storm that descended upon the low-lying Sea of Galilee. According to Mark, Jesus had spent much of the day teaching a large crowd on the seashore when He instructed the Twelve to go with Him by boat to another place. Other boats followed. On the trip, before the storm arose, He fell asleep "on a pillow" where He remained as the wind and waves increased in fury. When the angry waters threatened to swamp the boat, the disciples awoke Jesus, apparently to warn Him of the danger. At this point, instead of working to row the boat to safety, He took charge of nature, rebuking "the wind" and saying to "the sea, Peace, be still. And the wind ceased, and there was a great calm." One can only imagine the astonishment that is revealed in the words of the disciples to one another: "What manner of man is this, that even the wind and the sea obey him?" (Mark 4:35–41). It was one more step for the disciples—and a big one—in learning who Jesus truly is.

Power over Death

The one irreversible feature of human life is death. But in two notable acts that pointed to His own death and resurrection, Jesus showed His

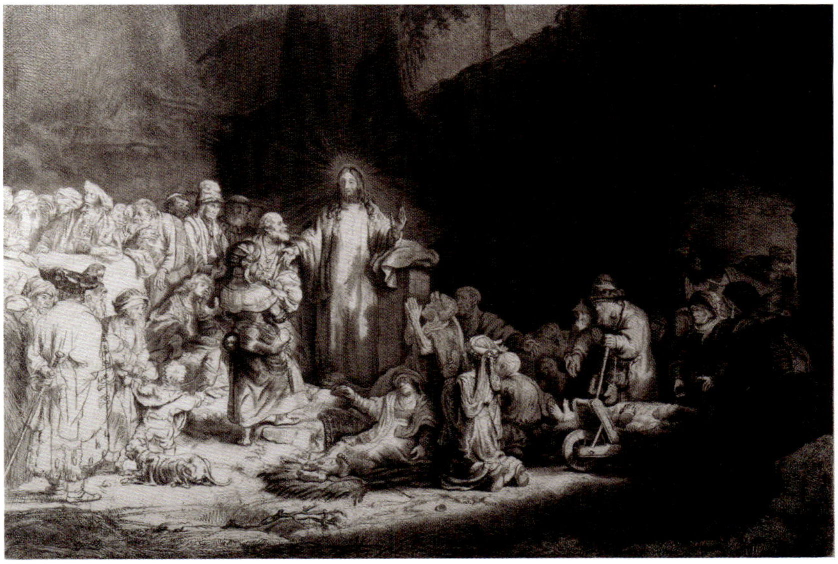

Figure 39. Rembrandt Harmenszoon van Rijn (1606–1669), *Christ Healing the Sick (The Hundred Guilder Print)*, ca. 1643–49, drypoint and burin, 11 1/8 x 15 1/2 inches. Private collection of Shawn and Andrea Merriman.

unequaled power to reverse the effects of death by restoring life. In the first case, narrated only by Luke, Jesus arrived at the town of Nain, which lies twenty miles uphill from Capernaum, just as a funeral procession was exiting the town. There, astonishingly, He raised the dead man to life. As background, on the day before, Jesus had healed a Roman centurion's servant who was gravely ill in Capernaum (see Luke 7:1–10). Then, apparently traveling through much of the night, He arrived just as neighbors were carrying the dead man, the only son of his widowed mother, to a burial place. In this light, much may be said about Jesus' knowledge of the widow's desperate situation and His evident compassion for her. In a tender act, Jesus approached the procession and said to the grieving woman, "Weep not," then "touched the bier: and they that bare him stood still. And he said, Young man, I say unto thee, Arise. And he that was dead sat up." Understandably, "there came a fear on all [the townspeople]: and they glorified God" (Luke 7:13–16). It was an unforgettable moment for the disciples; it was another disclosure of who Jesus is.

The second instance centers on Jesus' friend Lazarus, a citizen of the town of Bethany, which lay two miles east of Jerusalem over the Mount of Olives. According to John's Gospel, Lazarus became seriously ill, and his sisters sent word to Jesus, who was staying with disciples on the other side of the Jordan River, far from Bethany (see John 10:40).

When Jesus and His followers first heard of Lazarus' illness, Jesus commented, "This sickness is not unto death, but for the glory of God," meaning that Lazarus would not remain dead and that his resuscitation would point to God's glory. To His disciples' astonishment, Jesus inexplicably made no immediate effort to go to Bethany to see His friend but remained where He was for another two days. Then He began the long trek to Bethany, declaring to His followers, "Lazarus is dead" (John 11:4, 14).

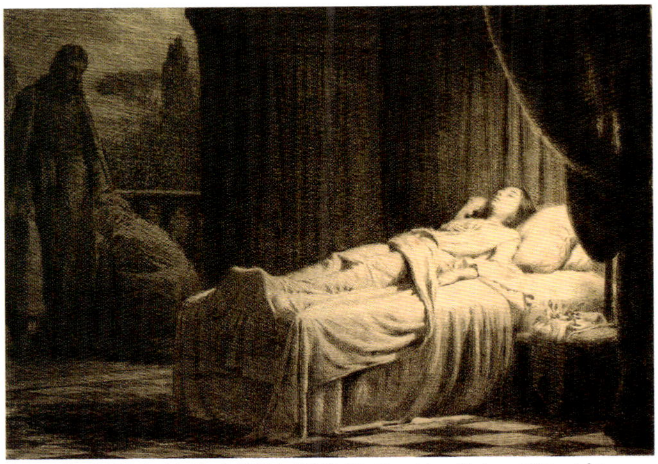

Figure 40. Carl Heinrich Bloch (1834–1890), *The Daughter of Jairus*, 1881, etching, 8 15/16 x 5 15/16 inches. Brigham Young University Museum of Art, purchased with funds provided by Robert and Lisa Wheatley.

When the party arrived in Bethany, they were told that Lazarus had indeed passed away—"four days" before their arrival, a period that in local belief meant his spirit had truly departed. When Jesus listened to Lazarus' sisters' lament about the loss of their brother, their sorrow must have weighed heavily on Jesus' soul, even though He knew what He would do. At last, He and the sisters went to the burial cave where Jesus ordered bystanders to take away the stone that lay across the entrance. Then, after praying, "he cried with a loud voice, Lazarus, come forth. And he that was dead came forth." Jesus once again had demonstrated His power over death by restoring life, pointing unmistakably to His own resurrection (see John 11:4–43).

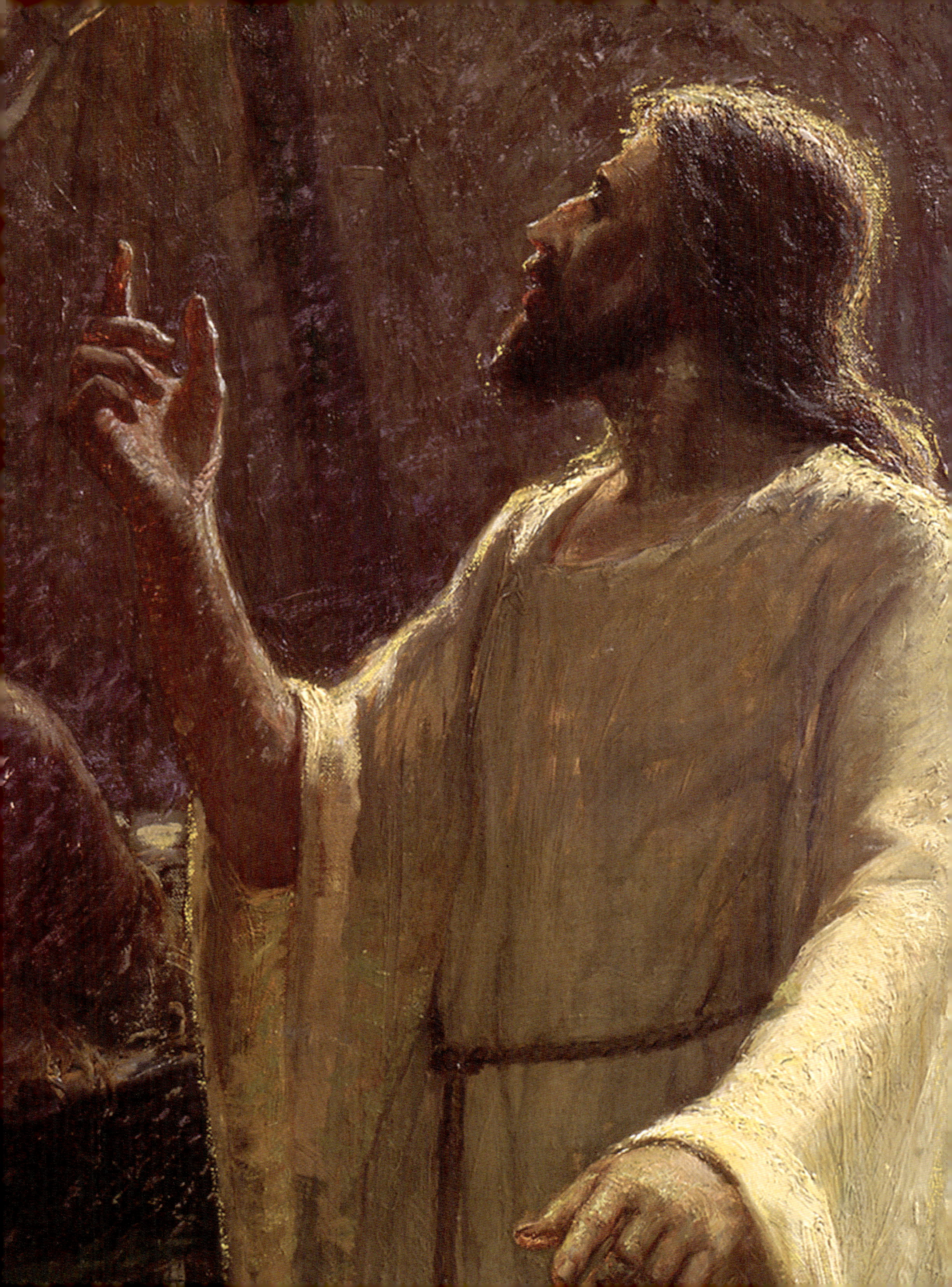

Chapter 7

Notable Moments

The Visitor came unrecognized into a village of lower Galilee called Capernaum, located on the edge of the northwestern shore of the freshwater lake. Villagers whom He passed most likely did not take notice as He walked along one of the narrow paths between small family dwellings that defined their town.

Any Visitor to Galilee would have instantly recognized that this was a Jewish village, constructed with basalt rock that is ubiquitous in the region. The architecture of the town stood in stark contrast to those places that displayed the typical characteristics of Greco-Roman culture across the Mediterranean world.

The visitor to Capernaum looked just like the residents—a poor Jewish laborer with calloused hands from years of hard work with stone and wood. But in their synagogue He spoke about a kingdom. They already knew about empires and kingdoms and authority and power, but, as He preached about the kingdom beyond this world, His words caused them to reflect that He was talking about something significantly different.

Present in the crowd was one poor soul, tormented by an unclean spirit, who cried out to the man. The man rebuked the unclean spirit, saying, "Hold thy peace, and come out of him" (Mark 1:25). When the spirit came out, the people "were all amazed, insomuch that they questioned among themselves, saying, What thing is this? what new doctrine is this? for with authority commandeth he even the unclean spirits, and they do obey him" (Mark 1:27). The Man who taught and healed was Jesus of Nazareth.

Those who met Jesus along the way and who opened their hearts, minds, and hands to Him were changed forever. Many of the resulting notable moments, including the one of His driving out the unclean spirit and events that followed, were recalled, remembered, and recorded.

The Calling of the Twelve

Early in His ministry, Jesus went into a mountain in Galilee "and calleth unto him whom he would: and they came unto him" (Mark 3:13). From those who began to follow Him, "he ordained twelve, that they should be with him, and that he might send them forth to preach" (Mark 3:14).

The Apostle Paul and the authors of the Gospels agree that Jesus created an inner circle of disciples commonly known as "the Twelve." They distinguished themselves from the other followers of Jesus because they had been specially chosen to participate in Jesus' ministry and were being prepared to lead the Church after His ascension into heaven.

However, even among the Twelve, three—Peter, James, and John—enjoyed a favored relationship with Jesus. They received special training and were included as witnesses of some of the most notable experiences in the Savior's ministry, including the raising of the daughter of Jairus and the Transfiguration (Figure 47); these three were also invited to be especially close to Jesus when He prayed in Gethsemane (see Mark 5:37–43; 9:2–8; 14:33–40).

Jesus' impact on people is demonstrated by the remarkable willingness of the Twelve to leave their occupations to literally follow Him. In doing so, they were transformed from common laborers, fishermen, and members of the royal bureaucracy to become Jesus' Twelve Apostles.

James Taylor Harwood (1860–1940), detail of *Come Follow Me*, 1922, oil on canvas, 51 x 41 ½ inches. Museum of Church History and Art.

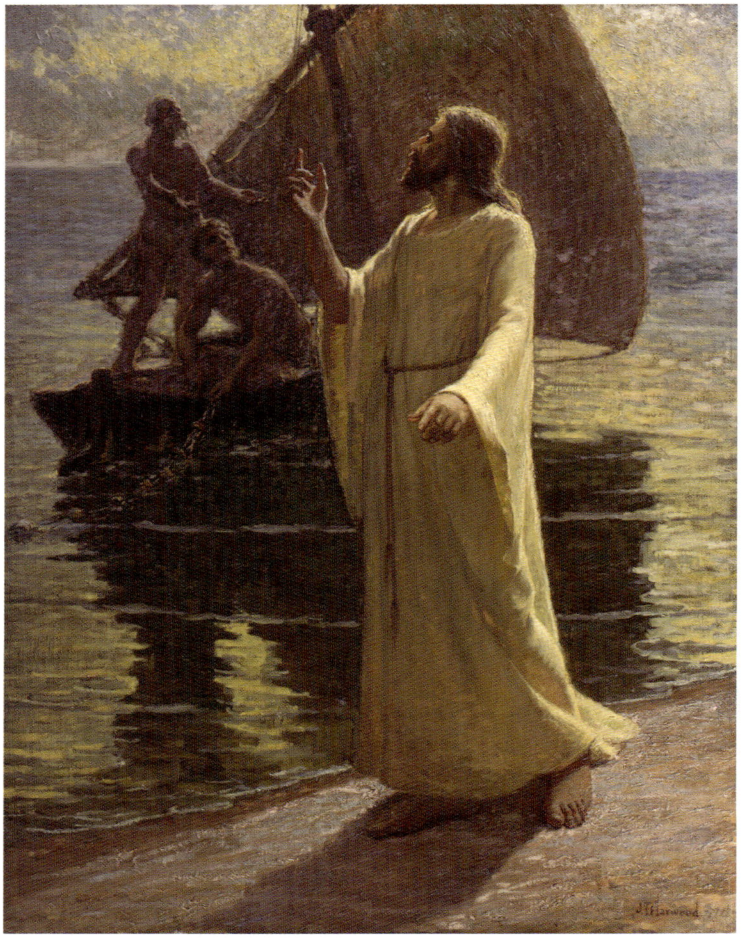

Figure 41. James Taylor Harwood (1860–1940), *Come Follow Me*, 1922, oil on canvas, 51 x 41½ inches. Museum of Church History and Art.

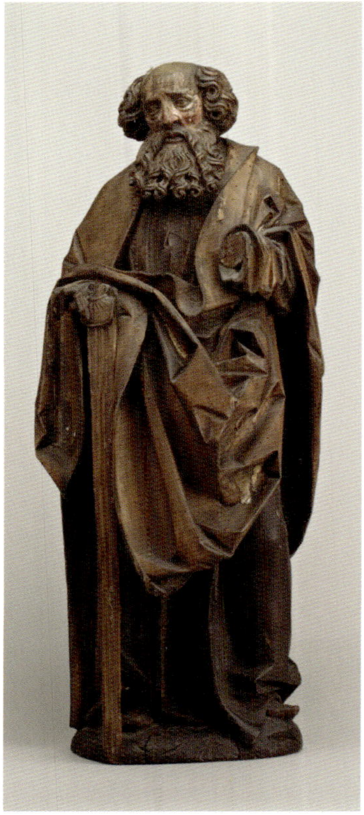

Figure 42. Workshop of Viet Stoss, *Saint* [Paul], late 15th century, wood, 34¼ x 15 inches. Brigham Young University Museum of Art, purchase/gift from Gloria Teichert, funds provided by Jack R. and Mary Lois Wheatley.

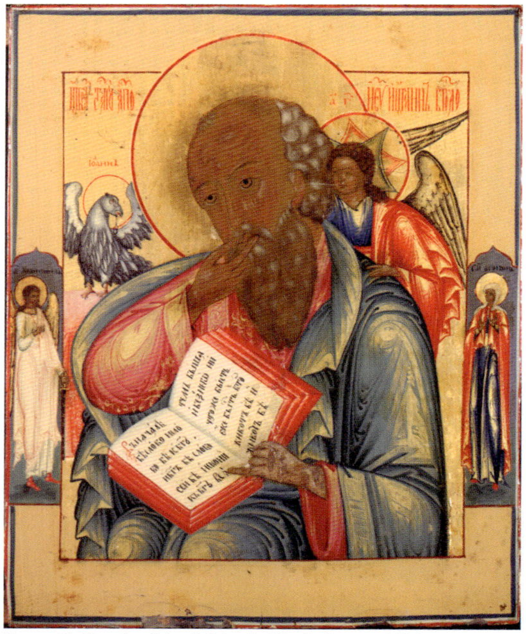

Figure 43. Yaroslav School, *John the Theologian*, ca. 1820, tempera on panel, 12⅛ x 10 1/16 x 1 inches. Brigham Young University Museum of Art, gift of Mr. and Mrs. Richard B. Oliver.

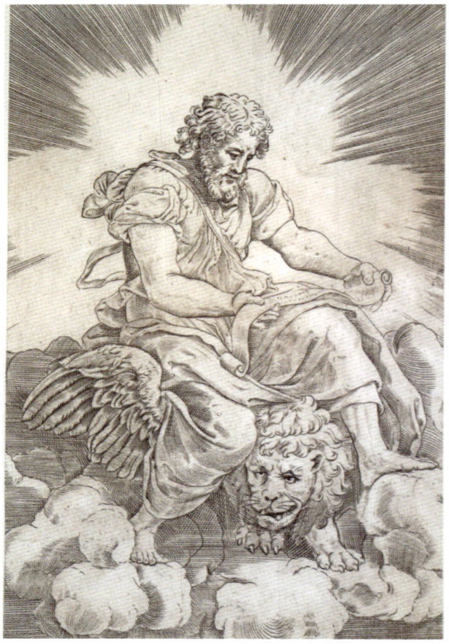

Figure 44. Anonymous, *St. Mark* (after Giulio Romano), 16th century, engraving, 8 x 5⅝ inches. Brigham Young University Museum of Art, purchase/gift from Mahonri M. Young Estate.

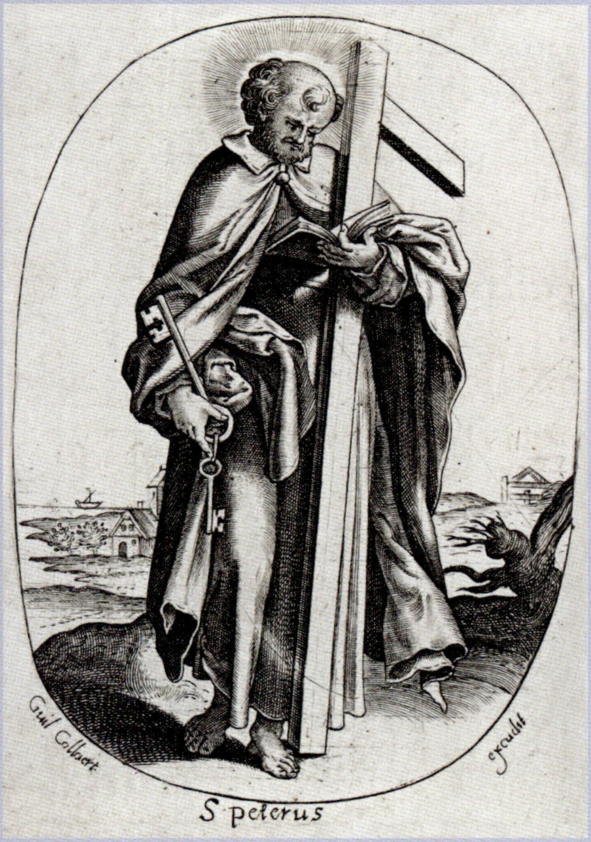

Figure 45. Guilliam Collaert (active 17th century), *St. Peter*, ca. 1650, etching, 3 9/16 x 2 9/16 inches. Brigham Young University Museum of Art, purchase/gift from Mahonri M. Young Estate.

Distinguishing Disciples

The apostles and other disciples often appear in company with Jesus in scenes of His ministry. For their identity to be recognized, artists developed specific motifs to distinguish these religious figures.[1] For instance, Peter is often depicted as an elderly, bearded man with a tonsure of white hair. Usually clothed in a blue or green robe with a gold mantle (Figure 46), he holds two keys (Figure 45), which symbolize the priesthood power that binds on earth and in heaven (see Matthew 16:19). The Apostle Paul is portrayed as a brown-bearded man holding a sword, the instrument of his martyrdom (Figure 42). Mary Magdalene, unfavorably regarded as a penitent prostitute and traditionally misinterpreted as the woman who washed Jesus' feet at the house of Simon the Pharisee (see Luke 7:37), is shown with long, flowing tresses and an alabaster jar (Figure 50).

Attributes were also assigned to each of the four Evangelists.[2] Matthew is often shown writing his Gospel at a desk, inspired by an angel or winged man. Mark is accompanied by a winged lion because his Gospel emphasizes the royal nature of Christ—"Lion to the house of Judah" (Hosea 5:14) (Figure 44). The ox, an animal sacrificed as a peace offering, is associated with Luke because his Gospel begins with a sacrificial ordinance in the temple. John is represented by an eagle, a symbol of divine inspiration by which he wrote the book of Revelation (Figure 43).[3]

1. These distinguishing attributes originated in the Byzantine era and were recorded in medieval painters' manuals. The use of such guidebooks continued through the eighteenth century when Dionysius of Fourna, a Greek monk and painter, produced the *Hermeneia*, one of the best known artists' manuals. In addition to prescribing conventions that represent holy beings and sacred events, this manuscript exhorted artists to develop their God-given talents, lest they fall under "condemnation [as] slothful servant[s]" (Dionysius of Fourna, *The Painter's Manual of Dionysius of Fourna*, trans. Paul Hetherington [London: Sagittarius Press, 1974], I–IV, 2).
2. The emblematic winged beings derive from visions recorded in Revelation 4:7–8 and Ezekiel 1:10–11.
3. George Ferguson, *Signs & Symbols in Christian Art* (New York: Oxford University Press, 1959), 75, 78–79, 81, and Duchet-Suchaux, *Bible and the Saints*, 140–41, 197, 221, 228–29, 240–41.

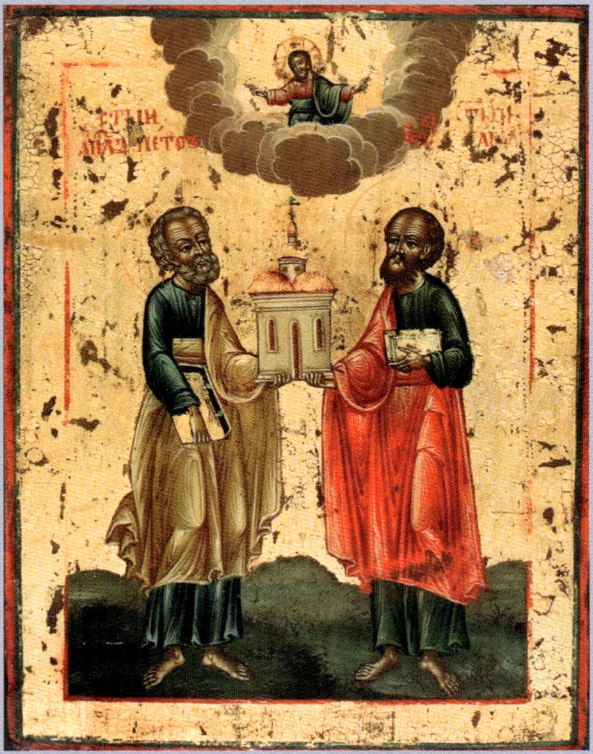

Figure 46. Russian icon, *Saints Peter and Paul*, ca. 1820, tempera on panel, 11 x 8 9/16 x 13/16 inches. Brigham Young University Museum of Art, gift of Mr. and Mrs. Richard B. Oliver.

The Transfiguration

Matthew, Mark, and Luke record in some detail an incident that took place upon a mountain where Jesus and His three chief disciples went to pray and where Jesus was transfigured (see Matthew 17:1–8; Mark 9:2–8; Luke 9:28–36). Peter, who was present on that transcendent occasion, recalls the events in his "farewell" letter (see 2 Peter 1:16–18). By all these accounts, the Transfiguration was one of the most important events in Jesus' mortal ministry and was orchestrated for the benefit of the disciples.

Because Mark's Gospel preserves Peter's reminiscences and, therefore, stands the closest to an eyewitness account of this event, we note his introduction: "And after six days Jesus taketh with him Peter, and James, and John, and leadeth them up into an high mountain apart." Finding themselves alone on this unnamed mountain, they were witnesses to Jesus, who "was transfigured before them. And his raiment became shining, exceeding white as snow; so as no fuller on earth can white them" (Mark 9:2–3). Clearly, these events were a stirring testimony of the divinity of Jesus. In this connection, we observe that Mark commences his Gospel with a dramatic announcement: "The beginning of the gospel of Jesus Christ, *the Son of God,*" boldly declaring Christ's divine lineage (Mark 1:1; emphasis added). Significantly, the Transfiguration account affirms this declaration, with the three disciples as witnesses, when they hear the voice of God declaring, "This is my beloved Son" (Mark 9:7).

One important reason for preserving this story is to demonstrate that Jesus, from a human point of view, was very ordinary, but He was, in fact, extraordinary, even divine. Those who met Jesus knew He spoke a Galilean dialect of Aramaic, the common language of His world. He ate the common food of His day and dressed in the common fashion. Chiseled into Jesus' mature face and imprinted onto His hands and feet must have been the effects of a village life of hard work, including extensive walking and manual labor. No one would have taken particular notice of Jesus without being prompted by the Spirit (see Luke 2:26–30), something Isaiah prophesied when he said of the coming Messiah, "He hath no form nor comeliness; and when we shall see him, there is no beauty that we should desire him" (Isaiah 53:2). Until His ministry of preaching, teaching, and healing brought Him notoriety, He did not attract undue attention. But this recognition was apparently not based on any special physical features; it was based on His words and deeds (see Acts 10:38). In other words, Jesus probably looked like many other first-century Mediterranean Jews.

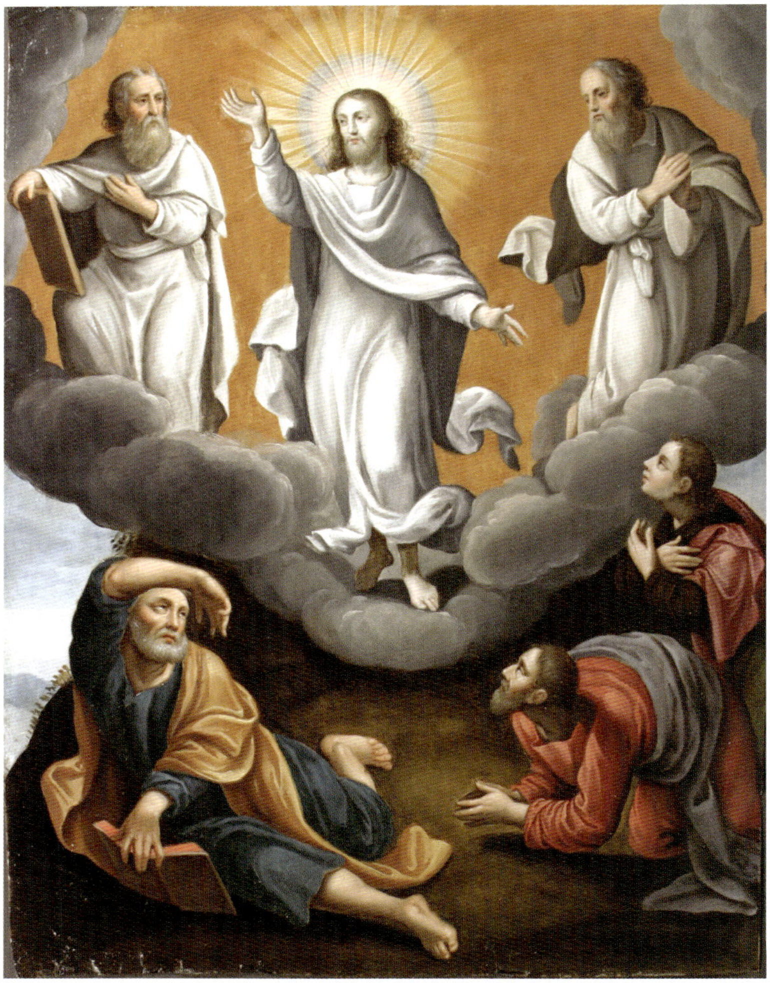

Figure 47. Anonymous (Spanish), *Transfiguration*, 17th century, oil on copper, 15¾ x 12 3/16 inches. Brigham Young University Museum of Art, gift of Jack Hopkinson.

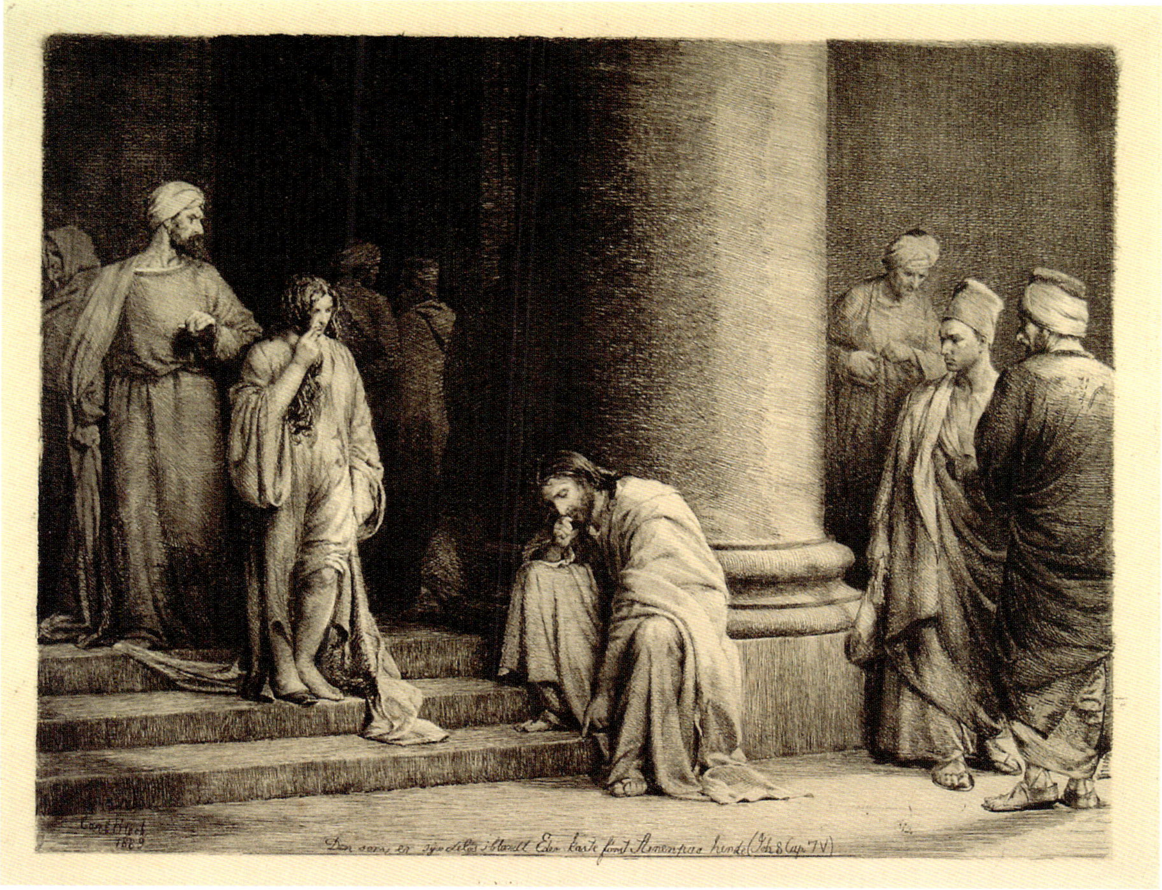

Figure 48. Carl Heinrich Bloch (1834–1890), *Christ and the Woman Taken in Adultery*, 1889, etching, 7¾ x 10 1/16 inches. Brigham Young University Museum of Art, purchased with funds provided by Robert and Lisa Wheatley.

Mark graphically reveals that the ordinary-looking son of a village carpenter was "transfigured." Jesus' glory revealed Him as God's "beloved Son," setting Him apart from all other humans. In an almost other-worldly note, we read that a cloud "overshadowed them: and a voice came out of the cloud, saying, This is my beloved Son" (Mark 9:7).

The Transfiguration also highlights Jesus' authority to interpret and add to Jewish scripture. In the absence of a prophet in Israel, various individuals or groups claimed exclusive privilege to interpret scripture. The Transfiguration answered the question definitively about who was empowered to interpret scripture and to speak for God. We note that Moses, representing the law, and Elijah, representing the prophets, were present on the mountain (see Mark 9:4). But the voice informs the disciples that they are to listen to Jesus, as we read, "This is my beloved Son: *hear him*" (Mark 9:7; emphasis added). The scene, adorned with the presence of Moses and Elijah and punctuated by God's voice, points to Jesus as God's mouthpiece, authorized to bring understanding to His recorded word and to present God's word anew.

Following the appearance of Elijah, Moses, and the cloud, Mark notes, "Suddenly, when they [Peter, James, and John] had looked round about, they saw no man any more, save Jesus only" (Mark 9:8). In one sense, the sight of Jesus alone underscores His superiority over the law and the prophets—their days had ended, and now was the time of the "beloved Son."

The Woman Taken in Adultery

The dramatic story about the woman taken in adultery could be called "Scribes, Pharisees, and a Woman," because it focuses on each (see John 8:1–11). The first scene of this important account bristles with drama. "Early in the morning he came again into the temple, and all the people came

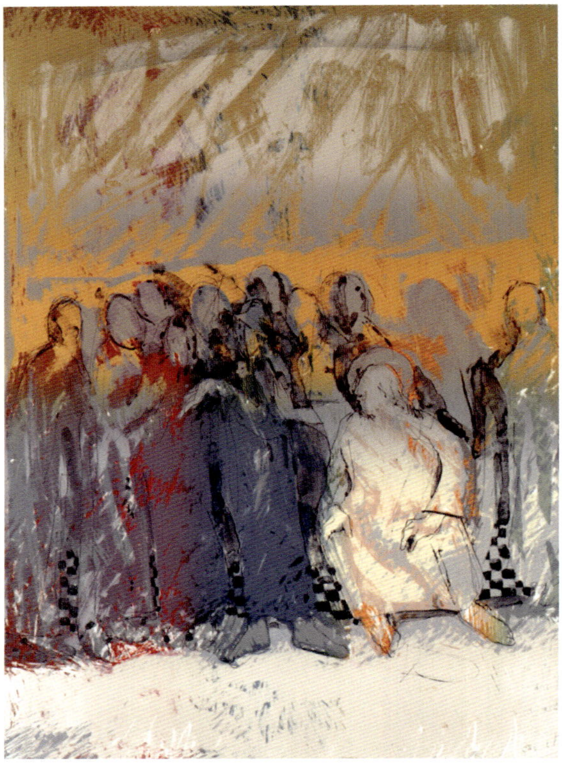

Figure 49. Bruce H. Smith (b. 1936), *Bait*, 1993, lithograph, 29¾ x 21⅞ inches. Brigham Young University Museum of Art.

unto him; and he sat down, and taught them. And the scribes and Pharisees brought unto him a woman taken in adultery; and when they had set her in the midst, They say unto him, Master, this woman was taken in adultery, in the very act" (John 8:2–4).

The absence of the man she had been with has often caught the attention of commentators. It seems that the officials were not interested in the woman but were interested in using her as a tool to entrap Jesus: "This they said, tempting him, that they might have to accuse him" (John 8:6). In this sense, they had arrogantly dehumanized her, turning her into an object for debate and discussion. Once and for all, Jesus challenged such attitudes in one of the most quiet but powerful scenes preserved in the New Testament.

Perhaps oddly, Jesus bent down and wrote on the ground with His finger, "as though he heard them not" (John 8:6). The later tradition that He wrote the names of those present and their sins is a fanciful creation to add color to a story that does not need any additional paint.

When the scribes and Pharisees continued to press Him for an answer, Jesus stood and addressed them directly, "He that is without sin among you, let him first cast a stone at her" (John 8:7). After Jesus finished this famous saying, "again he stooped down, and wrote on the ground" (John 8:8).

When the mean-spirited individuals in the crowd heard Him, they silently began to leave, "convicted by their own conscience" (John 8:9). Eventually, everyone was gone, leaving only Jesus and the woman. No pen or artist's brush can adequately capture the pathos of the moment—a sinful daughter of Abraham cowering before the sinless Son of God.

Jesus eventually stood up again and tenderly inquired, "Woman, where are those thine accusers? hath no man condemned thee?" and when she acknowledged all had gone, He replied, "Neither do I condemn thee: go, and sin no more" (John 8:10–11). In this tender and dramatic scene, depicting Jesus' unwillingness to condone the sin while forgiving the transgressor, John has left us a powerful testimony of the Master's perfect ability to balance justice and mercy.

The Woman Washing Jesus' Feet

Surprisingly, Jesus was invited to the home of a Pharisee named Simon to share a meal (see Luke 7:36–50). Rather than sitting, the guests and host reclined, typical of the period, at a low-level table that allowed them to stretch out their feet behind as they rested on an arm, typically the left arm, to partake of the meal set for them. In the first century, the home was a rather public place where people entered at will through open doors to visit and converse.

While Jesus, Simon, and the guests were eating, an unnamed woman—who should be distinguished from the women mentioned by Mark (see Mark 14:3–9) and John (see John 12:1–8)—came into the house, carrying "an alabaster box of ointment," which she used to anoint the reclining Savior's feet. Before doing so, she had "wash[ed] his feet with tears, and [wiped] them with the hairs of her head, and kissed his feet" (Luke 7:38).

Given the woman's reputation as a sinner, Simon was offended by the Savior's willingness to allow her to perform these somewhat audacious acts of kindness: "Now when the Pharisee which had bidden him saw it, he spake within himself, saying, This man, if he were a prophet, would have known who and what manner of woman this is that toucheth him" (Luke 7:39).

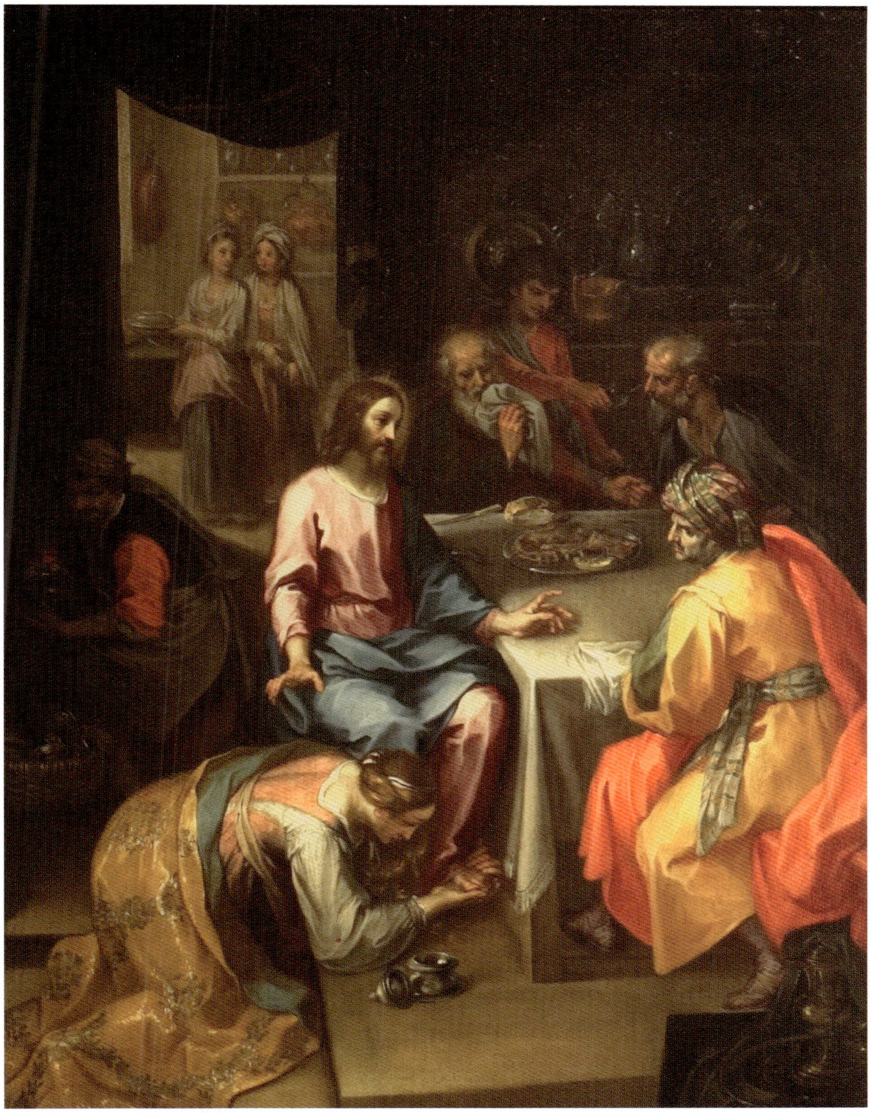

Figure 50. Francesco Vanni (1563–1610), *Christ in the House of Simon the Pharisee*, 1600, oil on canvas, 45 3/4 x 35 1/2 inches, gift of Robert B. Mayer, Snite Museum of Art, University of Notre Dame.

Jesus responded to the man's unspoken challenge by presenting one of His most loving parables—the parable of the two debtors (see Luke 7:41–43). In contrasting the debtors, Jesus made sure Simon understood that the one owed five hundred pence, which would take a common laborer five hundred days to earn. The other, Jesus stated, owed only fifty pence, a significantly lesser amount. The creditor, who found out that neither had anything to repay the debt, "frankly forgave them both" (Luke 7:42).

Then Jesus asked Simon, "Tell me therefore, which of them will love [the creditor] most?" (Luke 7:42). The answer was obvious; anyone at the meal could have responded correctly. Simon says what everyone must have been thinking: "I suppose that he, to whom he forgave most" (Luke 7:43).

Jesus acknowledged the correctness of Simon's response and then applied the parable to the situation at hand: "Seest thou this woman? I entered into thine house, thou gavest me no water for my feet: but she hath washed my feet with tears, and wiped them with the hairs of her head. . . . My head with oil thou didst not anoint: but this woman hath anointed my feet with ointment" (Luke 7:44–46).

Then Jesus came to the heart of the matter: "Her sins, which are many, are forgiven; for she loved much: but to whom little is forgiven, the same loveth little" (Luke 7:47). At this point Jesus turned from Simon to the woman: "And he said unto her, Thy sins are forgiven. . . . Thy faith hath saved thee; go in peace" (Luke 7:48, 50).

Each of the above incidents treasures up a precious moment that has been cherished and retold countless times; all were eventually recorded and preserved in the New Testament, allowing us to be present during some of the notable events that happened so many years ago when Jesus walked among us.

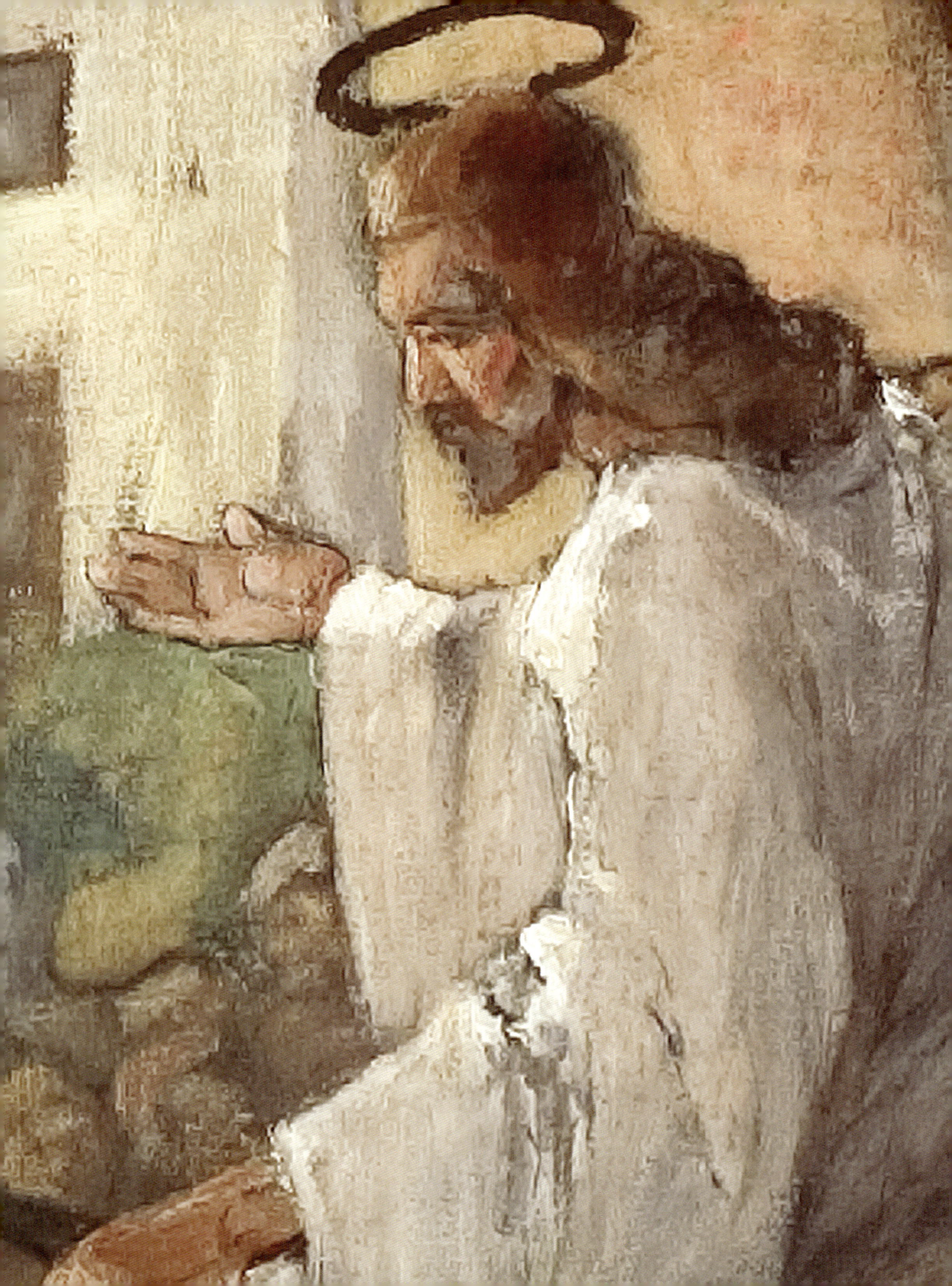

Chapter 8

In Jerusalem for the Last Time

In New Testament times, Passover was a joyful holiday that was anticipated annually. Jews from around the Mediterranean basin and the Near East made their way to the Holy City to celebrate this special day in the temple. Those left behind recalled and remembered in song and word and feasting what Jehovah had done for Israel so long before in their escape from ancient Egypt.

Jerusalem thronged with people during springtime, usually in March and April, who spoke different languages and dialects and who lived in scattered towns, cities, and even countries. However, these pilgrims who traveled to the temple for the special occasion of Passover were inseparably bound together by three commonly held commitments—their loyalties to Jehovah, the Torah, and the temple.

They came because the Lord commanded them in the Torah to come to Jerusalem to remember and worship. In the book of Deuteronomy they were instructed: "Remember that thou wast a servant in the land of Egypt, and that the Lord thy God brought thee out thence through a mighty hand and by a stretched out arm" (Deuteronomy 5:15). Additionally, the Lord commanded them to appear before Him at the temple on three annual occasions, including the Passover (see Exodus 23:14–17).

This holy day did help them remember—it was a sacred celebration reminding them who they were and what the Lord had done. Yet it also reminded them of their current political status—most of them lived in the Roman Empire and were subject to Roman authority and law. In the Promised Land, Jews lived under direct Roman control or were subject to one of Rome's client-kings. Many hoped for the coming of the Messiah, the "anointed" descendant of David, whom they hoped and prayed would deliver them and set up an independent kingdom of Israel again. It was in this setting that Jesus made His way to Jerusalem for the last time.

Triumphal Entry

According to the Gospels, Jesus rode a donkey, a symbol of kingship, on the final segment of a long journey that brought Him to Jerusalem at the time of Passover (Figure 51). When people heard that Jesus was on the way, they began to gather and "took branches of palm trees, and went forth to meet him" (John 12:13). In a scene that has inspired countless authors and painters, Jesus moved slowly among the throng with His face set toward Jerusalem to fulfill a mission of ultimate redemption. The scene is full of movement, noise, and action, with the people shouting, "Hosanna: Blessed is the King of Israel that cometh in the name of the Lord" (John 12:13).

Men, women, and children witnessed the fulfillment of ancient prophecy and seemingly could not contain themselves for joy (see Zechariah 9:9). Even those who had neither met Him nor heard Him preach knew about Jesus of Nazareth; they were aware of His amazing words and deeds. As they accompanied Jesus to Jerusalem, His jealous enemies also watched with envy: "Behold, the world is gone after him," they muttered (John 12:19).

Jesus knew this was an important moment

Minerva K. Teichert (1888–1976), detail of *Christ Entering Jerusalem*, 1916, oil on canvas, 58 1/4 x 40 inches. Museum of Church History and Art.

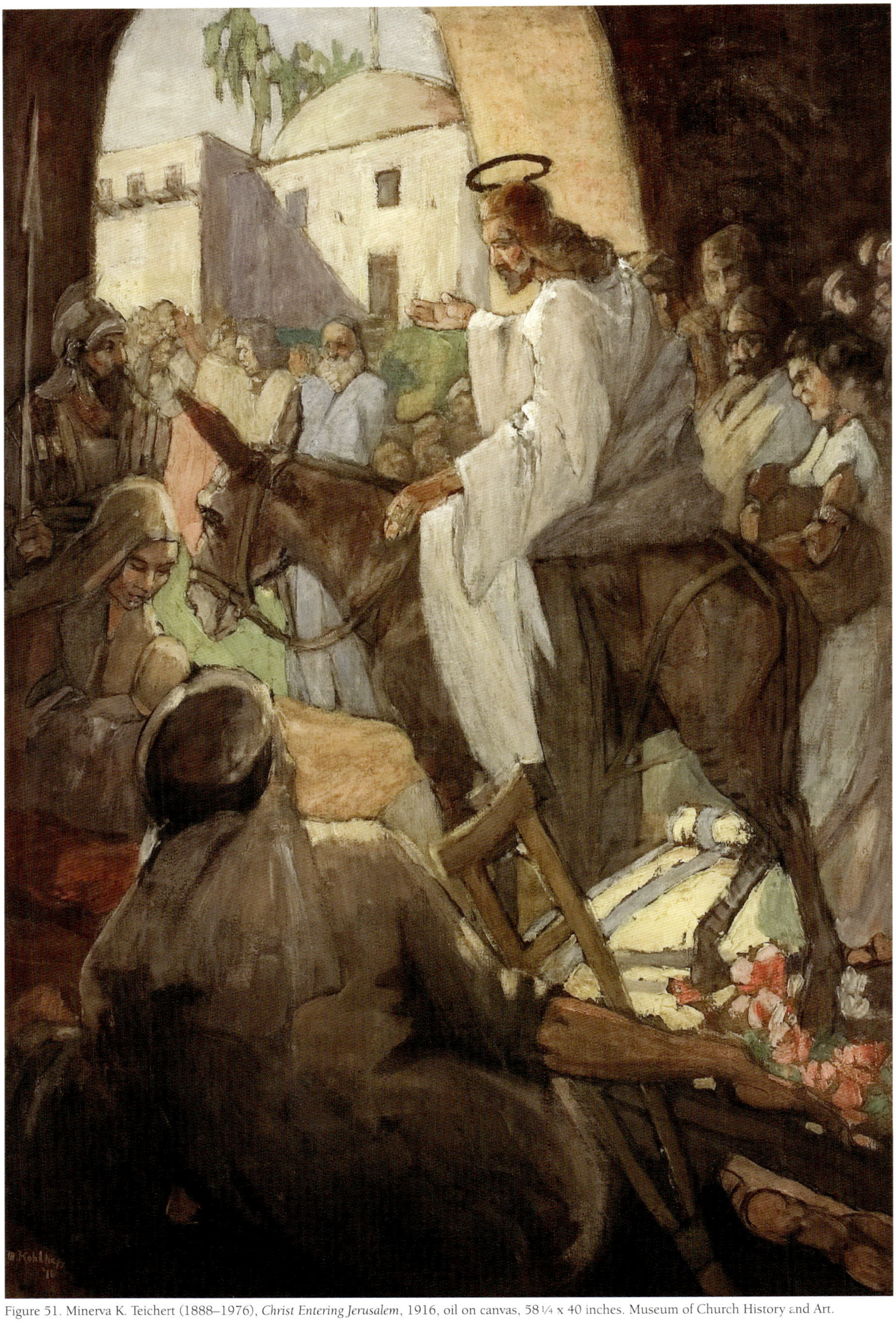

Figure 51. Minerva K. Teichert (1888–1976), *Christ Entering Jerusalem*, 1916, oil on canvas, 58 1/4 x 40 inches. Museum of Church History and Art.

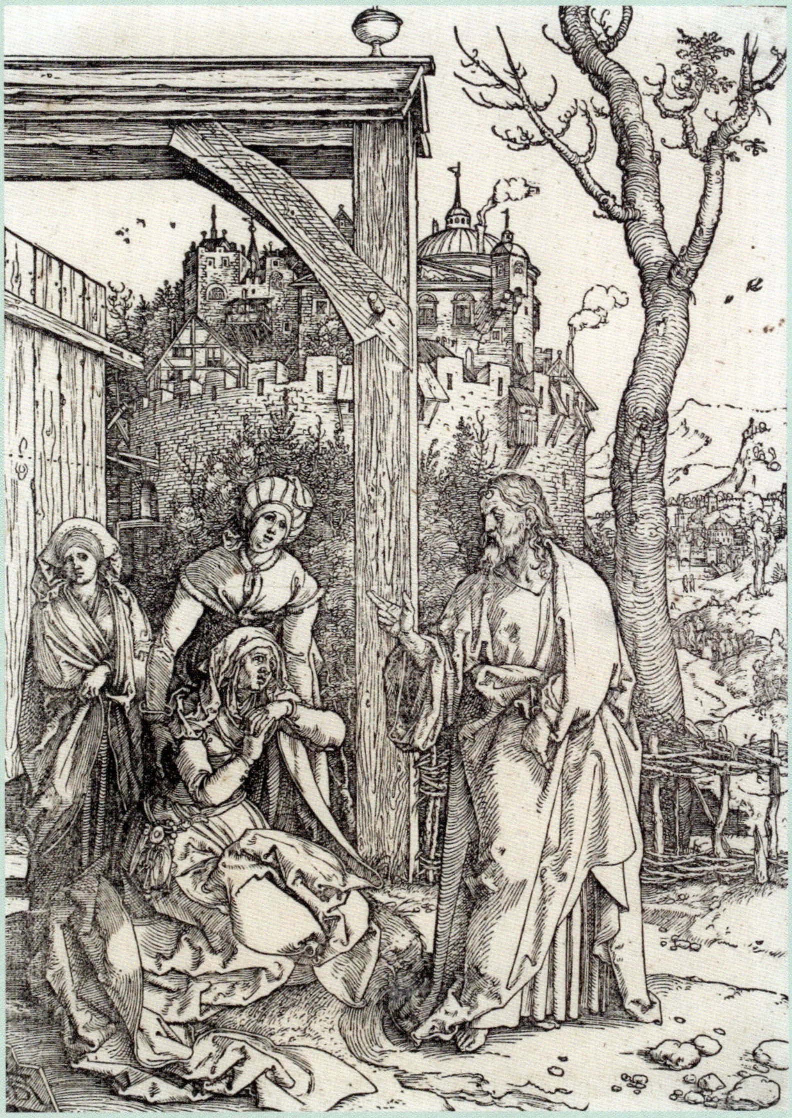

Figure 52. Albrecht Dürer (1471–1528), *Christ Taking Leave of His Mother,* from the *Life of the Virgin*, 1504–1505, woodcut, 11⅝ x 8³⁄₁₆ inches. Brigham Young University Museum of Art, purchase/gift from Mahonri M. Young Estate.

From Another Point of View

As we ponder how the disciples regarded their Lord, how Lazarus esteemed his friend, or how Mary felt about her Son, the Savior becomes a real figure with familial relationships and human experiences. This idea can be explored in Albrecht Dürer's series *Life of the Virgin*, which contains scenes of Christ's life as experienced by His mother.[1] In the intimate and anecdotal woodcut *Christ Taking Leave of His Mother* (Figure 52), Jesus gestures a sign of blessing to the grief-stricken Mary as He makes His way to the walled city of Jerusalem in the lofty distance. The large post of the gateway divides the compositional space, symbolically severing Jesus from His mother. She sinks to the ground in distress, anticipating the death of her Son. Her position prefigures her pose in Crucifixion scenes in which she collapses sorrowfully at the foot of the cross, tenderly supported by one of the Marys (Figure 76). In such scenes, artists emphasized the anguish of the Virgin, fulfilling Simeon's prophecy to Mary that "a sword shall pierce through thy own soul" (Luke 2:35). By considering the Savior's life through the eyes of those who interacted closely with Him, worshippers of Christ are better able to behold the magnitude of His sacrifice and further develop their relationship with Him.

1. Published in 1511, this series on the *Life of the Virgin* was composed of a title page and 19 woodcuts with Latin text written by Benedictus Chelidonius printed on the back of each print.

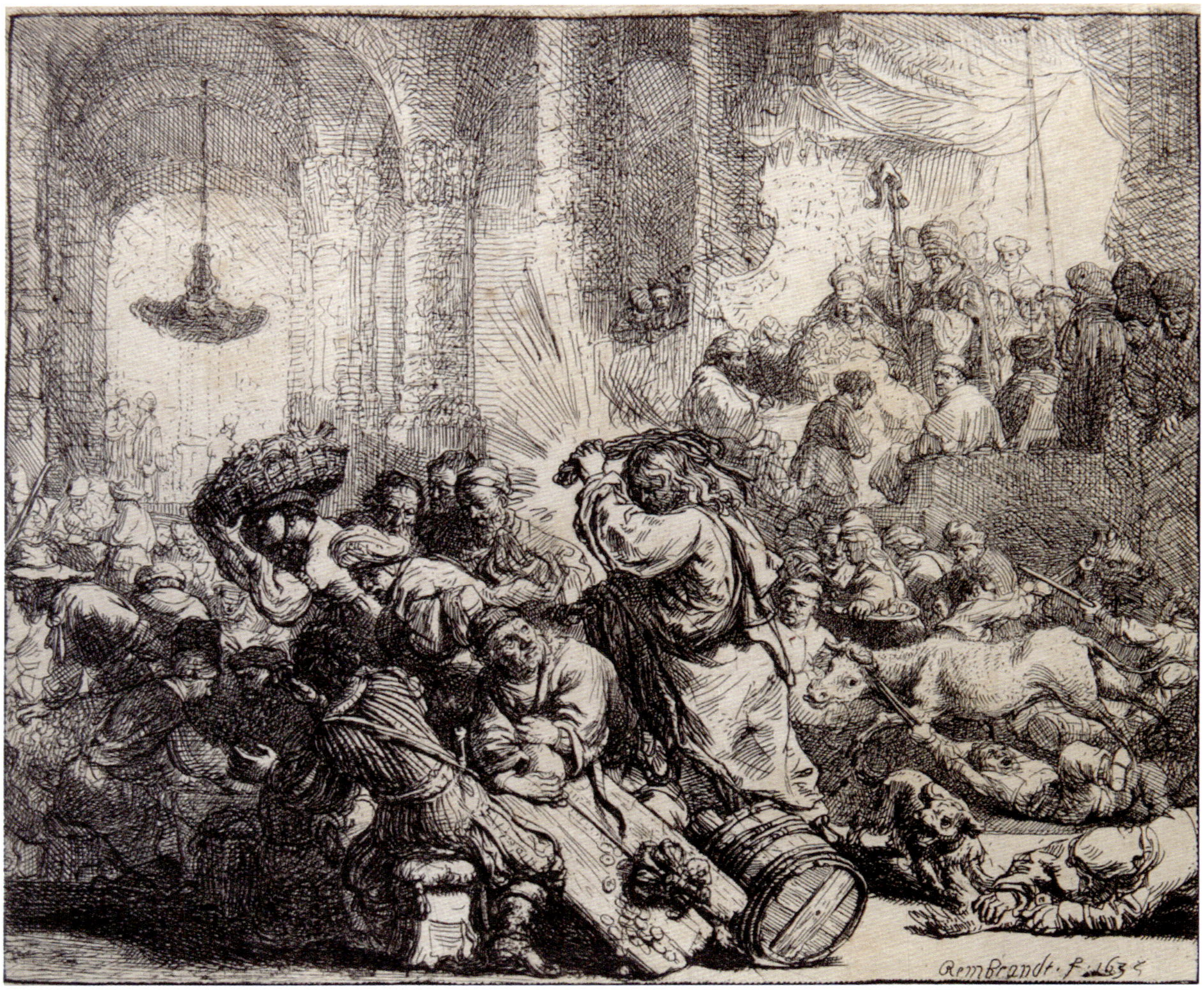

Figure 53. Rembrandt Harmenszoon van Rijn (1606–1669), *Christ Driving the Money Changers from the Temple*, 1635, etching, 5 7/16 x 6 3/4 inches. Private collection of Shawn and Andrea Merriman.

in His ministry that had begun with teaching and healing but that would now include suffering, death, and resurrection: "The hour is come, that the Son of man should be glorified," He observed (John 12:23).

The governor, Pilate, who lived in the provincial capital at Caesarea, came up to Jerusalem with his soldiers to watch over the feast. His arrival, and the visible presence of soldiers on the porticos overlooking the temple and throughout the city, were clear signs that Rome intended to keep Judea firmly under her eagle's wings. The waving of palm fronds by those accompanying Jesus, their shouts of biblical phrases, and the accompanying crush of the crowds as He and they entered one of the gates of the city undoubtedly came to the notice of the Romans.

At some point, the chief priests and some of the scribes and elders gathered to plan Jesus' arrest. Matthew reports that the conspirators "consulted that they might take Jesus by subtlety, and kill him" (Matthew 26:4). However, they agreed among themselves, "Not on the feast day, lest there be an uproar among the people" (Matthew 26:5).

They knew that Jesus was popular among the crowds. Even though many simply admired Him, others thought He was a prophet, and still others believed He was the long-awaited Messiah. Even then, those disciples who had confessed that He was the "anointed one" of God neither knew nor anticipated the events that would play out in Jerusalem by the end of the week.

We are not told exactly what happened, but apparently the Jewish leadership, with Roman authorization and knowledge, schemed to arrest Jesus at some point. Maybe they planned to wait for the highly emotional atmosphere that prevailed at Passover to dissipate, when the feast was completed and the crowded city had emptied of the masses. In the meantime, Jesus spent the next few days teaching in Jerusalem.

Teaching in the Temple

The synoptic Gospels report that it was during this time that Jesus entered the temple and cleansed it, apparently for a second time; John records an earlier cleansing (see John 2:13–17).

According to Luke, Jesus left the temple for the evening but returned on "one of those days" to teach again. Unlike the other Gospel accounts, Luke emphasizes that Jesus was "daily in the temple," preaching the good news of "the gospel" (Luke 19:47; 20:1; see also 21:37).

In fact, according to Luke, Jesus' ministry in Jerusalem was confined to teaching in the temple. Having assumed possession of the temple through His dramatic cleansing, Jesus now taught and preached in His Father's house. Eventually, in a tense and suspense-filled moment, Jesus was confronted by Jerusalem authorities, who demanded to know where He got the authority to do as He had done (see Luke 20:2).

Instead of immediately answering them or challenging their authority, He posed a counter question: "The baptism of John, was it from heaven, or of men?" (Luke 20:4). Sensing the dilemma and realizing the possible reaction of onlookers if they were to answer in a way that challenged John's authority, they refused to respond directly to the question. Obviously, if they accepted John's commission from God—John having declared Jesus to be greater than himself—such an acceptance would imply that they believed Jesus had been called of God to proclaim the "good news."

It must have been striking for those present to hear Him speak a parable about "a certain man" who planted a vineyard (see Luke 20:9–16). In telling the parable, Jesus predicts that, following the killing of the son by wicked tenants, the owner of the vineyard will come and destroy those murderous tenant farmers. The chief priests who opposed Jesus couldn't mistake the parable—it applied to them (see Luke 20:19).

The onlookers, when they hear of the coming destruction, pray that it will not happen. They are affected, nevertheless, by what their leaders do, and the conquest of Jerusalem will mean suffering or death for all its inhabitants.

Much earlier, Luke portrays the young twelve-year-old Jesus in the temple. Then Jesus had said to His mother and Joseph, "How is it that ye sought me? wist ye not that I must be about my Father's business?" (Luke 2:49). Now, at the end of His ministry and His life, Jesus was still about His Father's business by teaching, preaching, and healing as He prepared for the final act of His mission—the Atonement. For example, in the shadows of the temple, Jesus provides memorable teachings, including the saying about paying taxes to Caesar (see Luke 20:20–26) and the story of the widow's mite (see Luke 21:1–4).

Memorable and *amazing* may best describe Jesus' teachings during His final days in the temple.

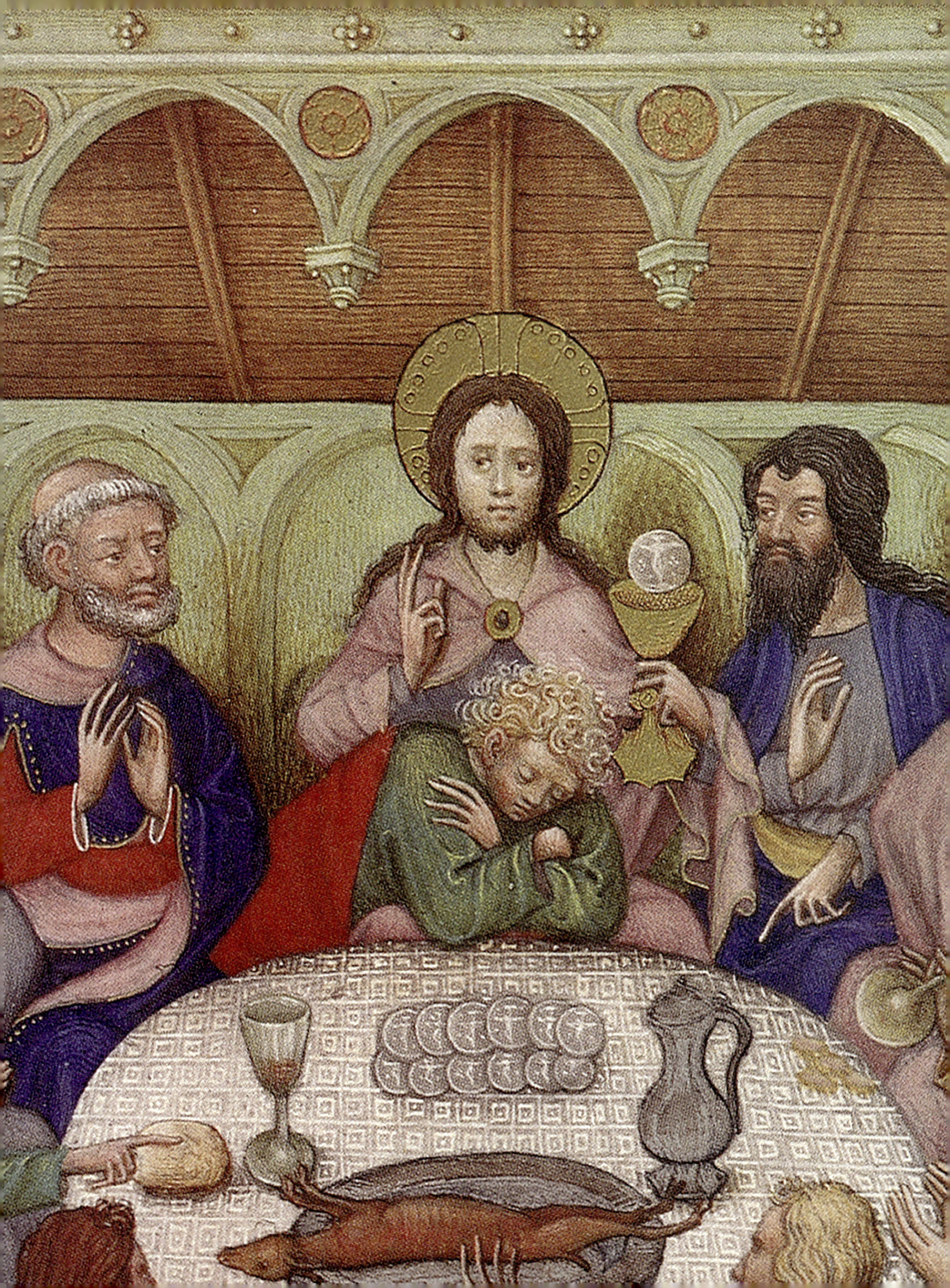

Chapter 9

The Last Supper

As an event, the Last Supper was a traditional meal celebrating the Passover. But in the Gospel accounts, every word, every act, and every miracle of Jesus point to this moment. Somewhere in Jerusalem, Jesus spent His last evening with His most trusted, most beloved disciples in "a large upper room" (Mark 14:15). The Coenaculum, a place name based on Jerome's *Latin Vulgate* term for upper room, and the name of the site most often identified as the original setting, is located on the southern spur of the upper city, on Mount Zion, between Herod's palace and the Gate of the Essenes. The spot was marked in Constantine's time by the Church of Holy Sion and appears on the "Madaba Map," the oldest extant map of the Holy Land. Tourists today visit an upper room in a building dating from the Crusader period; however, large, hewn stones called "ashlars," dating from the Roman period (which might have originally been Herodian temple stones that the Romans reused after destroying the temple), are located in the foundation of the building. Although standing just outside the Old City near Zion's Gate, this location was well within the ancient city walls of the first century.

What did Jesus and His friends eat on this important occasion? Was their meal a traditional Passover meal? These questions have held the interest of laymen and scholars alike. The synoptic Gospels suggest that the occasion was Passover (see Matthew 26:17–30; Mark 14:12–26; Luke 22:7–38), whereas John seems to indicate that Jesus died at the very moment when the Passover lambs were being ritually slaughtered in preparation for the annual feast (see John 18:28; 19:14).

Although identification of the specific location and timing eludes certainty, the Gospels witness that Jesus shared an important meal with His disciples, somewhere in Jerusalem, the evening before the day He was executed by the Romans.

Three Prophecies

One of the melancholy moments in the account of Jesus' last earthly meal centers on three prophecies about His impending death, all to be fulfilled before the night was over. They deal specifically with His closest disciples—Judas, the Twelve, and Peter.

The Savior's first prophecy describes Judas' treachery and betrayal. Mark notes that "in the evening he cometh with the twelve. And as they sat and did eat, Jesus said, Verily I say unto you, One of you which eateth with me shall betray me. And they began to be sorrowful, and to say unto him one by one, Is it I? and another said, Is it I? And he answered and said unto them, It is one of the twelve, that dippeth with me in the dish" (Mark 14:17–20).

Mark reports a second prophecy when Jesus states that "the sheep shall be scattered" (Mark 14:27). The Savior thus explicitly applies Zechariah's prophecy to his closest associates: "Awake, O sword, against my shepherd, and against the man that is my fellow, saith the Lord of hosts: smite the shepherd, and the sheep shall be scattered" (Zechariah 13:7).

Detail of *Last Supper,* from *Das Turin-Mailänder Stundenbuch* (f. 90), ca. 1389, illuminated manuscript facsimile (1994), 11 x 8 inches. Rare Books Division, Special Collections, J. Willard Marriott Library, University of Utah; after the Fine Art Facsimile edition by Faksimile Verlag Luzern.

The third prophecy follows immediately after Peter takes exception to Jesus' words about the scattering of sheep (see Mark 14:29). Jesus sadly predicts that Peter, and he alone, would deny Him three times: "Jesus saith unto him, Verily I say unto thee, That this day, even in this night, before the cock crow twice, thou shalt deny me thrice. But he [Peter] spake the more vehemently, If I should die with thee, I will not deny thee in any wise. Likewise also said they all" (Mark 14:30–31). Jesus is very specific—this very night—and then becomes more precise by saying "before the cock crow twice." Peter's response requires the most powerful adverb available, rendered in English as "vehemently."

Some Latter-day Saints have wondered whether Peter was, in fact, "commanded" to deny the Lord to preserve Peter's life so he could lead the Church following Jesus' departure. Asking new questions of the text is an important way to engage with the scriptures. However, the text ultimately speaks for itself, and the combined evidence is that Jesus was sure: "*All ye* shall be offended because of me this night: for it is written, I will smite the shepherd, and the sheep of the flock shall be scattered abroad" (Matthew 26:31; emphasis added). Peter was among those who were to be offended.

Additionally, the *Gospel of Judas,* which was published in 2006, raises questions about whether Jesus commanded Judas to betray Him. Here, it is not a matter of interpretation of the text, for the canonical Gospels agree that Judas was influenced by Satan when he "handed" Jesus over to His enemies (see, for example, John 13:2). In this case, the matter hinges upon whether the earliest sources, the canonical Gospels, are the most reliable. The *Gospel of Judas* is a late document, most likely with no connection to any eyewitness of the Last Supper. Therefore, this document may tell us something about second- and third-century Christianity but most likely provides no first-hand information about Jesus' last Passover.

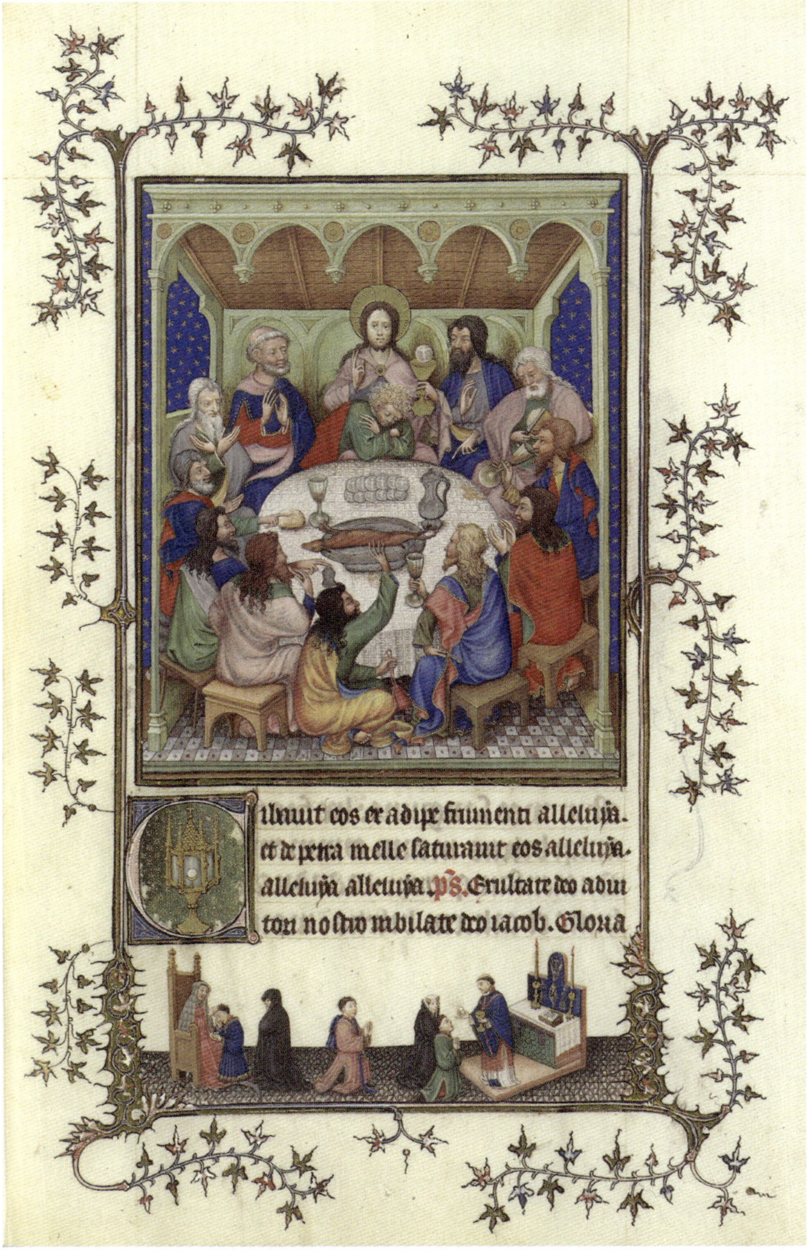

Figure 54. *Last Supper,* from *Das Turin-Maïlander Stundenbuch* (f. 90), ca. 1389, illuminated manuscript facsimile (1994), 11 x 8 inches. Rare Books Division, Special Collections, J. Willard Marriott Library, University of Utah; after the Fine Art Facsimile edition by Faksimile Verlag Luzern.

The Sacrament of the Lord's Supper

The Last Supper institutes the observance of the sacrament (Eucharist), the partaking of the bread and wine as prescribed by Jesus in Matthew 26:26–28. Interpreting this scripture in 1215, the Catholic Church initiated the doctrine of transubstantiation, which taught that the bread and wine of the Eucharist were literally transformed into Christ's flesh and blood. Symbolically illustrating this doctrine, a crucifix is imprinted on each wafer in the *Last Supper* from *Das Turin-Maïlander* manuscript (Figure 54). Here the paschal lamb displayed on a serving dish in the center of the table not only marks this as the Passover meal, but also prefigures Christ's atoning sacrifice as the Lamb of God. At other times a fish, the early Christian symbol of Christ, appears on the table (Figure 56).[1]

Other images of the Last Supper concentrate on the moment when Christ announces that one of His apostles will betray Him. In these depictions, the apostles turn to one another in disbelief, as shown by their facial expressions and questioning gestures. Judas, characterized by his dark hair and beard, is often identified by his placement apart from the others or by his dipping a morsel of bread into the bowl (Figure 55). Sometimes he holds a purse, referring to his stewardship over the apostles' communal monies or alluding to his betrayal of Christ for thirty pieces of silver (Figure 54). John the Beloved is also easily recognized by his clean-shaven face and long hair. He is usually seated next to Christ with his head resting on Jesus' breast as described in John 13:23. Following established conventions, the other Apostles are also distinguished by their physical features and by their placement within the group. By the late Middle Ages, artists often combined the two motifs of the Last Supper and the washing of the apostles' feet into one event.

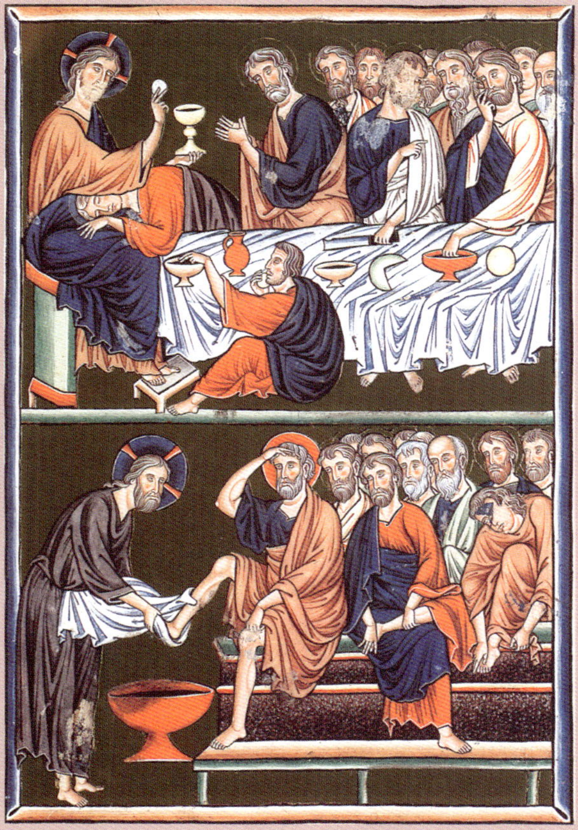

Figure 55. *Last Supper and Washing of the Disciples' Feet*, from *Der Ingeborg Psalter de Danemark* (f. 23r), ca. 1195, illuminated manuscript facsimile (1985), 11 ¾ x 7 ½ inches. L. Tom Perry Special Collections, Harold B. Lee Library, Brigham Young University, Provo, Utah; ADEVA, Akademische Drück- u. Verlagsanstalt, Austria.

Personal Devotion

Lavishly illustrated liturgical texts, psalters, gospels, and Books of Hours were popular during the Middle Ages and commonly used by the clergy and laity for daily reading and meditation (Figures 54, 55, 56, and 58). These devotional books were manifestations of an individual's commitment to piety. For example, a Book of Hours, often described as a "late medieval best-seller,"[2] was a personal prayer book containing calendars of religious feasts, scriptural passages, images, and specific prayers to be said during different hours of the day. By faithfully reciting these prescribed prayers, believers thought their time spent in purgatory could be shortened. In some instances, worshippers meditated on an image of Christ while repeating the prayer over and over to obtain absolution of their sins.

With the advent of the printing press in 1440, Books of Hours could be produced in large quantities, making inexpensive copies available to the middle classes. The more exquisitely ornamented books, however, were reserved exclusively for royalty and the aristocracy. Often painted with brilliant colors and embellished with precious gold or silver leaf, the richly decorated folios emphasized the treasured and sacred nature of these prayer books. Frequently, these luxurious manuscripts included images of the book's owner participating in the sacred events portrayed within its pages (Figure 55).

1. The Greek word for fish, *ichthys*, was an acronym for *Iesus Christos Theou Yios Soter* (Jesus Christ, Son of God, Savior).
2. Beth Williamson, *Christian Art: A Very Short Introduction* (Oxford: Oxford University Press, 2004), 23.

The Sacrament

The betrayal, the offense and scattering, and the denial are significant aspects of the story; but the fact that Jesus would atone for the sins of humankind is the main story. In this salvific act, Jesus offers His life willingly to inaugurate a new covenant (testament); thus, the chief focus of the synoptic Gospels rests not on Jesus' woeful prophecies that involved His disciples but on the institution of the sacrament, known as the Lord's Supper. In this sense, the portrayal of the Last Supper is more a celebration of the beginning of the new symbol of deliverance—the sacrament—than it is a dramatic rendering of peripheral events.

By the time Jesus met with His disciples on that momentous evening, all the guests were reclining at their dinner, as was the custom of the time. People in the city had adopted the Roman custom of the *triclinium*, a Latin word that suggests couches arranged on the outward three sides of a U-shaped table. In this arrangement, the three-sided table left the middle open for serving those who were dining. Apparently, the custom of the day was that the guest of honor was to recline at the head of the table, opposite the door. This setting may help illuminate several passages of scripture regarding the Last Supper story.

First, people reclining to eat were in a position that someone could reach their feet easily (see John 13:3–5). Second, after bathing His disciples' feet, Jesus announces the betrayal. John tells us that "there was leaning on Jesus' bosom one of his disciples, whom Jesus loved. Simon Peter therefore beckoned to him, that he should ask who it should be of whom he spake" (John 13:23–24). We can imagine Jesus reclining at dinner with John on one side and Judas on the other. As the treasurer of the Twelve ("Judas had the bag"; see John 13:29), Judas probably had a place of honor on one side of Jesus; some suggest the left side. From a reclining position on Jesus' right side, John easily could lay his head onto Jesus' bosom. Peter, however, is far enough way that he has to nod, signal, or, as the King James Version translates John's Greek word, "beckon" to the disciple leaning upon Jesus' breast to obtain information.

Mark provides many details of Jesus' words and acts during the meal, including: "And as they did eat, Jesus took bread, and blessed, and brake it, and gave to them, and said, Take, eat: this is my body. And he took the cup, and when he had given thanks, he gave it to them: and they all drank of it. And he said unto them, This is my blood of the new testament, which is shed for many" (Mark 14:22–24). Here, anticipating His suffering and death, Jesus speaks of a new testament, or covenant, that replaces the old. Yet Jesus' death is not the end. To make this point, He virtually swears an oath, "Verily I say unto you," showing that He has unshaken faith in the promises of His Father: "I will drink no more of the fruit of the vine, until that day that I drink it new in the kingdom of God" (Mark 14:25).

At this point, we might recall Jesus' earlier teaching that "whosoever of you will be the chiefest, shall be servant of all. For even the Son of man came not to be ministered unto, but to minister, and to give his life a ransom for many" (Mark 10:44–45). *Diakonein*, a Greek verb meaning "to minister" (serve), had a distinct secular meaning, denoting waiting at tables, but in Hellenistic Jewry, this usage was broadened to cover various ways to provide a service. Eventually, within the first-century church, the word took on added meaning, as it was used specifically for religious activity. The shift in meaning from its original Greek usage to the ecclesiastical one by the early Christians can be understood best in light of the accounts of the Last Supper.

Here the teaching and the reality combine as Jesus "serves" His disciples the emblems that represent His "service" for humankind. The Last Supper is seen as a *diakonia*, performed on behalf of the disciples. The same theme, readiness to serve, is discernible in John's portrayal of the Last Supper when he describes the washing of feet (see John 13:1–15).

In the end, the synoptic Gospels' narration of the institution of the sacrament contrasts dramatically Jesus' life-giving sacrificial offering with Judas' life-taking offering to the chief priests. The Last Supper, which promises that the Passion will mediate a new covenant between the Father and His children, shapes the climactic finale of a ministry in which every action effectively announced, promised, and offered salvation. Even here, in the face of His own impending death, Jesus continues to serve by offering salvation through the sacramental bread and wine.

John's Contribution

John begins his account of Jesus' last poignant gathering with His disciples by saying, "Now before the feast of the passover, when Jesus knew that his hour was come that he should depart out of this world unto the Father, having loved his own which were in the world, he loved them unto the end" (John 13:1).

Compared to the other Gospels, John's report provides an extended recitation of what Jesus did and, particularly, said during this gathering the night before He died (see John 13–17). The fundamental theme of these chapters appears in the very first verse of chapter 13, as recited above: "Having loved his own which were in the world, he loved them unto the end." In light of the deep concern He demonstrated for His friends, it is no wonder that He prepares them for the shock of His death by warning them not to fall into despair and disillusionment: "A little while, and ye shall not see me: and again, a little while, and ye shall see me. . . . I say unto you, That ye shall weep and lament, but the world shall rejoice: and ye shall be sorrowful, but your sorrow shall be turned into joy" (John 16:19–20).

In the end, Jesus gathered the Twelve and very possibly some of His most intimate disciples, including women, for a dinner held in a large upper room somewhere in Jerusalem on Thursday evening. This important gathering has been depicted, based on the written accounts preserved in the New Testament, by countless artists over time and remains one of the most poignant events preserved in the scriptures.

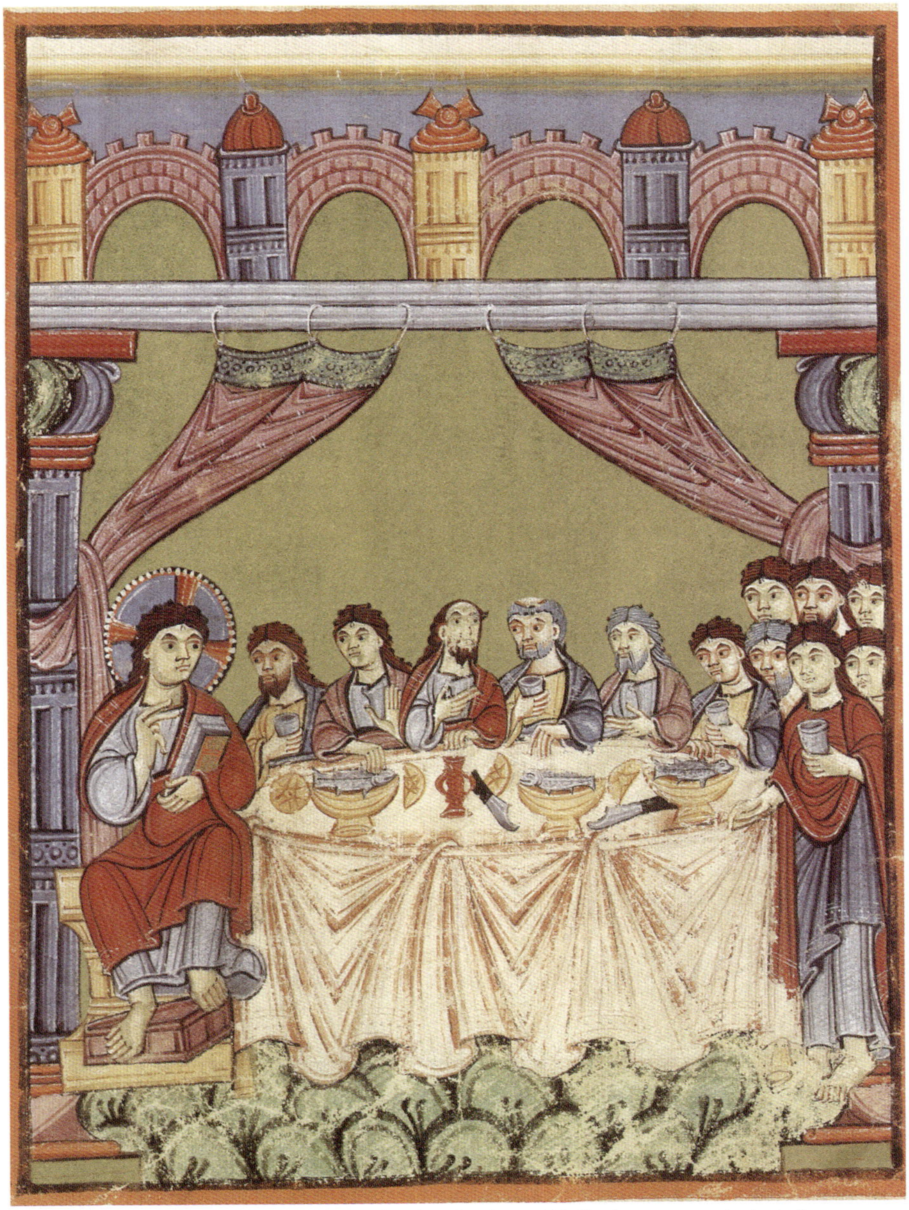

Figure 56. *Last Supper*, from the *Gospel Harmony of Eusebius* (f. 32), ca. 1050, illuminated manuscript facsimile (1991–92), 13 1/4 x 9 3/8 inches. Rare Books Division, Special Collections, J. Willard Marriott Library, University of Utah; ADEVA, Akademische Drück- u. Verlagsanstalt, Austria.

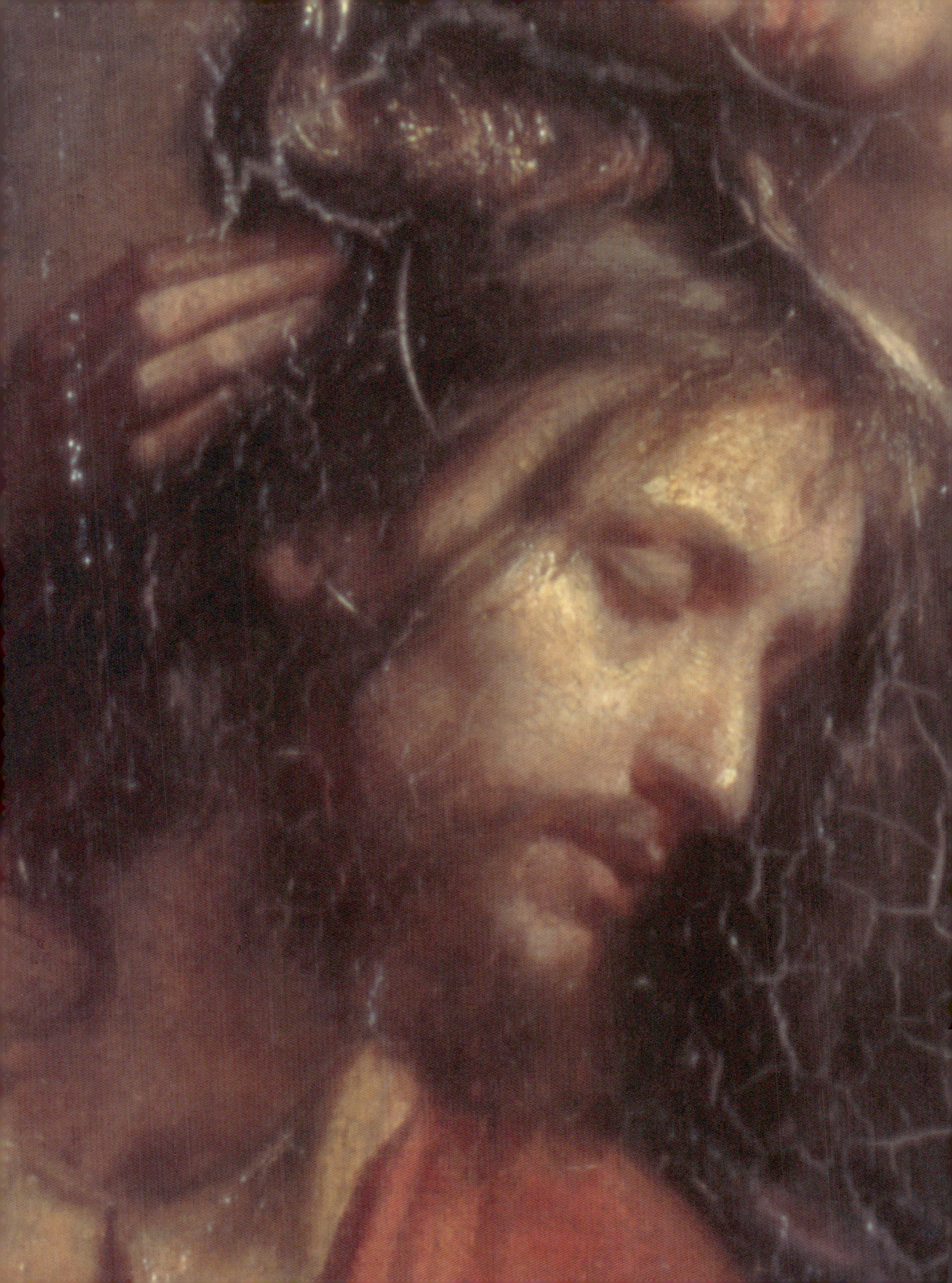

Chapter 10

Gethsemane

Gethsemane. The name evokes feelings of reverence and awe at what the Savior faced in this place. Lying just outside the city walls of Jerusalem, below the hill whereon the temple rose and near the bottom of the Mount of Olives, Gethsemane was the place of Jesus' most intense suffering. The adjoining valley, called Kidron in the New Testament era, bore the name "Valley of Jehoshaphat" from an earlier age and, according to the prophet Joel, is to be the place of the last judgment (see Joel 3:12).

Positioned on the western slope of the Mount of Olives, as the synoptic Gospels indicate, Gethsemane was called "a garden" in John's gospel (John 18:1), though it was transformed into something more lofty by Jesus' suffering there. In characterizing the locale, Matthew and Mark simply repeat a term for a private piece of ground (see Matthew 26:36; Mark 14:32). Both Luke and John designate it "the place" (Luke 22:40; John 18:2), a label that hints the earliest Christians knew the spot. The designation "the place" also bonds Gethsemane to Old Testament references to sacred places, conferring an air of dignity and sanctity onto events occurring that Thursday night.

The name *Gethsemane* itself means "olive press" and adds import to the fact that the agonies Jesus suffered pressed "great drops of blood" from Him (Luke 22:44), doubtless staining His clothing. The modern discovery of the remnants of ancient olive presses in a nearby cave points to the presence of an olive grove in the area.

The Eleven, of course, followed the Savior to this spot. Because it was customary for Jesus and His closest followers to retreat to this locale, as the Gospels remind us, it was easy for Judas to guess correctly where he and the arresting party would find Him (see Luke 22:39; John 18:2). Why was this spot among olive trees a regular haunt? Because it probably offered a resting and sleeping place when Jesus and the Twelve were visiting the city (see Luke 21:37), much closer than the home of Lazarus, which stood two miles away in Bethany, on the other side of the Mount of Olives, where they had lodged the night after the triumphal entry (see Matthew 21:17; Mark 11:11). After all, during festivals the city's lodging facilities bulged with visitors. The presence of a cave at the base of the Mount of Olives, which evidently served as an oil-pressing facility during the autumn harvest, would have offered to them a warm, dry place to sleep, out of the cold spring air of that Passover season (see John 18:18) and may help to explain the Gospels' expression "*into* the mount of Olives" when describing Jesus' arrival at Gethsemane (see Matthew 26:30; Mark 14:26; Luke 22:39; emphasis added).

Though only later copies of Luke's Gospel record that Jesus bled through the pores of His skin in Gethsemane, such intense suffering is confirmed in sources outside the New Testament, including early Christian authors who were evidently summarizing a fuller version of Luke's Gospel. Moreover, according to a prophecy uttered about 125 B.C. by an angel in the New World, the Savior, in His agony, was to "suffer temptations, and *pain of body*, . . . even more than man can suffer, except it be unto death; for behold, *blood cometh from every*

Carl Heinrich Bloch (1834–1890), detail of *Christ in the Garden of Gethsemane*, 1879, oil on canvas, 21 1/4 x 16 1/8 inches. Ny Carlsberg Glyptotek, Copenhagen.

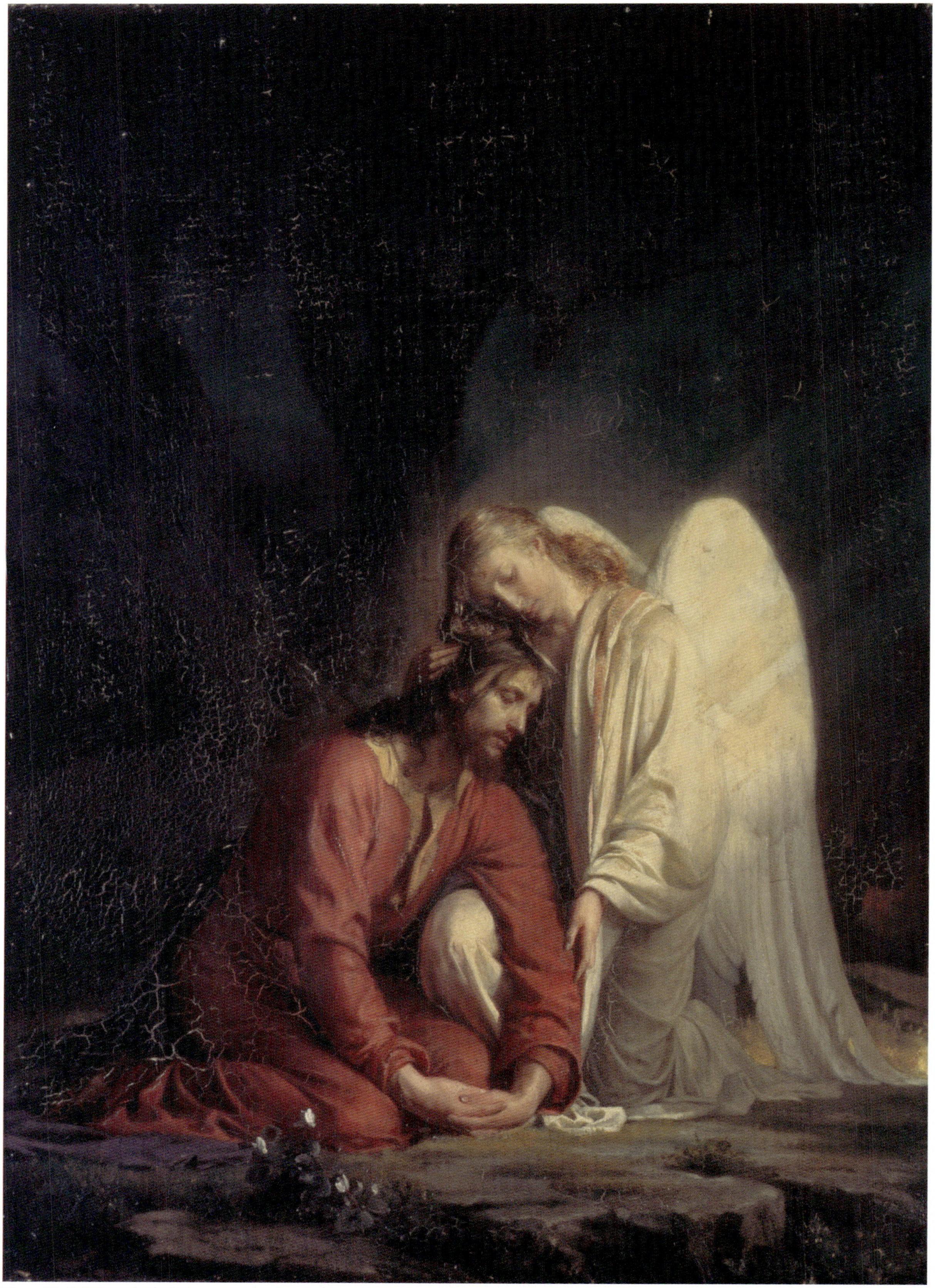

Figure 57. Carl Heinrich Bloch (1834–1890), *Christ in the Garden of Gethsemane*, 1879, oil on canvas, 21 1/4 x 16 1/8 inches. Ny Carlsberg Glyptotek, Copenhagen.

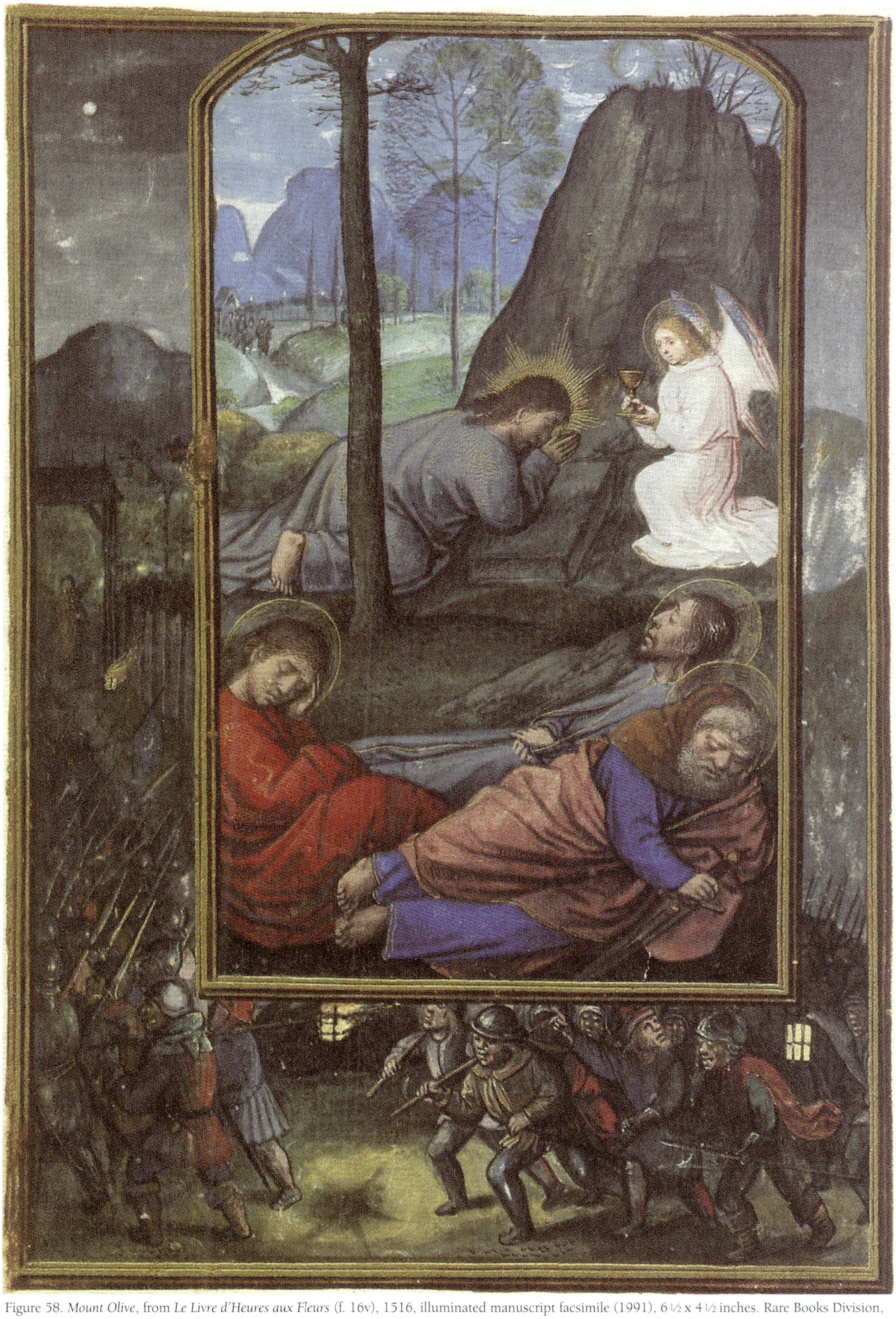

Figure 58. *Mount Olive*, from *Le Livre d'Heures aux Fleurs* (f. 16v), 1516, illuminated manuscript facsimile (1991), 6 ½ x 4 ½ inches. Rare Books Division, Special Collections, J. Willard Marriott Library, University of Utah; after the Fine Art Facsimile edition by Faksimile Verlag Luzern.

pore, so great shall be his anguish for the wickedness and the abominations of his people" (Mosiah 3:7; emphasis added). This stark picture is mirrored in the pain-laced reminiscences of the Savior Himself who, when looking back 1,900 years, poignantly recalled His wrenching "suffering [which] caused myself, even God, the greatest of all, to tremble *because of pain*, and *to bleed at every pore*, and *to suffer both body and spirit*" (Doctrine and Covenants 19:18; emphasis added).

That the Savior suffered intensely in Gethsemane appears both in the dark description of His experience and in His ache-drenched words to the three apostles, Peter, James, and John. Mark's account is the most vivid. According to his report, before Jesus left the three apostles, He "began to be sore amazed, and to be very heavy" (Mark 14:33). One suspects that, even though Jesus had prepared for this moment for eons of time, effectively "from the foundation of the world" (Moses 7:47; also 5:57), the scourge of sin and pain that fell on Him in that moment—"the wickedness and the abominations of his people" (Mosiah 3:7)—surprised even Him. For He immediately confided to the three, "My soul is exceeding sorrowful unto death" (Mark 14:34). Mark's notation that Jesus was "sore amazed" and "very heavy" might be rendered "astonished" and "deeply stressed," plainly hinting that Jesus was suddenly engaged in an almost overpowering inner struggle, which His words "exceeding sorrowful unto death" confirm. Only gradually, with enormous difficulty, did He wrestle down His anguish, gaining control of Himself in a monumental effort hinted at in the imperfect tense of the verbs that describe His repeated and continual actions in the garden: "He went forward a little [time after time], and fell

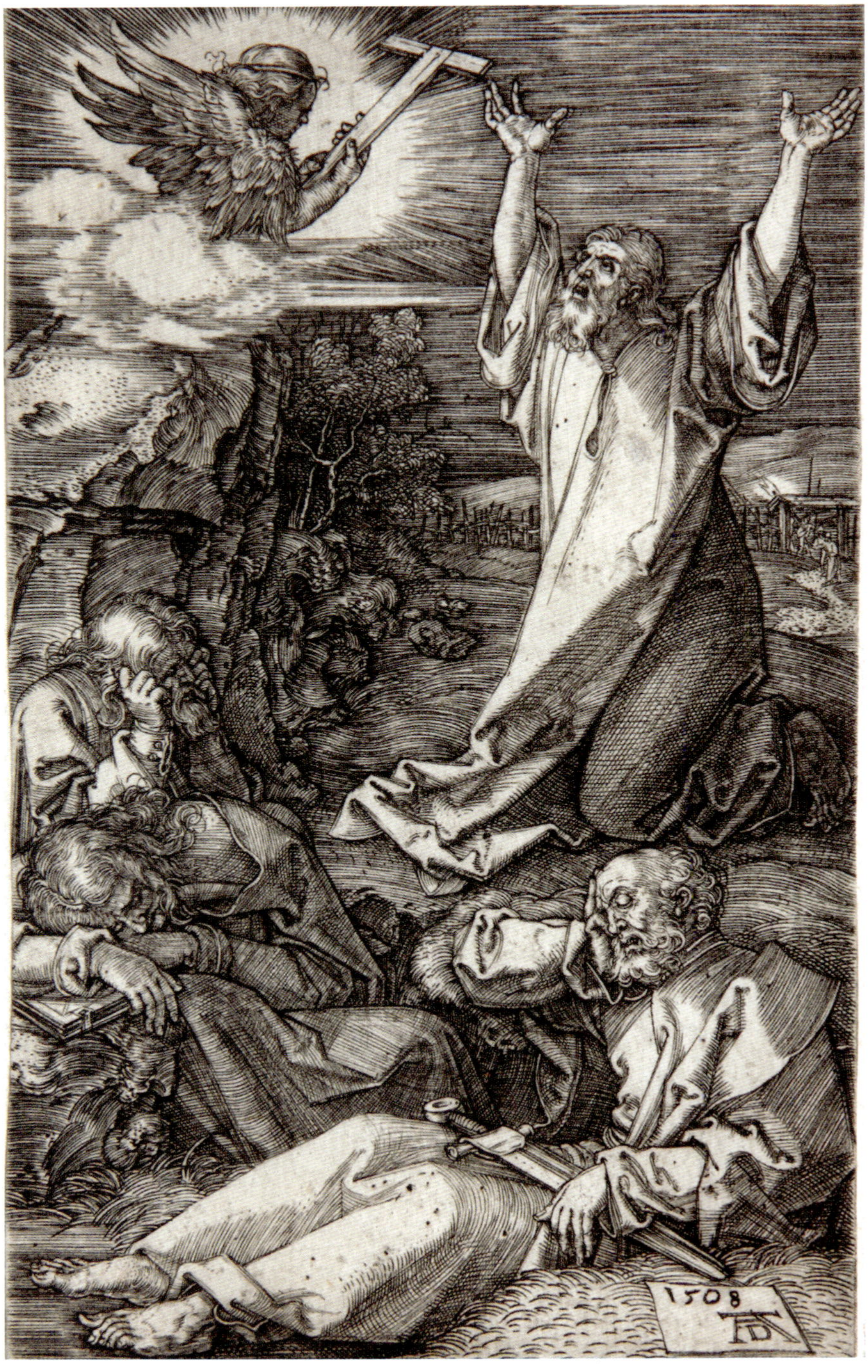

Figure 59. Albrecht Dürer (1471–1528), *Agony in the Garden*, from the *Engraved Passion*, 1508, engraving, 4 5/8 x 2 13/16 inches. Private collection of Shawn and Andrea Merriman.

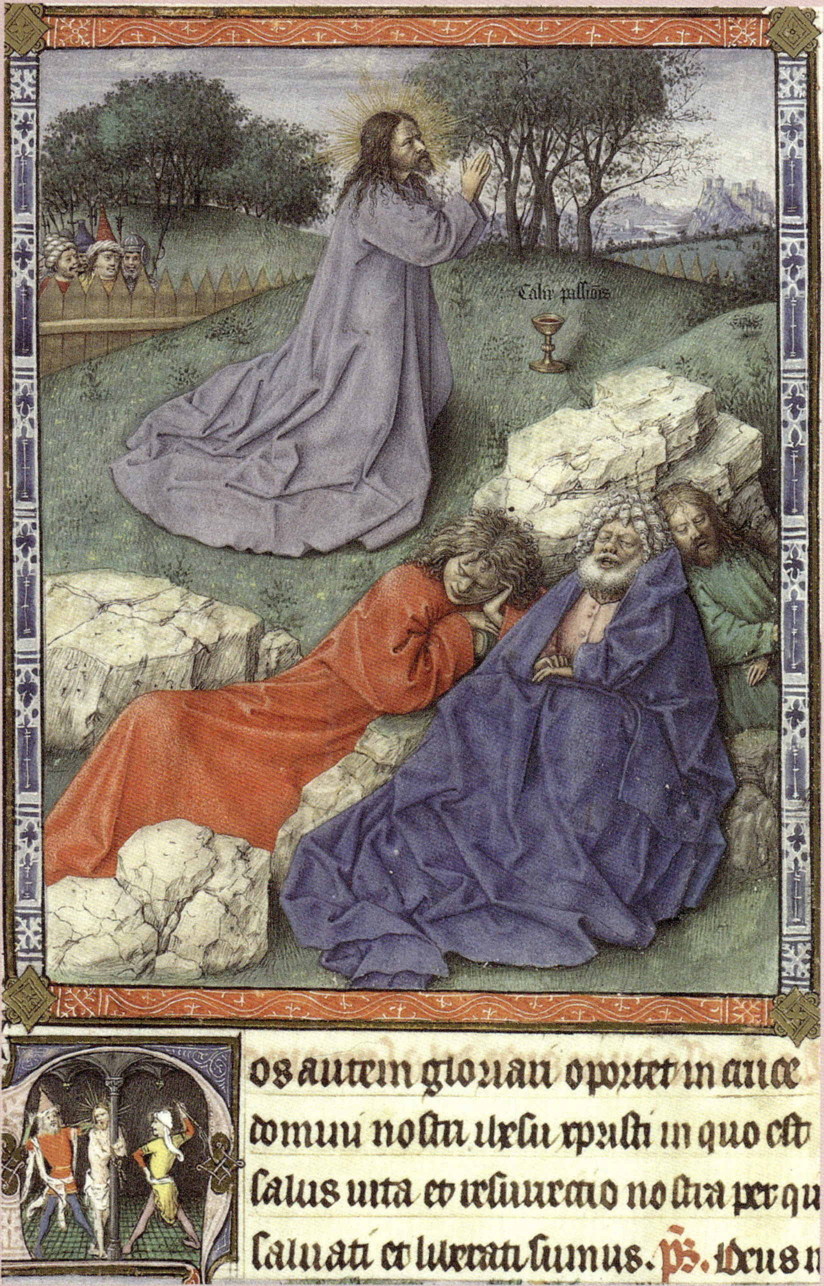

Figure 60. *Mount Olive, Flagellation and Way of the Cross*, from *Das Turin-Maïlander Stundenbuch* (f. 30v), ca. 1389, illuminated manuscript facsimile (1994), 11 x 8 inches. Rare Books Division, Special Collections, J. Willard Marriott Library, University of Utah; after the Fine Art Facsimile edition by Faksimile Verlag Luzern.

Agony in the Garden

Most Christian denominations regard Christ's prayer in the Garden of Gethsemane as merely a plea to the Father to strengthen Him for the imminent suffering of Calvary rather than a central act of the Atonement. Given this predominant Christian view, there are relatively few images of the agony in the garden in comparison with those of His suffering on the cross.

By the time of the Renaissance, traditional conventions had been established for depicting Christ's prayer in the Garden of Gethsemane. Christ is often shown on or beside a rock formation, perhaps referencing Him as "the rock of our salvation" (Psalm 95:1). In the scriptural accounts, He is shown either prostrate on the ground (see Matthew 26:39) or kneeling in earnest prayer while sweating great drops of blood (see Luke 22:41). In *Das Turin-Maïlander* manuscript (Figure 60), the chalice placed on the ground in front of Christ alludes to His entreaty to the Father, "If thou be willing, remove this cup from me: nevertheless not my will, but thine, be done" (Luke 22:42). In *Le Livre d'Heures aux Fleurs* and in Dürer's engraving of *Agony in the Garden* (Figures 58 and 59), the angel brings the chalice or the cross to Jesus, offering Him "the dregs of a bitter cup" (Alma 40:26). Peter, James, and John, recognizable by their physical appearances, are shown sleeping in the foreground. In the distance is the approaching band of soldiers and men commissioned by the chief priests, carrying torches, weapons, and staves (Figures 58 and 60).

One of the most poignant moments during Christ's agony in the garden is the appearance of the angel who came "unto him from heaven, strengthening him" (Luke 22:43). So sensitively interpreted by Carl Heinrich Bloch in *Christ in the Garden of Gethsemane* (Figure 57), the angel tenderly embraces the Savior as the Lord takes upon Himself the sins and infirmities of all mankind. This tangible interaction with Christ prompts recollection of His counsel to "succor the weak, lift up the hands which hang down, and strengthen the feeble knees" (Doctrine and Covenants 81:5).

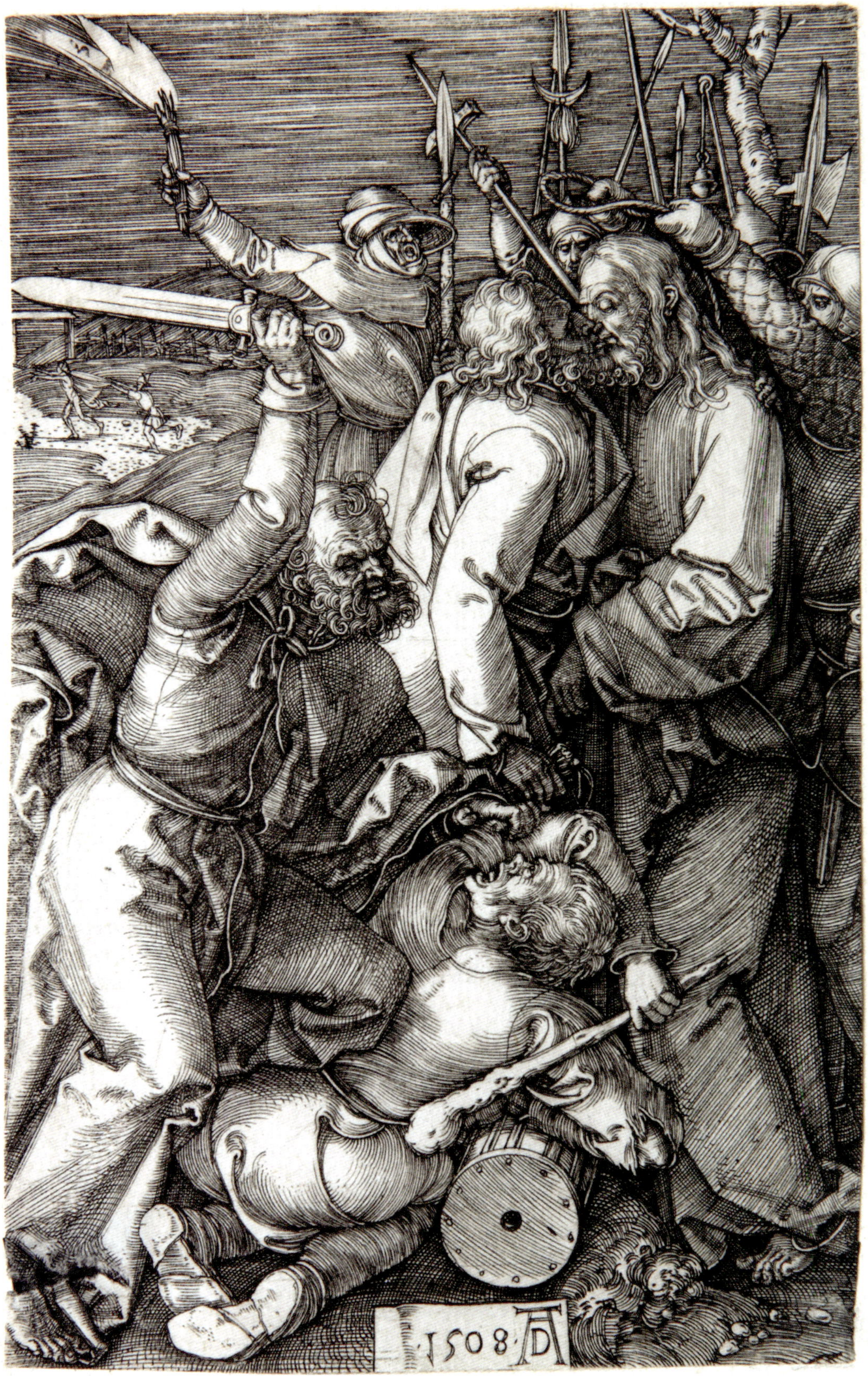

Figure 61. Albrecht Dürer (1471–1528), *Betrayal of Christ*, from the *Engraved Passion*, 1508, engraving, 4¾ x 3 inches. Private collection of Shawn and Andrea Merriman.

on the ground [repeatedly], and prayed [again and again]" (Mark 14:35).

The words of Jesus to His three chief apostles, after returning to them from His horrific initial struggles in Gethsemane, also betray the engulfing suffering that had convulsed Him. In a statement that brims with meaning, He alludes to the blinding intensity of His own agony when He says, "Watch and pray, that ye enter not into temptation: the spirit indeed is willing, but the flesh is weak" (Matthew 26:41; see also Mark 14:38). He had just learned for Himself how frightfully weak His flesh really was, bringing Him to beg of His Father that mercifully "the hour might pass," leaving the "cup" undrunk (Mark 14:35–36).

The graphic reports of the Savior's agony in Gethsemane, taken from the New Testament, naturally informed how artists portrayed Christ during the agonizing hours before His arrest. A second dimension of their art had to do with light and dark. Because Jesus' tormenting experience occurred during the Passover festival, the moon was full, brightening the night. It seems probable that the full moon had risen high enough in the sky so that, when He and His apostles reached Gethsemane, its soft light was beginning to stretch down the western slopes and into the recesses of the Mount of Olives. Thus, the muted, white-gray light of the moon washed across Gethsemane that night.

A third aspect that art often accounts for is the weariness of the apostles, a condition that the three synoptic Gospels report (Figures 58, 59, and 60). The Gospel of Mark records that, after arriving at Gethsemane with the Eleven Apostles, Jesus separated out Peter, James, and John, taking them farther into the garden. He then instructed them to "watch" while He "went forward" (Mark 14:34–35). The Gospels also report that, on three occasions that night, Jesus found these three chief apostles sleeping, unable to "watch with [Him]" (Matthew 26:40). To be sure, they would have witnessed His initial struggles before they dropped off to sleep. But their slumber meant that Jesus' awful suffering occurred in isolation, unobserved by others in this world.

The precise location of Gethsemane remains unknown. It would have lain "over the brook Cedron" when coming from the city (John 18:1)—that is, on the east side of the stream. The modern church buildings that rise near the base of the Mount of Olives all rest on medieval foundations where later Christians thought Gethsemane lay. Presumably, the place would have been near one of the three trails that ascended the Mount from the Kidron Valley, all of which begin in this general area. Thus, the general locale where Gethsemane is currently thought to lie may be correct. For some reason, Christian pilgrims seem not to have been particularly curious about the place of Gethsemane. Instead, their focus was the top of the Mount of Olives where they met in large groups on the Tuesday before Easter and read together Jesus' sermon wherein He prophesied about the fate of Jerusalem and events of the last days (see Matthew 24–25).

When Queen Helena, mother of the Emperor Constantine, came to Jerusalem and its environs in A.D. 326, she was interested not in the location of Gethsemane but three other spots: the place of Jesus' birth, the place of His death and burial, and the place of His ascension into heaven. At her order, magnificent church buildings were erected over these spots that she and others identified, whereas Gethsemane seems to have been completely neglected, thus leaving for a later day any attempts to determine its locale.

The name *Gethsemane*, as already noted, means "olive press." The prefixing term *geth-* or *gath-* means "press." The root *-semane*, related to the Hebrew term for oil, *šemen*, has to do with olives. The symbolism of Jesus' entering a place named for a press, and then being squeezed so hard that blood oozed from the pores of His skin, cannot be missed. But what of the reddish color of blood when compared to the golden color of olive oil? Is there any metaphorical connection between these elements? The answer is no and yes. No, there is no apparent connection between the colors red and gold. And no known authors have tried to suggest a connection. But, yes, there is a connection between the color of olive oil when first pressed and the color of blood. For olive oil, when squeezed from olives crushed in a press, bears a distinctive red color that, in the traditional way of producing olive oil, stains any stone on its way to a storage vat. Thus, both the name *Gethsemane* (olive press) and its earliest product (reddish liquid) tie to the Savior's experience in that place.

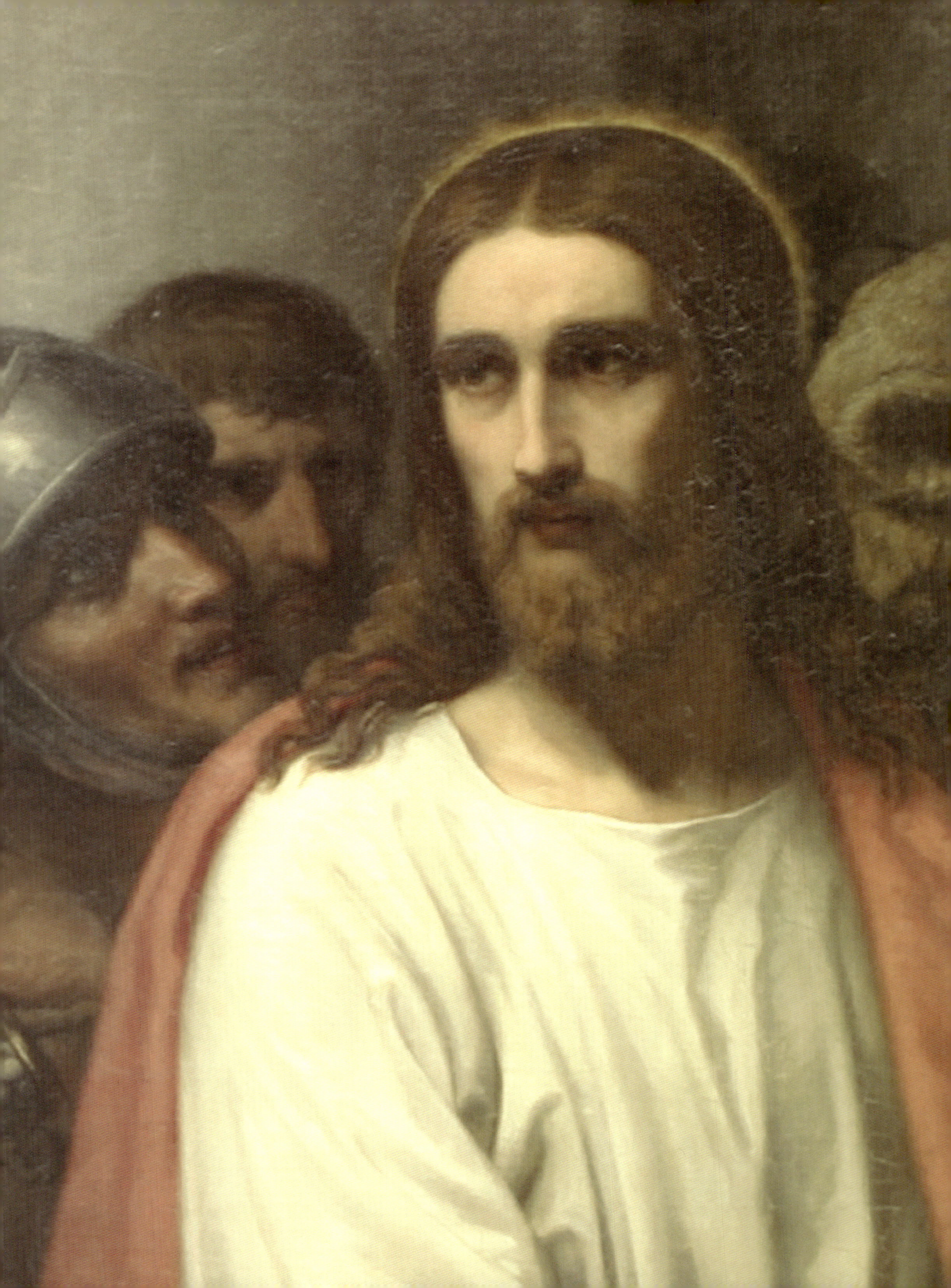

Chapter 11

Trials

On a moonlit night, a crowd from the Jewish high priest, including a Roman tribune and soldiers, marched down the Kidron Valley and paused before the entry to Gethsemane. There they met the man Jesus and arrested Him, binding Him for the forced trek to the house of the high priest. Within a half hour of reentering Jerusalem, the arresting party arrived at the high priest's home. There the long night and morning of Jesus' hearings began before various religious and civil authorities. With imaginative success, art has tried to capture the Gospels' vivid depictions of Jesus' hearing before Jewish authorities, Peter's denial, and finally the trial before Pontius Pilate, the Roman governor.

The Hearing before Jewish Authorities

Although details differ among the Gospels, all repeat the story of a hearing before Jewish authorities at the high priest's home. The hearing was not a formal trial; rather, it consisted of a preplanned effort to establish Jesus' guilt and to determine grounds for an accusation before Pilate, the Roman prefect. John's account is the most brief and reports that the arresting crowd took Jesus first to Annas, formerly the high priest of the temple, and then to his son-in-law Caiaphas, the current high priest (see John 18:13–14, 19–24). Although John preserves little of what was said, he does recount an earlier meeting wherein the authorities came to a somewhat official decision that they get rid of Jesus because He was a threat to their relationship with the Roman government and to their own personal positions of influence (see John 11:47–53). In the end, they would settle on little more than a charge of blasphemy, a charge that held little interest for the Romans.

It is the synoptic Gospels that preserve the fullest record of the nighttime hearing. Although each records the events of the hearing differently, common elements emerge. First, as John reports, the authorities had already reached the dark decision to seek Jesus' death. Hence, they were anxious to establish His guilt.

Second, in their urgency to prove Jesus' culpability, they sought testimony from questionable people, including false witnesses, an act that clearly put them in violation of the Mosaic law (see Deuteronomy 19:16–19). This part of the proceedings shows the desperation that authorities felt to do something with Jesus after He was finally in their grasp.

Third, their intense interest in whether Jesus claimed to be the Messiah shows both strident opposition and a peculiar curiosity. It is doubtful that any of Jesus' interrogators had met Him personally. Both knowing His reputation as a teacher and miracle worker, and sensing that He was an unusual personality, their curiosity must have been at a high pitch when at last they found themselves in the same room with Him. It is this wide-eyed curiosity that seeps into the high priest's last question, "Art thou the Christ, the Son of the Blessed?" (Mark 14:61).

Fourth, in seeking to establish Jesus' guilt, the authorities finally got witnesses to say that Jesus had spoken against the temple, a crime in their culture because it undercut the faith

Ary Scheffer (1795–1858), detail of *Denial of Peter,* 1855, oil on canvas, 59 7/8 x 74 1/16 inches. Brigham Young University Museum of Art, gift of Donald Greenwood.

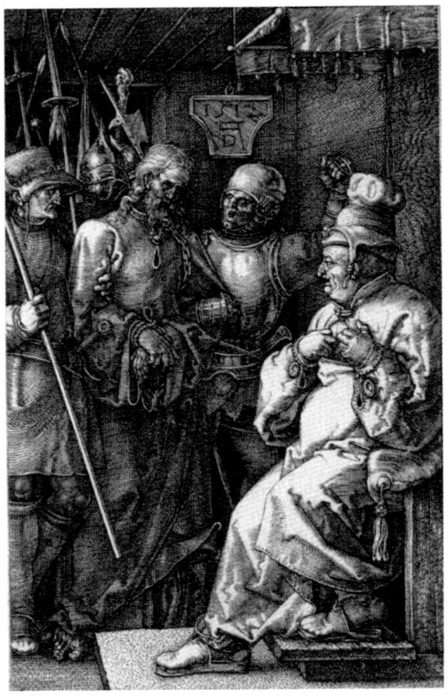

Figure 62. Albrecht Dürer (1471–1528), *Christ Before Caiaphas*, from the *Engraved Passion*, 1512, engraving, 4 11/16 x 2 15/16 inches. Private collection of Shawn and Andrea Merriman.

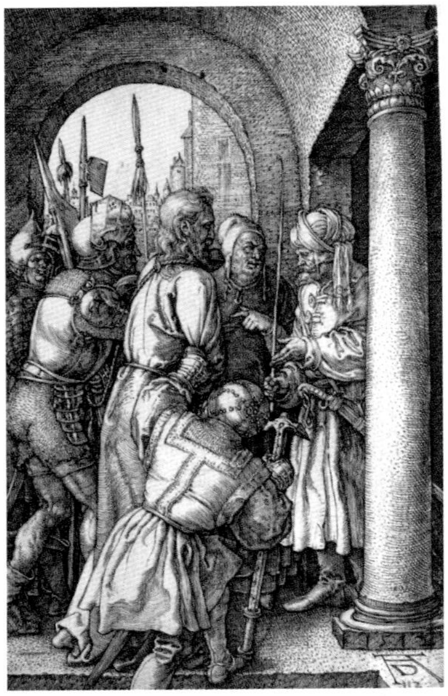

Figure 63. Albrecht Dürer (1471–1528), *Christ Before Pilate*, from the *Engraved Passion*, 1512, engraving, 4 11/16 x 3 inches. Private collection of Shawn and Andrea Merriman.

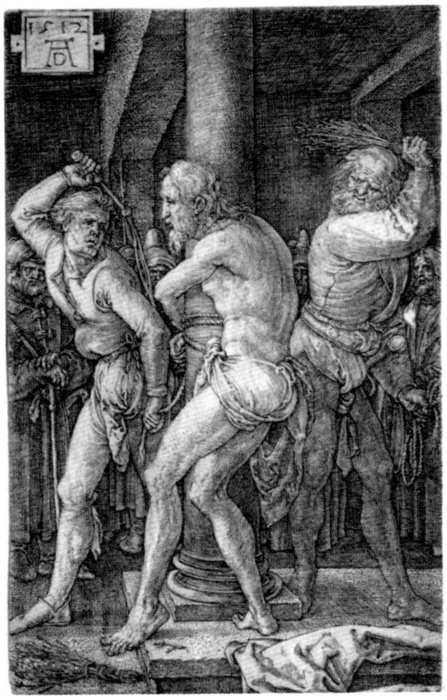

Figure 64. Albrecht Dürer (1471–1528), *Flagellation*, from the *Engraved Passion*, 1512, engraving, 4 3/4 x 2 15/16 inches. Private collection of Shawn and Andrea Merriman.

inherited from their ancestors and besmirched the most important symbol of God's loving kindness to them, the temple.

Fifth, it was the high priest who, after silently watching the parade of witnesses, demanded that Jesus respond to the charges: "Answerest thou nothing? what is it which these witness against thee?" (Mark 14:60).

Sixth, when Jesus responded "I am" to the question of whether He was "the Son of the Blessed" (Mark 14:62), the high priest tore his robes, a dramatic demonstration that he thought Jesus guilty and an act that may have been customary in serious legal cases.

Although the legality of these proceedings has been written about almost endlessly, there are dimensions that clearly do not fit within the bounds of Mosaic law. This earlier law of Moses stood as a quiet but ever-present sentinel that looked out for the rights of the accused in capital cases. And certainly two of its legal guarantees were violated in Jesus' hearing, whether we consider the event a formal trial or not.

Besides the regulation against lying statements from false witnesses, already mentioned, the Mosaic law required that, if a person were suspected of bearing false witness or giving conflicting testimony, those judging the case "shall make diligent inquisition" of any witness so that "thou put the evil [person] away from among you," thus protecting the rights of the accused (Deuteronomy 19:18–19). According to the New Testament reports, the authorities held no such inquiry. To be sure, the Gospel writers were not focusing on the legal niceties of the hearing, but their accounts preserve the dishonorable climate of the affair (see Matthew 26:57, 59–68; 27:1; Mark 14:53, 55–65; 15:1; Luke 22:54, 63–71; John 18:13–14, 19–24).

Peter's Denials

One of the best documented incidents from the Gospels has to do with Peter's three denials. Although "all the disciples forsook [Jesus], and fled" (Matthew 26:56), Peter had enough courage to follow the arresting crowd to the home of the high priest. According to John, another disciple of Jesus (Nicodemus?) used his influence to admit Peter into the courtyard of the home where others were warming themselves over a fire in the cold night air (see John 18:15–16, 18).

As in the case of the hearing before Jewish authorities, so the synoptic Gospel accounts of Peter's denials exhibit differences. But even these differences underscore an intense interest in the defining lesson in ultimate loyalty for Peter, a loyalty that puts another person's well-being above

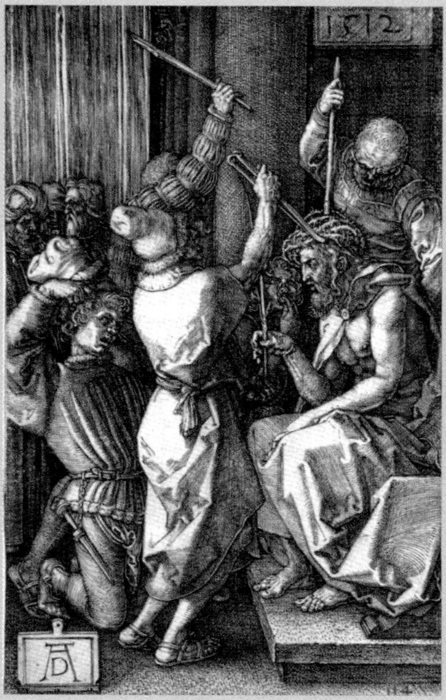

Figure 65. Albrecht Dürer (1471–1528), *Christ Crowned with Thorns,* from the *Engraved Passion*, 1512, engraving, 4 3/4 x 2 15/16 inches. Private collection of Shawn and Andrea Merriman.

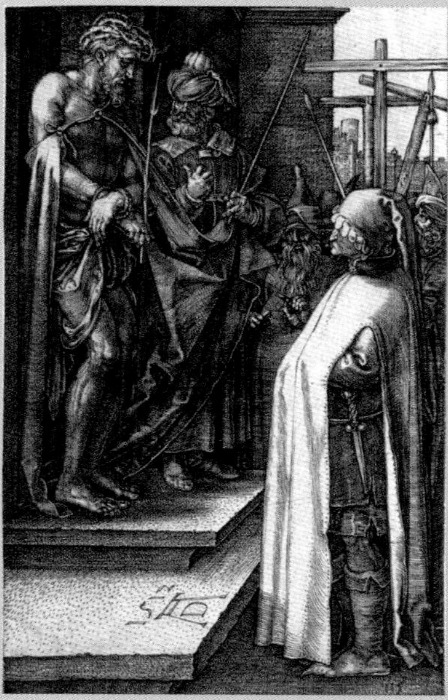

Figure 66. Albrecht Dürer (1471–1528), *Ecce Homo,* from the *Engraved Passion*, 1512, engraving, 4 11/16 x 3 inches. Private collection of Shawn and Andrea Merriman.

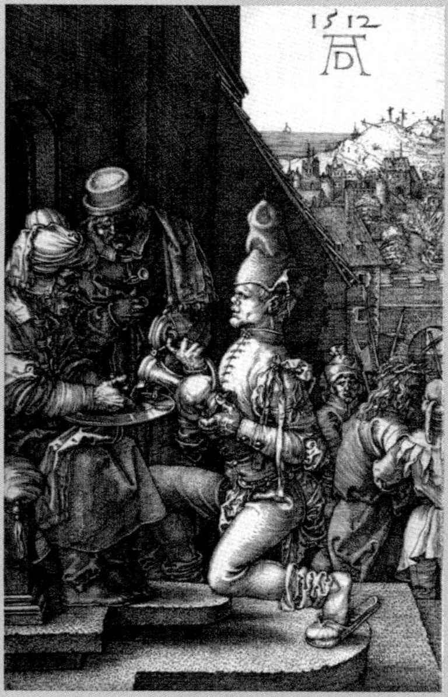

Figure 67. Albrecht Dürer (1471–1528), *Pilate Washing His Hands,* from the *Engraved Passion*, 1512, engraving, 4 11/16 x 3 inches. Private collection of Shawn and Andrea Merriman.

Narrative Imagery

Various methods of teaching have been used during the centuries to convey the stories and meanings of the scriptures. One approach has been the narrative cycle, which has been a popular practice since the fifth century. These consecutive scenes illustrating biblical stories were placed on church walls as mosaics or frescoes. "Constantly in view," these cycles were intended to "encourage fear and faith toward God."[1] They were initially thought to function as books for the illiterate, visually teaching what some were incapable of reading. However, more recent scholarship suggests that these cycles served more often as reminders and guides for the literate. This is confirmed by the Venerable Bede, an eighth-century monk of the monastery of Wearmouth-Jarrow, who asserted that images could "recall to the memory of the faithful" the events and teachings of the Bible.[2] Eventually, theologians accepted both of these functions—to educate and to remind—as a justification for the use of images in facilitating spiritual enlightenment.

On a smaller scale, narrative series of woodcuts or engravings, such as those by Albrecht Dürer, were produced for the church laity as well as for connoisseurs and collectors. In addition to his well-known woodcuts of the *Life of the Virgin* (Figures 2 and 52), Dürer completed several series on the Passion, drawing on the detailed, often graphic, accounts found in the synoptic Gospels. Published in book form in 1511, Dürer's woodcut series, the *Large Passion,* included an explanatory Latin text accompanying each image. He also published the *Engraved Passion* (1513) (Figures 59, 61, 62–67, 70, 77, 78, 80, 85, 88), a series of sixteen small engravings, and another series, the *Small Passion,* of thirty-seven woodcuts that chronicled the redemption of man, from the fall of Adam, through the life of Jesus, to the last judgment. These violent and explicit images of the Passion were meant to stir the mind and the emotions of the viewer and encourage contemplation of Christ's suffering.

1. *Luther's Works* (Philadelphia: Westminster Press), 43:43, quoted in John Dillenberger, *Images and Relics: Theological Perceptions and Visual Images in Sixteenth-Century Europe* (New York: Oxford University Press, 1999), 92–93, n. 32.
2. Williamson, *Christian Art: A Very Short Introduction*, 67.

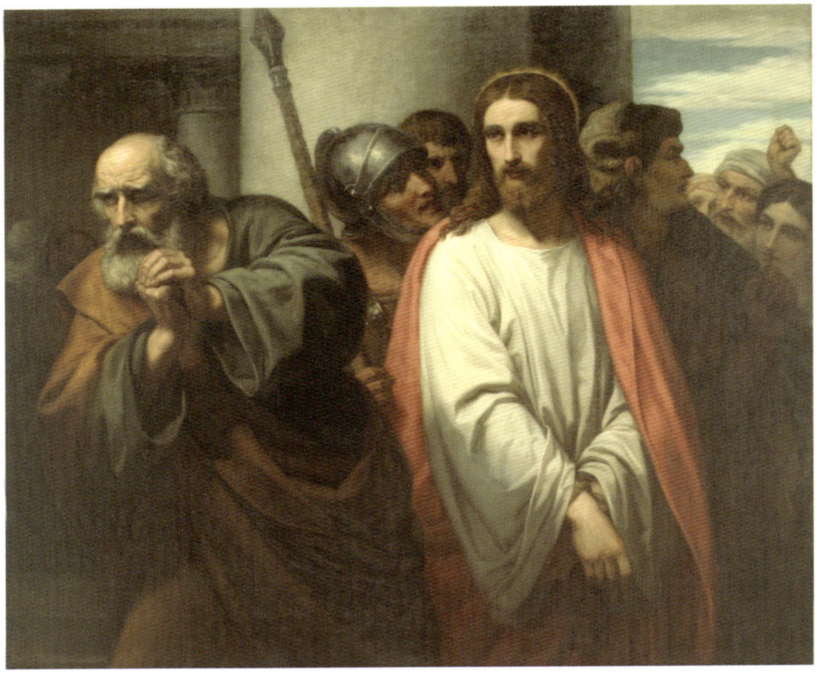

Figure 68. Ary Scheffer (1795–1858), *Denial of Peter*, 1855, oil on canvas, 59 7/8 x 74 1/16 inches. Brigham Young University Museum of Art, gift of Donald Greenwood.

one's own. Just a few hours before, Jesus had emphasized this virtue, applying it to Himself: "Greater love hath no man than this, that a man lay down his life for his friends" (John 15:13). But the principle applies to all, not just to Jesus, a point that Peter would come to understand in personal, conscience-wrenching terms.

All reports agree that the first person to recognize Peter as a follower of Jesus was a servant girl in the high priest's household, which shows that such young women had chores that took them throughout the city and allowed them to observe what was going on. Peter, as we know, denied to her that he knew Jesus. We can only imagine what guilt surged through his mind and heart. His thoughts, according to Matthew and Mark, caused him to withdraw from the group huddled around the warming fire. Peter did not have much time for reflection. In three reports, we read that another person pointedly asked him whether he was one of Jesus' followers. According to Matthew, Peter "denied with an oath" that he knew the Master (Matthew 26:72).

The stage was now arranged for the final denial. The synoptic Gospels hint that Peter had said enough during the night's conversations to betray his Galilean accent. Hence, his speech brought about the final attempt to identify him as one of Jesus' followers: "Surely thou art one of them: for thou art a Galilean" (Mark 14:70). To the persons who approached him, Peter responded by invoking a curse on himself and swearing an oath, "I know not the man" (Matthew 26:74). As soon as the words were out of his mouth, a rooster crowed. Peter's mind ran to Jesus' prophetic utterance that, before the cock crowed, Peter would deny Him three times. In Luke's words, "Peter went out, and wept bitterly" (Luke 22:62). Peter's heart would not be fully healed until the resurrected Savior would show His confidence in the senior apostle by charging him with feeding His flock (see John 21:15–17). For the moment, Peter was completely crestfallen (see Matthew 26:58, 66–75; Mark 14:54, 66–72; Luke 22:54–62; John 18:15–18, 25–27).

An especially poignant detail about Peter's denials appears in Luke's Gospel. Accordingly, as soon as the rooster crowed, "the Lord turned, and looked upon Peter" (Luke 22:61). The remark bears the signs of an eyewitness account. It is impossible to say where Jesus was at this moment, whether being led through the courtyard or standing at a window that looked onto the courtyard. The glance that passed between the two must have served to make Peter's grief even more sharp and deep (Figure 68).

The Trial before Pilate

One of the lingering questions is whether Jewish authorities had power to execute a person convicted of a capital crime. The customary form of execution since Old Testament days was by stoning, a practice that continued into the Christian era. The New Testament record points to instances of stoning. Stephen, the first Christian martyr, died in this way at the hands of an angry crowd (see Acts 7:58–60). In a second example, a mob had seized the Apostle Paul and was dragging him out of the temple grounds for a vigilante-style execution when a squad of Roman soldiers rescued him (see Acts 21:30–34). A key passage is John's account, which holds that Jewish authorities needed to turn to the Roman governor for executing Jesus because they lacked authority to carry out a death sentence (see John 18:31).

It is striking that the governor Pilate judged Jesus to be innocent. He saw through the legal façade spun by Jewish authorities. The question naturally arises, Why, then, did he order Jesus' execution?

According to John, the authorities brought Jesus to Pilate while it "was early" and then, for religious reasons, remained outside his Jerusalem residence "lest they should be defiled . . . [so] that they might eat the passover" (John 18:28). What were the charges? The Gospels enumerate several accusations, the most compelling recorded by Luke: "We found this fellow perverting the nation, and forbidding to give tribute to Caesar, saying that he himself is Christ a King" (Luke 23:2). When Pilate questioned Jesus, He replied almost not at all. It is clear that Jesus was in charge of the interview, even through His silence. It was the same when Pilate sent Him to Herod Antipas, the tetrarch of Galilee, who was in Jerusalem for the festival. Evidently, Herod judged Him to be innocent because he sent Him back to Pilate without accusation (see Luke 23:7–11).

In an apparent effort to free Jesus, Pilate offered to set Him free in keeping with a custom of freeing a prisoner at the feast. His mistake was to offer a choice between prisoners, Jesus or a convicted insurrectionist named Barabbas, whose name, ironically, means "son of the father." The authorities were not to be deterred from their determined course. They chose Barabbas, even knowing his unsavory character. Then they demanded loudly that Jesus be crucified. Even though Pilate had been slow coming to this decision, perhaps because of a message from his wife about a troubling dream concerning Jesus that had invaded her slumber (see Matthew 27:19), he seemingly succumbed to the mounting pressure from the clamoring crowd of authorities and supporters and finally gave the order to crucify Jesus.

Both in prophecy and in the records, what came next was most vicious—the scourging (see Isaiah 53:5; 1 Nephi 19:9; 2 Nephi 6:9; Mosiah 3:9; 15:5; John 19:1). The intent of this beating, which sometimes killed a condemned prisoner, is to weaken him so that death by crucifixion will come more quickly. The whip itself consists of several leather strands into whose flying ends are tied bits of metal and bone, which tear and lacerate the flesh.

In an act designed to mock and humiliate their prisoner, the soldiers dressed the newly beaten and quivering Jesus in a purple robe and pressed a crown of thorns onto His head. All was complete. The prisoner was now ready for execution (see Matthew 27:26–31; Mark 15:15–20; Luke 23:25; John 19:16).

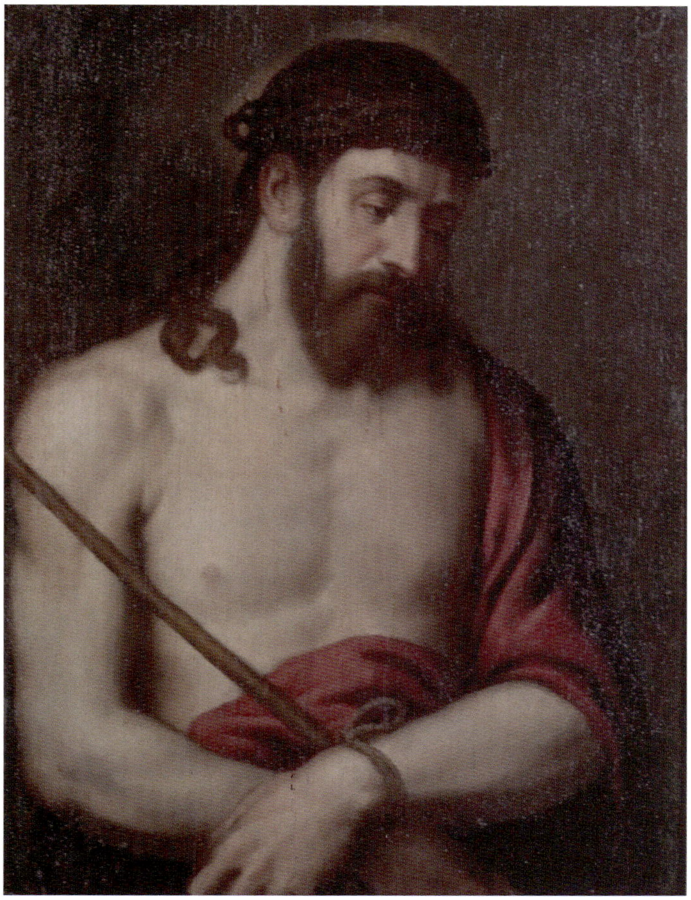

Figure 69. Workshop of Titian (1488–1576), *Ecce Homo*, 16th century, oil on canvas, 42 x 38 inches. Brigham Young University Museum of Art, purchase/gift from Gloria Teichert, funds provided by Jack R. and Mary Lois Wheatley.

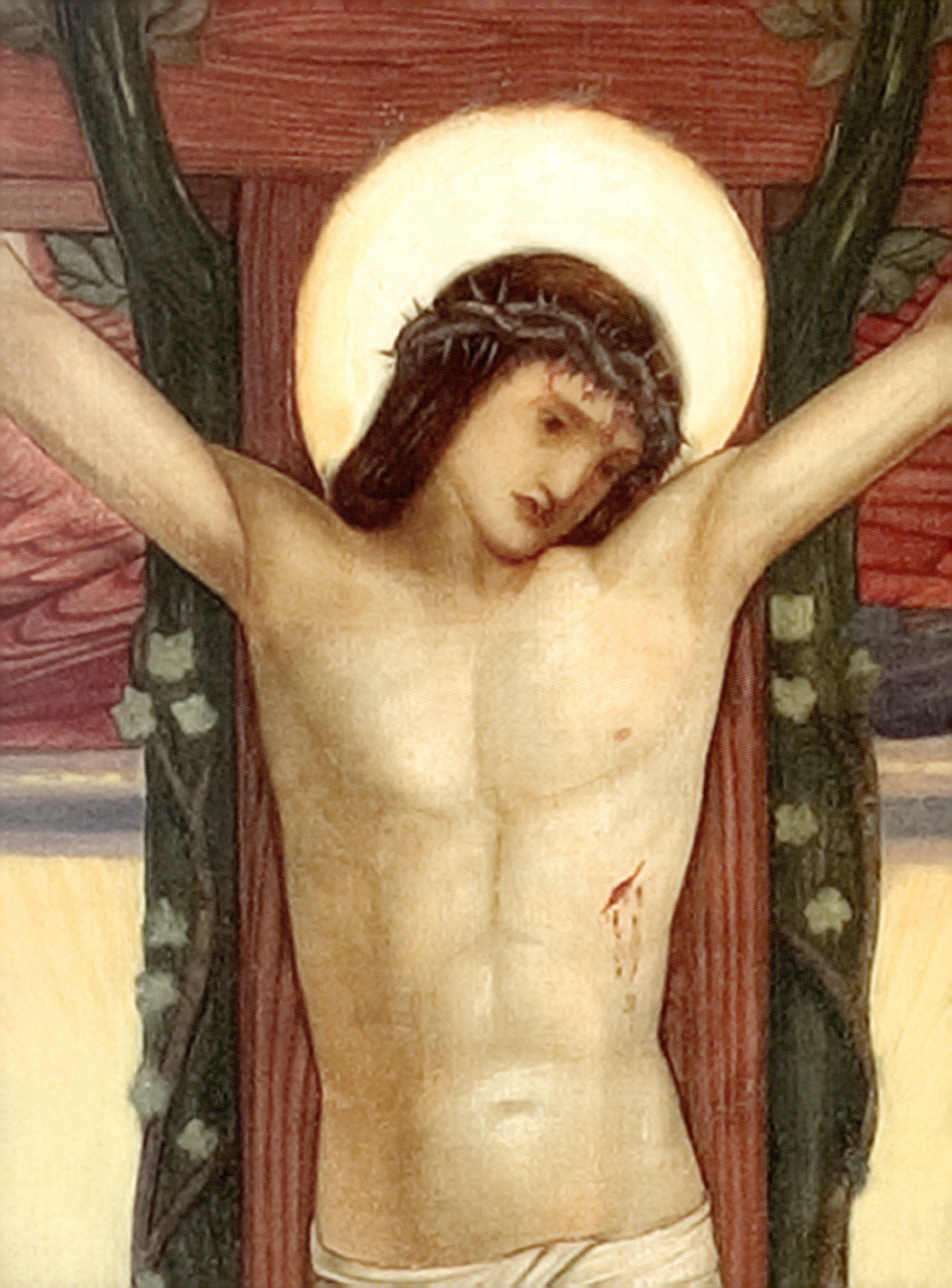

Chapter 12

Crucifixion

The cross is the most enduring symbol in Christendom. As a symbol, it points in two directions. First, it looks backward over the events of Jesus' life and ministry that have brought Him to His agonizing crucifixion, seeing Him as Examplar, Teacher, Nurturer, Son, and Brother. In this sense, the cross casts a dark shadow that, ironically, sets into relief the enlightening goodness that radiated from Jesus.

Second, the cross looks to the future, beyond His suffering, to the tomb, specifically the empty tomb on Sunday morning, when His resurrection breaks apart the otherwise unbreakable bands of death and pierces the impenetrable barrier that has separated God and His children for eons of time. In this sense, the cross is an instrument of healing, now and forever. We thus see the cross in an ever-shining arc of light as a tree of life. Drawing upon this meaning, Jesus declared, "As Moses lifted up the serpent in the wilderness, even so must the Son of man be lifted up: that whosoever believeth in him should not perish, but have eternal life" (John 3:14–15).

The Realities of Crucifixion

Stripped of clothing in an ultimate act of humiliation, Jesus was executed by the slow, cruel method of Roman crucifixion—a most extreme form of punishment reserved for slaves, dangerous and violent criminals, and political enemies of Rome. With a few faithful friends and family watching, Jesus died an agonizing and painful death that is perhaps impossible to describe or depict adequately. What is often lost on us is the fact that no one living in the first century expected the Messiah to suffer, let alone die.

Those followers standing near His cross certainly were stunned and shocked. Jesus, they thought, was the promised Messiah. His triumphal entry into Jerusalem earlier in the week seemed only to confirm their hopes and dreams about redemption and rescue from their enemies. Following Jesus' nighttime arrest, their world was now turned upside down. The events that followed were full of pain and sorrow, seemingly tragic beyond description.

Aside from His glorious resurrection, Jesus' crucifixion is the singular, most prominent event in the Gospel accounts. It is certainly one of the facts of the story that is not seriously challenged by anyone. Jesus' death at Passover by this cruel form of punishment is one of the most incontrovertible facts in all of history.

Neither the Gospel narratives nor Paul, nor even Josephus, provide intricate details of the execution. Crucifixion was not administered in identical ways in every case. The basic aspects of Jesus' crucifixion were undoubtedly known by those who first read and heard the stories about Him, but eyewitnesses to Jesus' death have left us to our own imagination in reconstructing the details of the brutal event. Therefore, we must leave room for potential, significant variations in the story as we take into account local and individual circumstances of executions

Bernard Sleigh (1872–1934), detail of *The Crucifixion–A Triptych*, 1906, oil on canvas, 84 x 32 inches. Brigham Young University Museum of Art, purchased with funds provided by the Campbell Family Foundation and Verla Birrell.

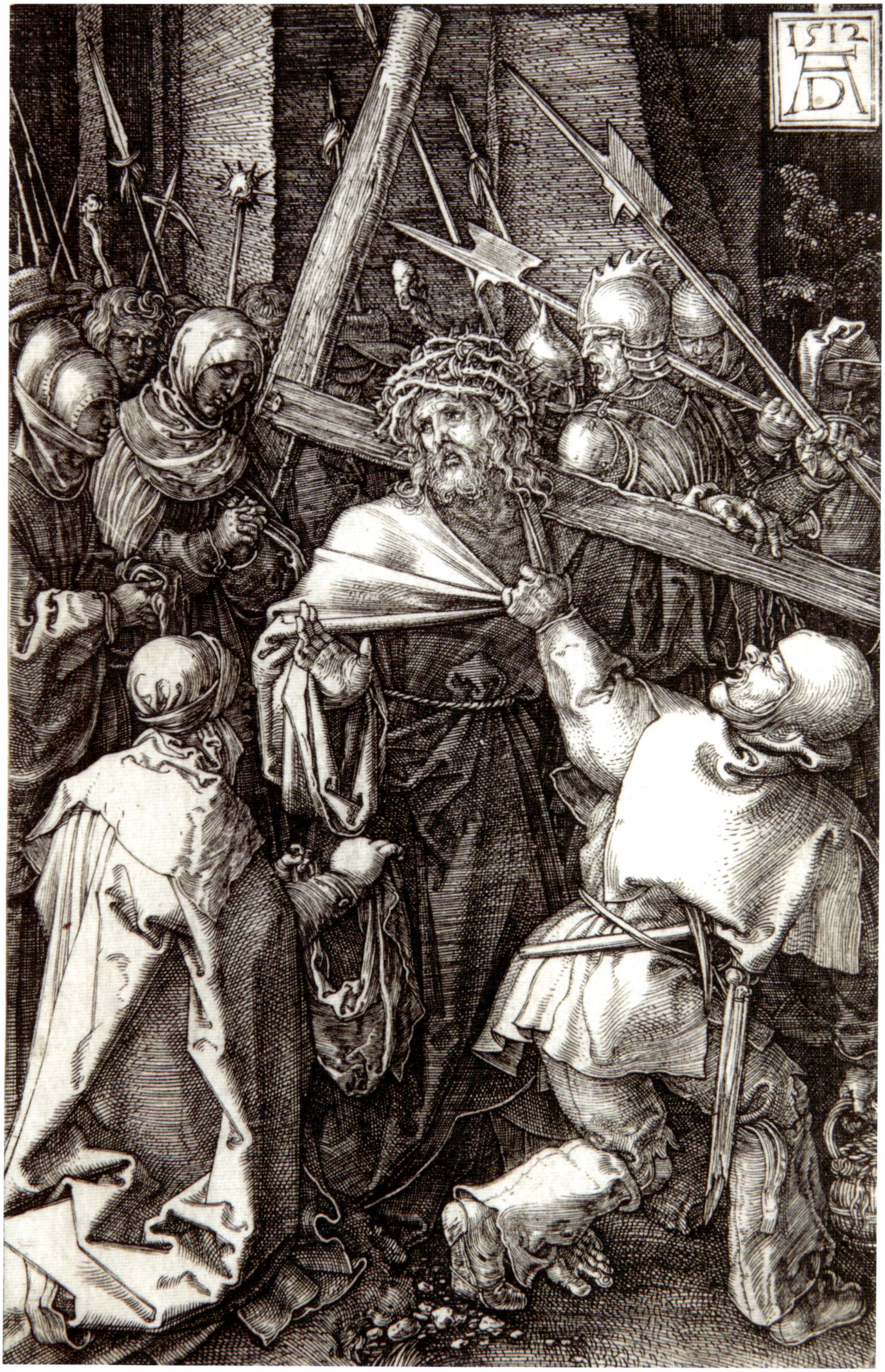

Figure 70. Albrecht Dürer (1471–1528), *Bearing of the Cross*, from the *Engraved Passion*, 1512, engraving, 4 11/16 x 3 inches. Private collection of Shawn and Andrea Merriman.

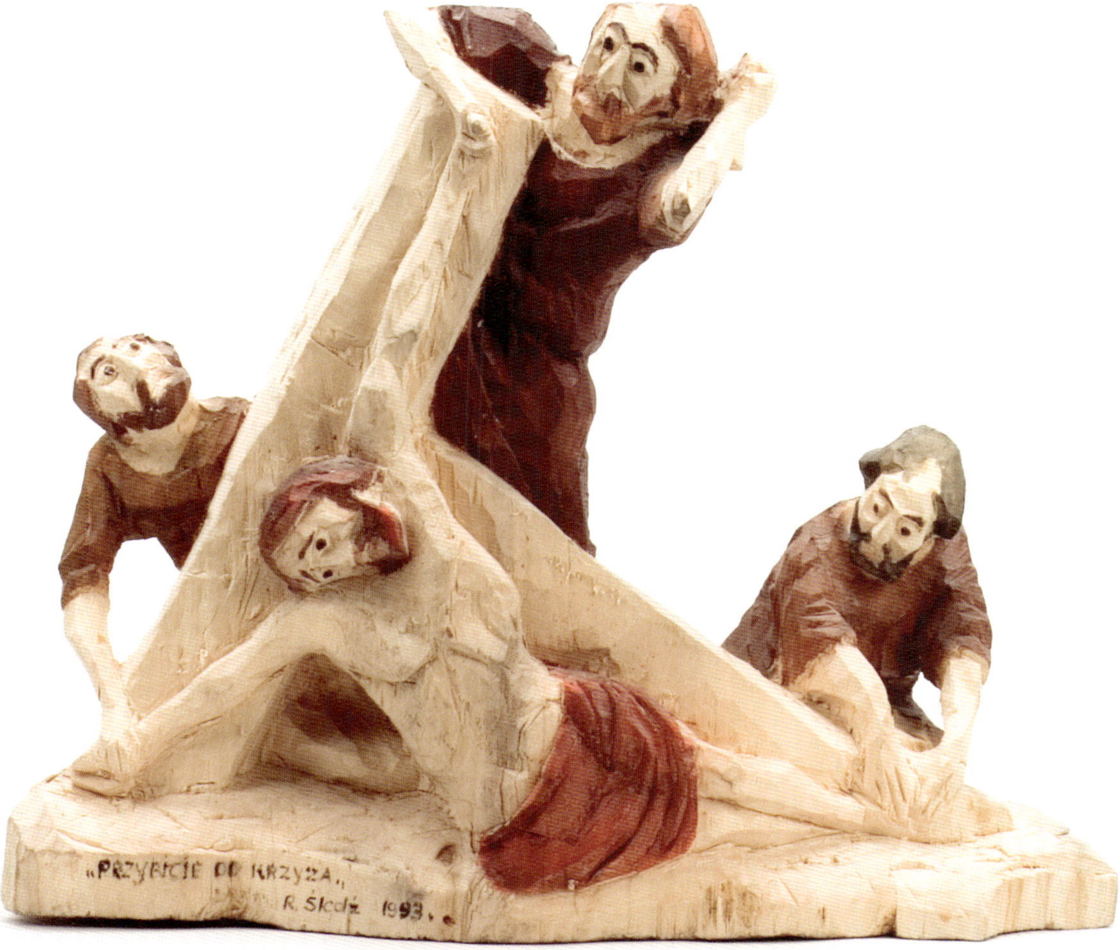

Figure 71. Roman Śledź (b. 1948), *Christ Nailed to the Cross*, 1993, polychrome wood, 11 inches (height). Private collection of Walter and Mary Whipple.

in general in trying to reconstruct the intricate details of Jesus' death on the cross.

Crucifixion inflicted unspeakable pain and physical suffering on the condemned. The stench, screams, and horrible sights of the public place of execution on the outskirts of Jerusalem offered a grotesque counter image to the elegance and architectural splendor of the magnificent Herodian Temple and the Roman streets, pools, plazas, and other places in this largest city in the Roman province of Judea. The crosses planted outside the city walls of Jerusalem, as in other Roman cities throughout the Empire, warned potential enemies, runaway slaves, and rebellious religionists of what could happen to them. By publicly displaying a naked victim at a prominent place such as a

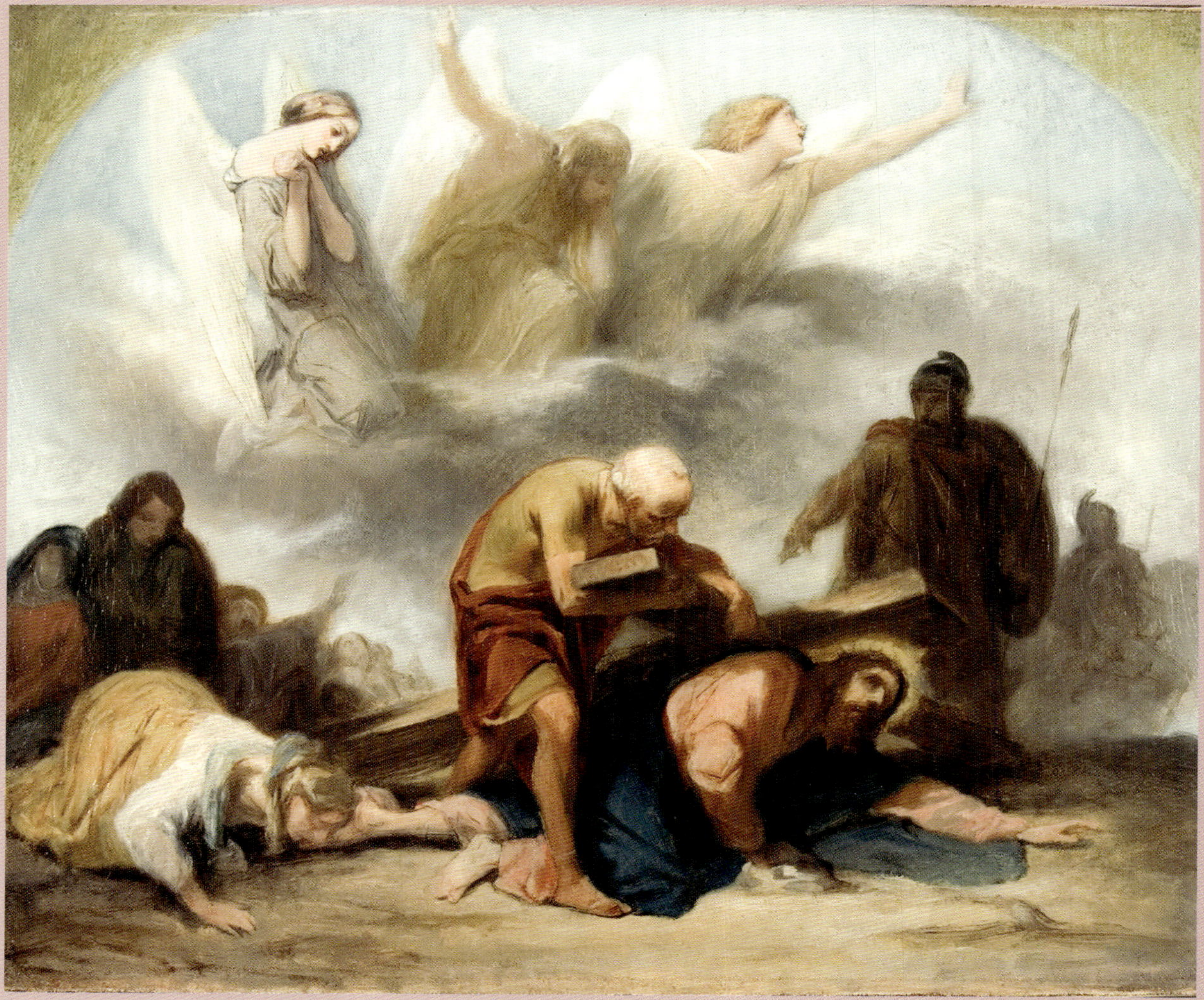

Figure 72. Octave Tassaert (1800–1874), *The Road to Calvary*, 19th century, oil on canvas, 13 x 16 inches. On loan from Mr. and Mrs. Noah L. Butkin, Snite Museum of Art, University of Notre Dame.

Counter-Reformation Art

In response to the accusations leveled against the Catholic Church during the Reformation, Pope Paul III called the Council of Trent in 1545 to define the doctrine and authority of the Roman Church. At the last session of the council in December 1563, Pope Pius IV issued an edict to counter Protestant claims of Catholic idolatry. The edict justified the use of sacred imagery as an aid in communicating with Deity and for religious instruction of the laity. Through art "the people are instructed and confirmed, in remembering and daily calling to mind the Articles of Faith . . . admonished of the Benefits and Gifts which are conferred upon them by Christ . . . [and] stirred up to adore and love God, and exercise and delight in Godliness."[1]

The council's revitalized emphasis on sacred images fostered a dynamic and theatrical art style, which sought to enrapture viewers and reestablish emotive relationships between the worshipper and God. This Baroque style, sometimes labeled as an emotional assault of the senses,[2] was intended to move viewers to devotion and to restore and strengthen the faith of believers.

The Crucifixion: Condemnation or Salvation?

The Crucifixion, understood in greater and lesser degrees throughout the history of Christianity, was a recurrent theme in Counter-Reformation art. These brutal images at times seemed contradictory in purpose. Some were intended to stir up guilt in the sinner for causing the suffering of Christ, whereas others were meant to offer hope to the believer through the healing power of the Atonement. The first of these purposes inspired an image type called the

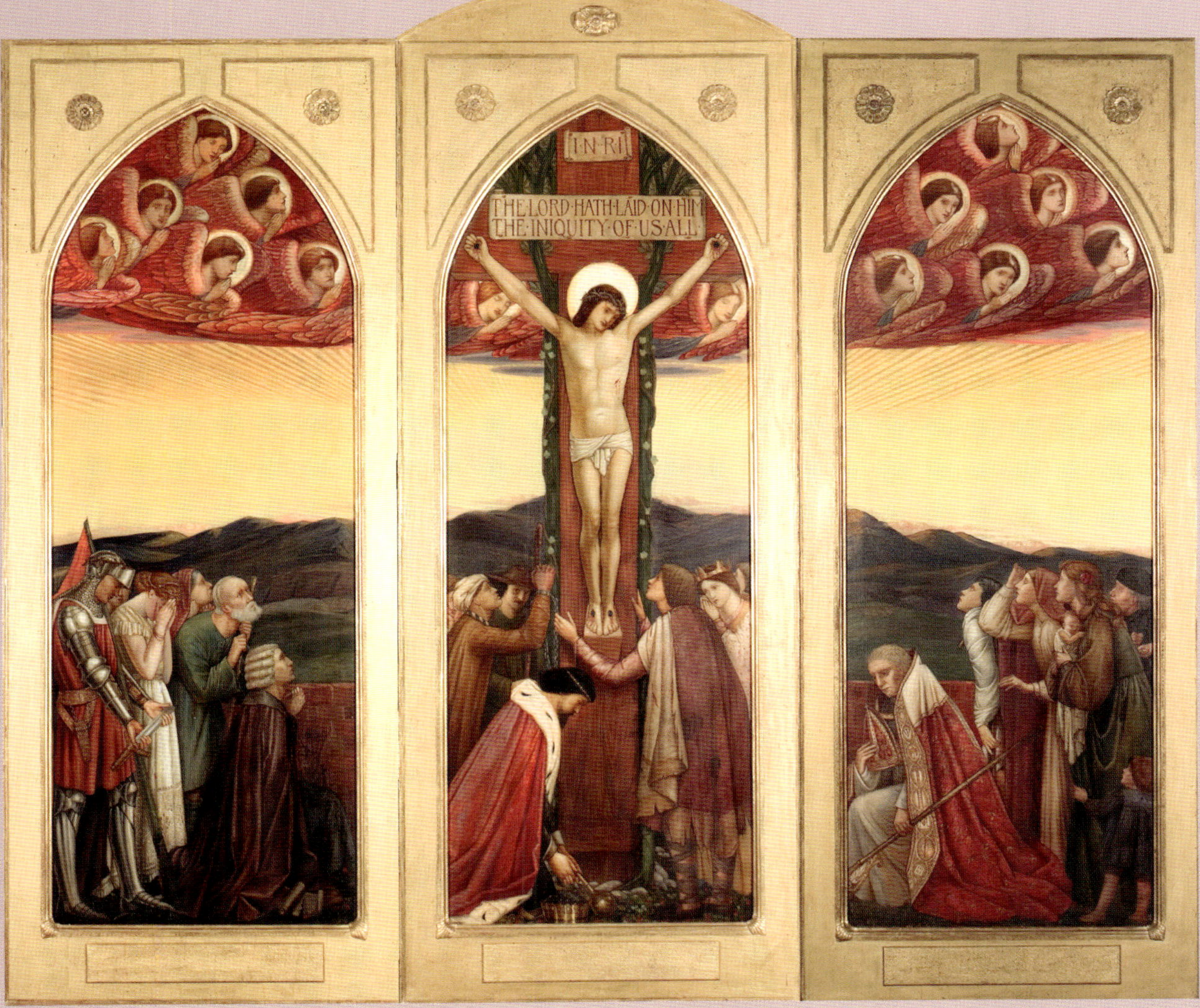

Figure 73. Bernard Sleigh (1872–1954), *The Crucifixion—A Triptych*, 1906, oil on canvas, 84 x 32 inches. Brigham Young University Museum of Art, purchased with funds provided by the Campbell Family Foundation and Verla Birrell.

Suffering Christ or Man of Sorrows in which Christ, surrounded by the instruments of the Passion, displays the wounds of the Crucifixion. These pictorial representations were developed from the Catholic doctrine of "Perpetual Passion," an idea popularized in the fourteenth and fifteenth centuries. Affirming man's culpability in the eternal suffering of Christ, these images were intended to elicit strong feelings of remorse on the part of the sinner and to be a deterrent to further transgressions. In Albrecht Dürer's *Title Page: The Mocking of Christ* from the *Large Passion* series (Figure 74), Christ confronts the viewer as He displays the wounds in His hands and feet while seated on the lid of the sepulcher. This visual message was supplemented with a devotional poem in which Christ appeals to the viewer to cease from the sins that cause Him to suffer anew:

These cruel wounds I bear for thee, O man,
And cure thy mortal sickness with my blood.
I take away thy sores with mine, thy death
With mine—a God Who changed to man for thee.
But thou, ingrate, still stabb'st my wounds with sins;
I still take floggings for thy guilty acts.
It should have been enough to suffer once
From hostile Jews; now, friend, let there be peace![3]

A second purpose inspired crucifixion images that communicated salvation rather than condemnation. An excellent example of this is Bernard Sleigh's *The Crucifixion—A Triptych* (Figure 73), an altarpiece commissioned for the chapel in London's Holloway Prison. The inscription at the head of the cross, "THE

LORD HATH LAID ON HIM THE INIQUITY OF US ALL," made it particularly poignant for its imprisoned viewers. Cognizant of his audience, Sleigh includes a man in chains at the foot of the cross who pleads for forgiveness and mercy.

The painting also portrays a wide range of both historical and symbolic figures dressed in contemporary costume who worship the Savior. Standing immediately to the left of the cross, the artist appears as a shepherd, most likely referring to the role of the shepherds at Christ's birth and also to the artist's own Welsh ancestors who were shepherds for many generations.[4] The artist's wife, Stella, and their two young children are pictured on the far right. By appearing as participants in the worship of the crucified Christ, the artist and his family invite believers to do likewise and place themselves within the context of the scene.

To expand this universal implication, Sleigh also incorporates four figures symbolic of key entities of society: a knight (military), a judge (law), a king (government), and a bishop (religion). Each bows his head or knee to the Savior, offering up an emblem of his earthly power and authority. The knight holds out a broken sword, symbolic of the end of all war (see Isaiah 2:4). The torn scroll placed before the judge and the removed crown of the king signify Christ as the new judge, lawgiver, and king (see Isaiah 33:22). The bishop, too, removes his miter and lowers his crosier, submitting to the supreme "Bishop of [our] souls" (1 Peter 2:25). By transforming the Crucifixion into a contemporary event and representing this cross-section of mankind, the work engages the viewer in an intimate manner.

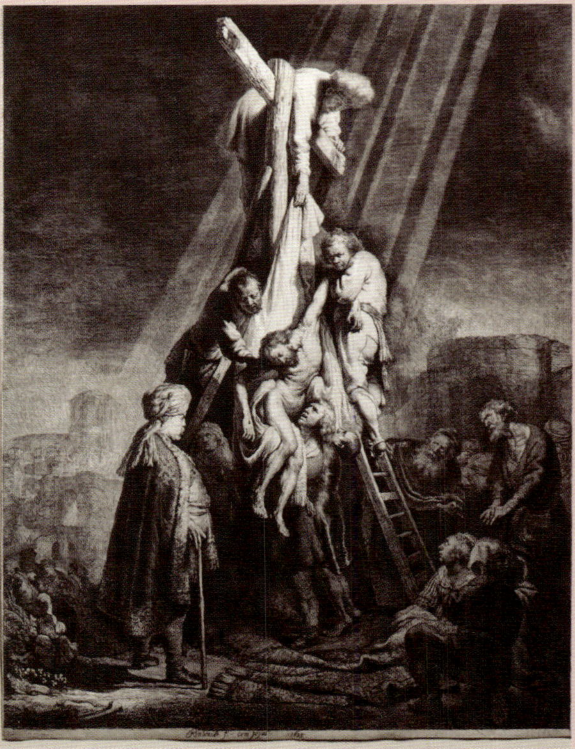

Figure 75. Rembrandt Harmenszoon van Rijn (1606–1669), *The Descent from the Cross by Torchlight*, 1654, etching and drypoint, 8 3/16 x 6 3/8 inches. Private collection of Shawn and Andrea Merriman.

Both the condemning and saving types of crucifixion images were intended to educe emotional responses from the viewer: one draws in the believer with guilt, while the other draws in the believer with love. Although these two approaches seem diametrically opposed, they both anticipate the same result of encouraging believers to "come unto Christ" (Jacob 1:7).

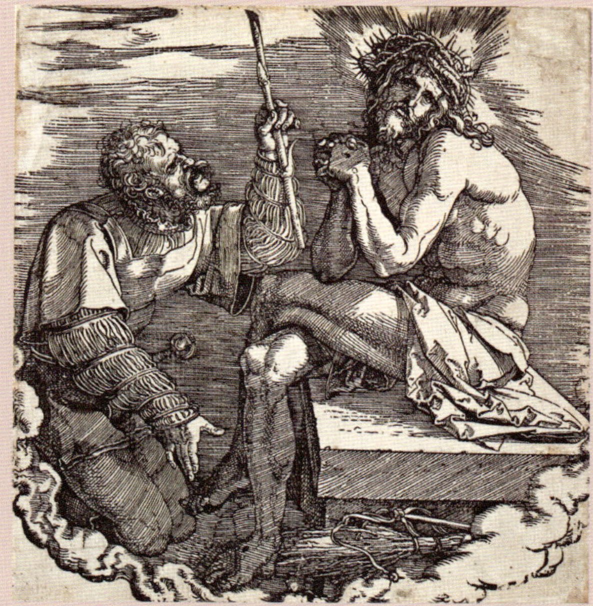

Figure 74. Albrecht Dürer (1471–1528), *Title Page: The Mocking of Christ*, from the *Large Passion*, 1511, woodcut, 7 5/8 x 7 7/16 inches. Brigham Young University Museum of Art, purchase/gift from Mahonri M. Young Estate.

1. "Concerning the Invocation, Worship, and Relicks of the Saints, and Holy Images," in *The Canons and Decress of the Council of Trent: Celebrated under Paul III, Julius III, and Pius IV, Bishops of Rome* (Ann Arbor, MI: University of Michigan, 1999– [Early English Books Online]), Digital version of: Early English Books, 1641–1700; 1057:2.
2. Williamson, *Christian Art: A Very Short Introduction*, 64.
3. These verses, written by Benedictus Chelidonius, were added to the title page of the 1511 edition of the *Large Passion* series (Erwin Panofsky, *Albrecht Dürer*, vol. 1 [Princeton, NJ: Princeton University Press, 1945], 139).
4. Bernard Sleigh, "Memoirs of a Human Peter Pan," unpublished autobiography, 1941–42. Information provided by Roger Cooper.

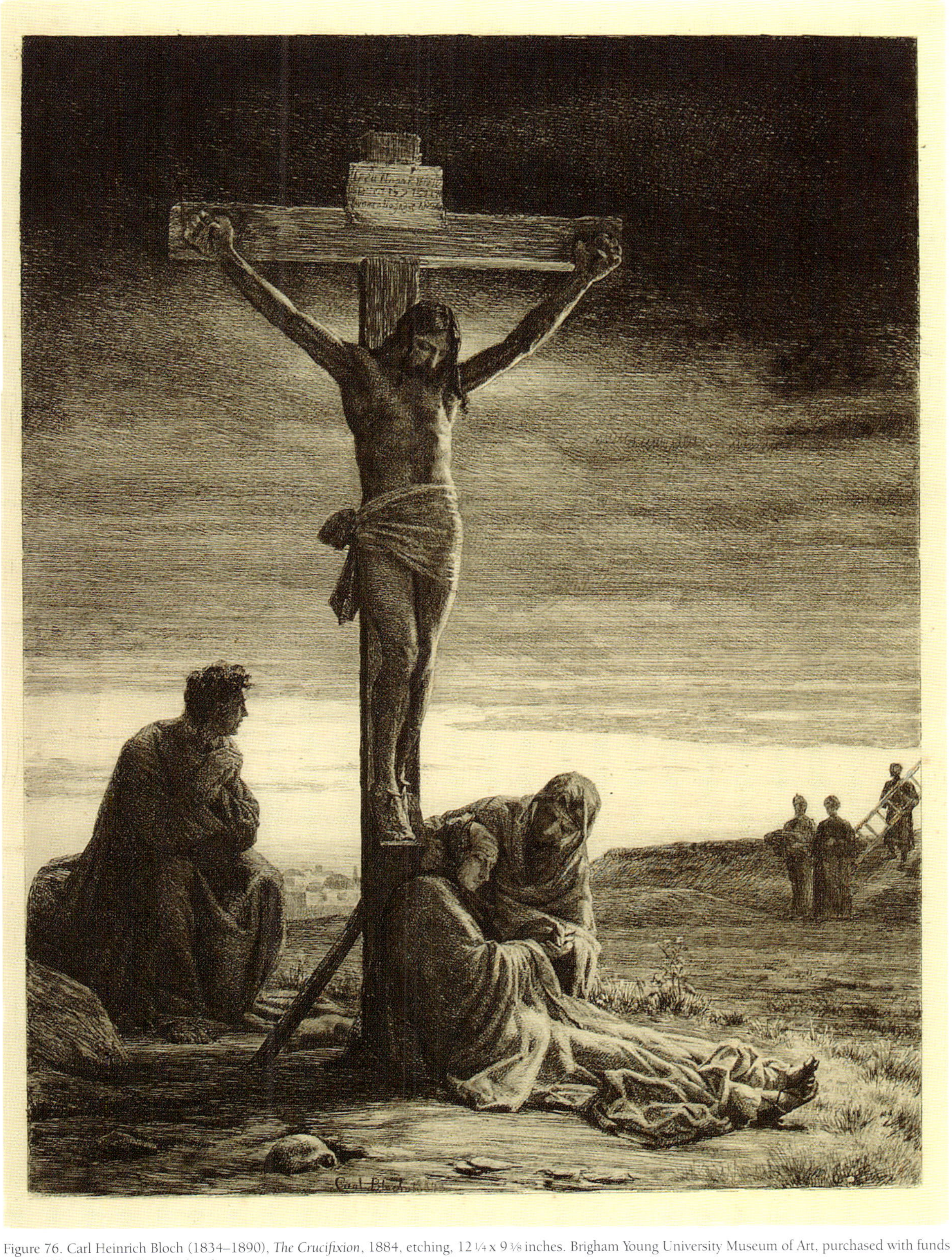

Figure 76. Carl Heinrich Bloch (1834–1890), *The Crucifixion*, 1884, etching, 12 1/4 x 9 3/8 inches. Brigham Young University Museum of Art, purchased with funds provided by Robert and Lisa Wheatley.

crossroads, a crowded highway, theater, or high ground, the Romans also ensured the condemned would suffer utmost humiliation.

Death by crucifixion was not meant to be quick. It generally slowly transformed anyone branded as an enemy of the Roman order from a living, breathing person into a very bruised and battered corpse. Crucifixion often, as with other forms of execution, involved pitiless maltreatment, public abasement, and lack of burial.

Distorted Views of Jesus' Crucifixion

The visual image of a "green hill" for Jesus' crucifixion is not based on the biblical text. Rather, it is a fictional notion popularized in a beautiful and reverential hymn written in the nineteenth century by Cecil Frances Alexander, "There Is a Green Hill Far Away" (*Hymns*, no. 194). In reality, the terrain surrounding the city of Jerusalem is stony, stark, and barren. Mark's account does not give directions to the hill where Jesus was executed but merely states that He was brought "unto the place Golgotha, which is, being interpreted, The place of a skull" (Mark 15:22).

We cannot possibly know exactly what the original audience who first heard and read the story of Jesus' crucifixion thought and felt as they heard about, read about, or discussed the account. One thing is certain—their mental image of crucifixion was not based on paintings, movies, and sculptures to which we are exposed and which often feature aspects that fall under the heading of artistic interpretation.

Sometimes, to distinguish Jesus from the two other men who were being crucified, artists and film directors depict the other men as being

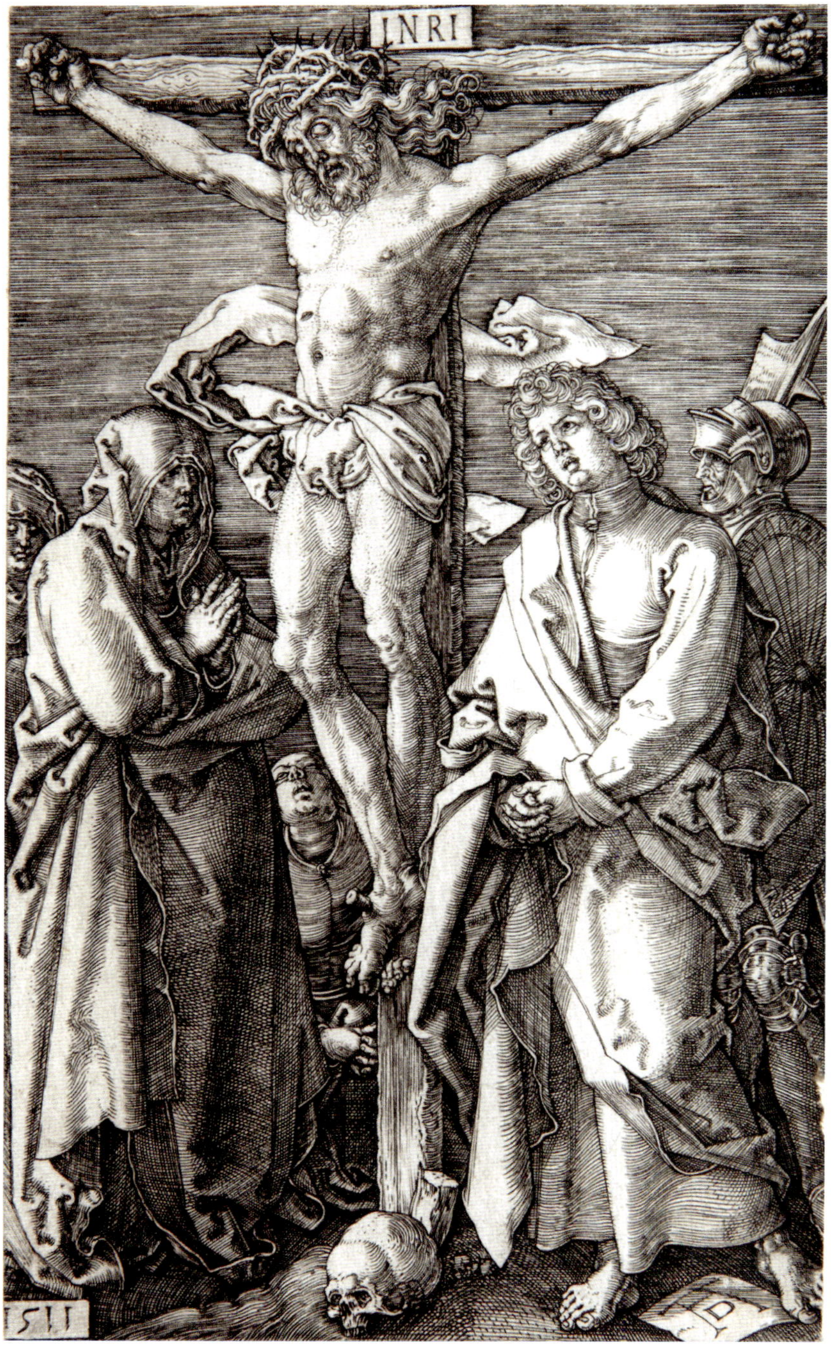

Figure 77. Albrecht Dürer (1471–1528), *Crucifixion*, from the *Engraved Passion*, 1511, engraving, 4 3/4 x 2 15/16 inches. Private collection of Shawn and Andrea Merriman.

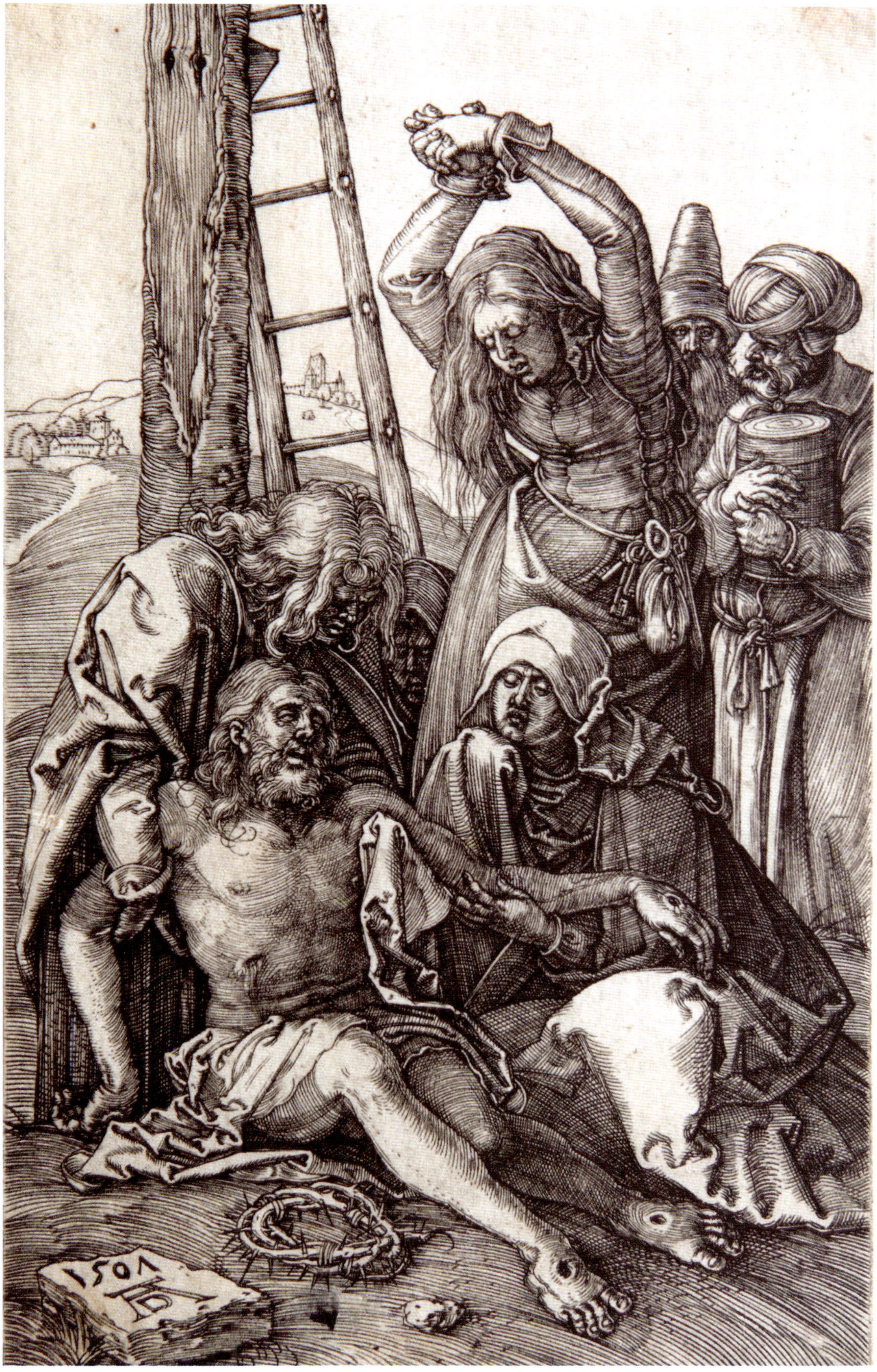

Figure 78. Albrecht Dürer (1471–1528), *Lamentation over Christ*, from the *Engraved Passion*, 1507, engraving, 4 3/8 x 2 13/16 inches. Private collection of Shawn and Andrea Merriman.

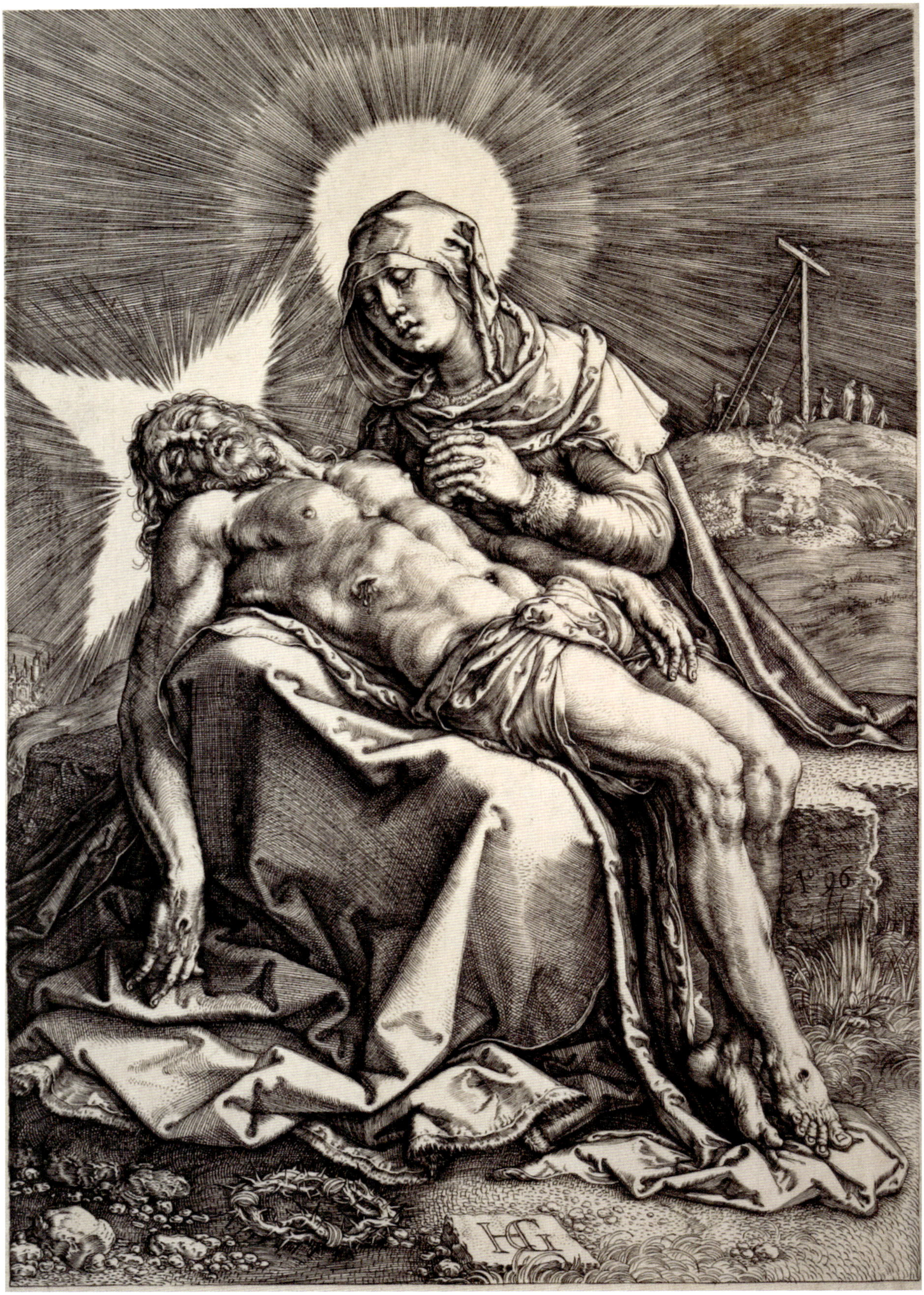

Figure 79. Hendrik Goltzius (1558–1617), *Lamentation of the Virgin*, 1596, engraving, 6 7/8 x 4 15/16 inches. Brigham Young University Museum of Art, purchase/gift from Mahonri M. Young Estate.

tied, not nailed, to their crosses. Although history contains examples of victims being tied to a cross to lengthen the process of death, nothing in the New Testament indicates that such was the case. Because Jesus was nailed to the cross, we should assume that the two criminals executed with him were also nailed.

Other artistic developments over the centuries have also shaped our present mental images of Jesus' crucifixion. One frequent image we are correctly exposed to is the piercing of Jesus' feet, generally the right foot placed over the left, with one large spike penetrating both feet. However, artists leave us to puzzle over whether the nails pierced Jesus' hands only, His wrists only, or both His hands and wrists. Another common image that is typically and unrealistically distorted is the size, shape, and construction of the cross. The depiction and use of the cross through crucifixes, as opposed to the doctrine of the cross, was a late development in Christianity.

Our Participation in the Crucifixion

Despite the visual images of the event, whether correctly or incorrectly captured by artistic endeavors, the story carries power independent of all images so that we can be present on the fateful Friday afternoon in Jerusalem.

Jesus' terrible scourging, His slow, agonizing march to the place of execution, His humiliating stripping before He was nailed to the cross, the mocking by those present, including at least one of those executed with Him, His final words, including those directed toward the beloved disciple and His own mother, and other singular aspects of the horrible crucifixion form a conglomerate of individual, unforgettable events that can each be visualized, described, and experienced vicariously through personal mental images and artistic endeavors. Each recorded moment tells a poignant story and provides the basis for word-pictures and visual images to help us interpret the words of the scriptures and appreciate the dimensions of the Atonement. More important, however, is the meaning of His life that we should search for within these awful and unforgettable events.

The sorrows and disappointments, pains and anguish, and sufferings and deaths of previous generations were bound up in this day. The answer to all the voices that had been crying for redemption, rescue, justice, and forgiveness was echoed in Jesus' final declaration, "It is finished" (John 19:30).

In the end, the Roman soldier, who had presumably witnessed numerous executions like this one at Golgotha, noticed something remarkably different, causing him to proclaim, "Truly this was the Son of God" (Matthew 27:54). The various facets of the Crucifixion should help us draw similar conclusions, along with attendant implications for our discipleship.

Jesus' Burial

We typically do not appreciate the fact that, in one last act of humiliation, the Romans generally forbade the proper burial of the condemned. Either the body was left on the cross to become the food of wild dogs and birds or was thrown into a mass grave, denying family and friends a place to remember their loved one with certainty.

However, it was Passover in Judea, and Pilate made an exception to the rule. We know such exceptions were occasionally made because we have at least one example of the burial of a crucified victim in Judea during the first century. When the Lord's body was taken from the cross, Joseph of Arimathaea "wrapped it in linen," a common burial cloth of the period made of flax from either Egypt or Jericho. The body was then taken to a new tomb, "hewn in stone, wherein never man before was laid" (Luke 23:53). Luke continues, "And the women also, which came with him from Galilee, followed after, and beheld the sepulchre, and how his body was laid. And they returned, and prepared spices and ointments; and rested the sabbath day according to the commandment" (Luke 23:55–56). We have no reason to doubt the reality of Jesus' hasty burial in the empty tomb,

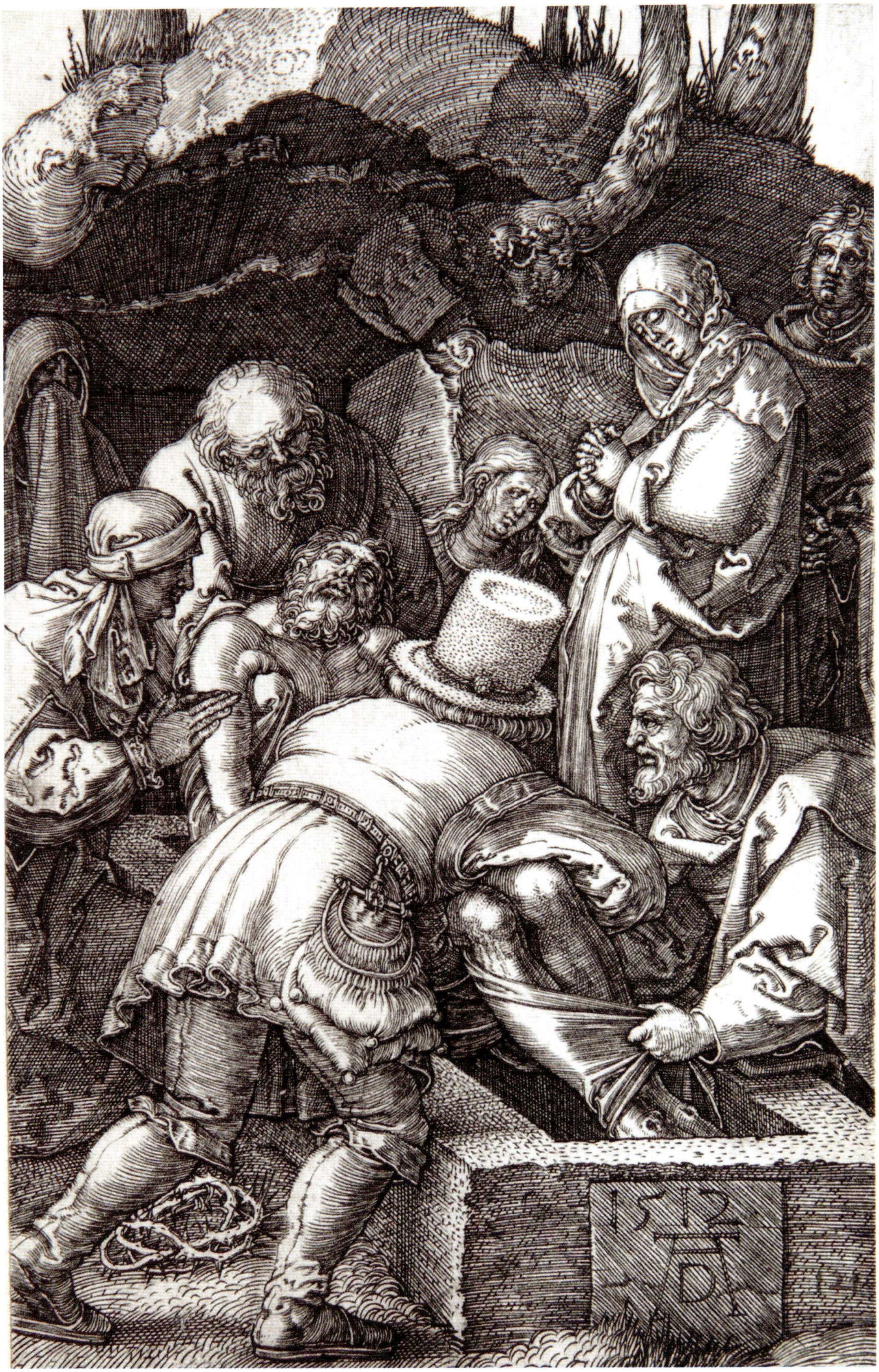

Figure 80. Albrecht Dürer (1471–1528), *Entombment*, from the *Engraved Passion*, 1512, engraving, 4 5/8 x 2 7/8 inches. Private collection of Shawn and Andrea Merriman.

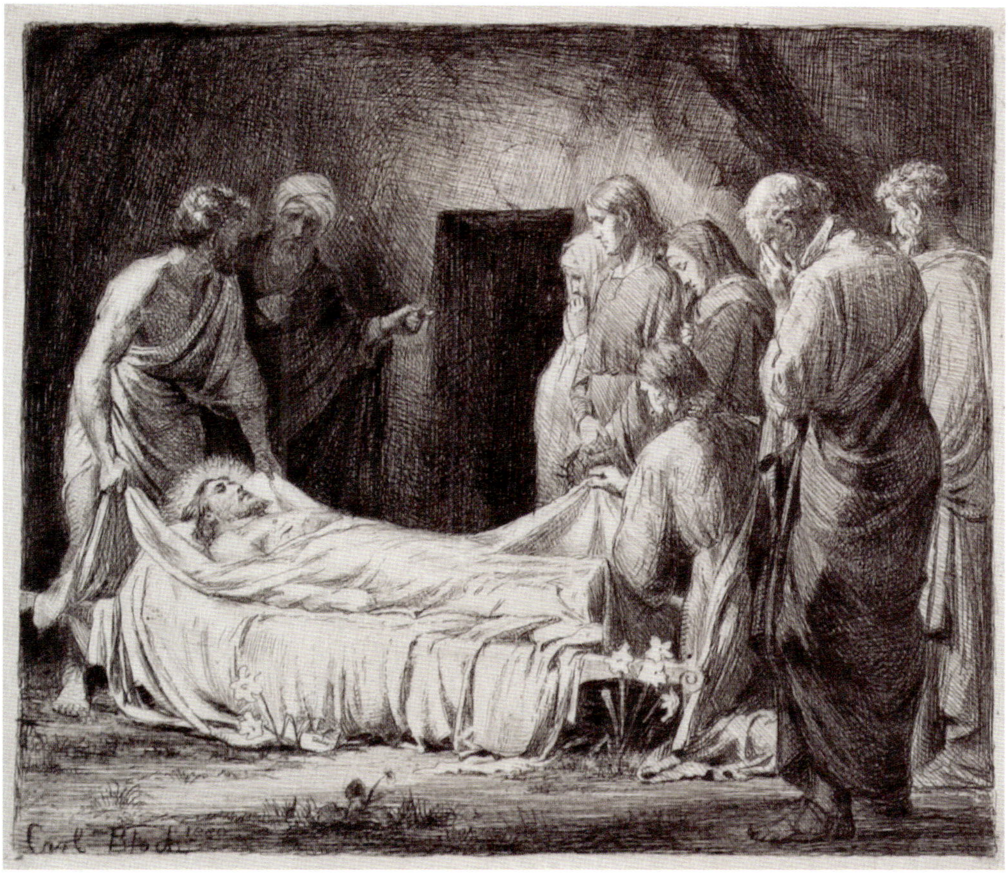

Figure 81. Carl Heinrich Bloch (1834–1890), *The Entombment*, 1880, etching, 3 13/16 x 3 5/16 inches. Brigham Young University Museum of Art, purchased with funds provided by Robert and Lisa Wheatley.

with the attendant easing of the horrible scenes of the Crucifixion from our minds.

Within a very short time, Jesus had been tried, executed, and buried near the Holy City. Capturing those events in art, like others in Jesus' life and ministry, has resulted in unparalleled human efforts to help past, present, and future generations of both believers and nonbelievers remember those days in creative, confirming, and artistic ways of adoration.

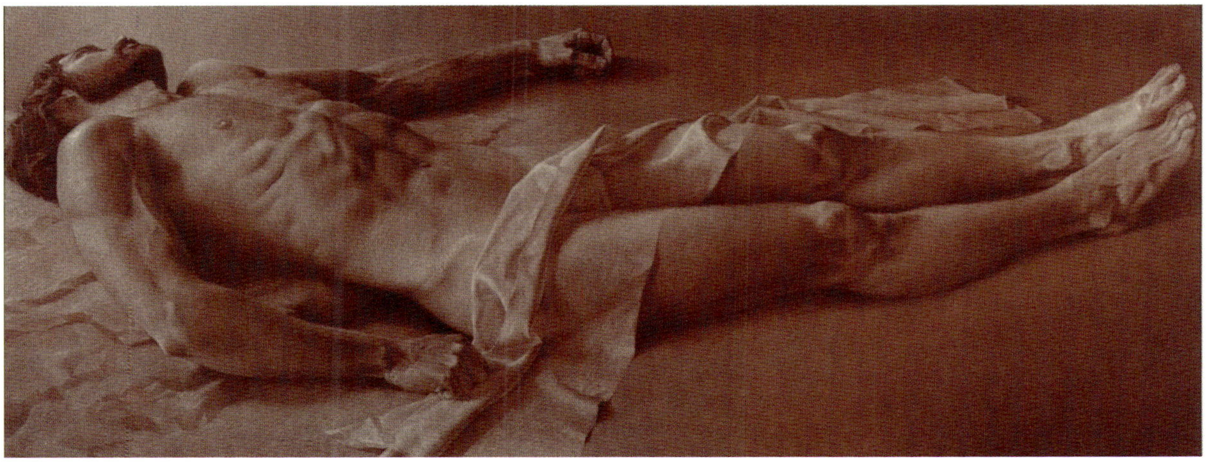

Figure 82. Kent Goodliffe (b. 1946), *Through Death Came Life*, 1979, prismacolor pencil, 11 7/16 x 29 1/8 inches. Brigham Young University Museum of Art.

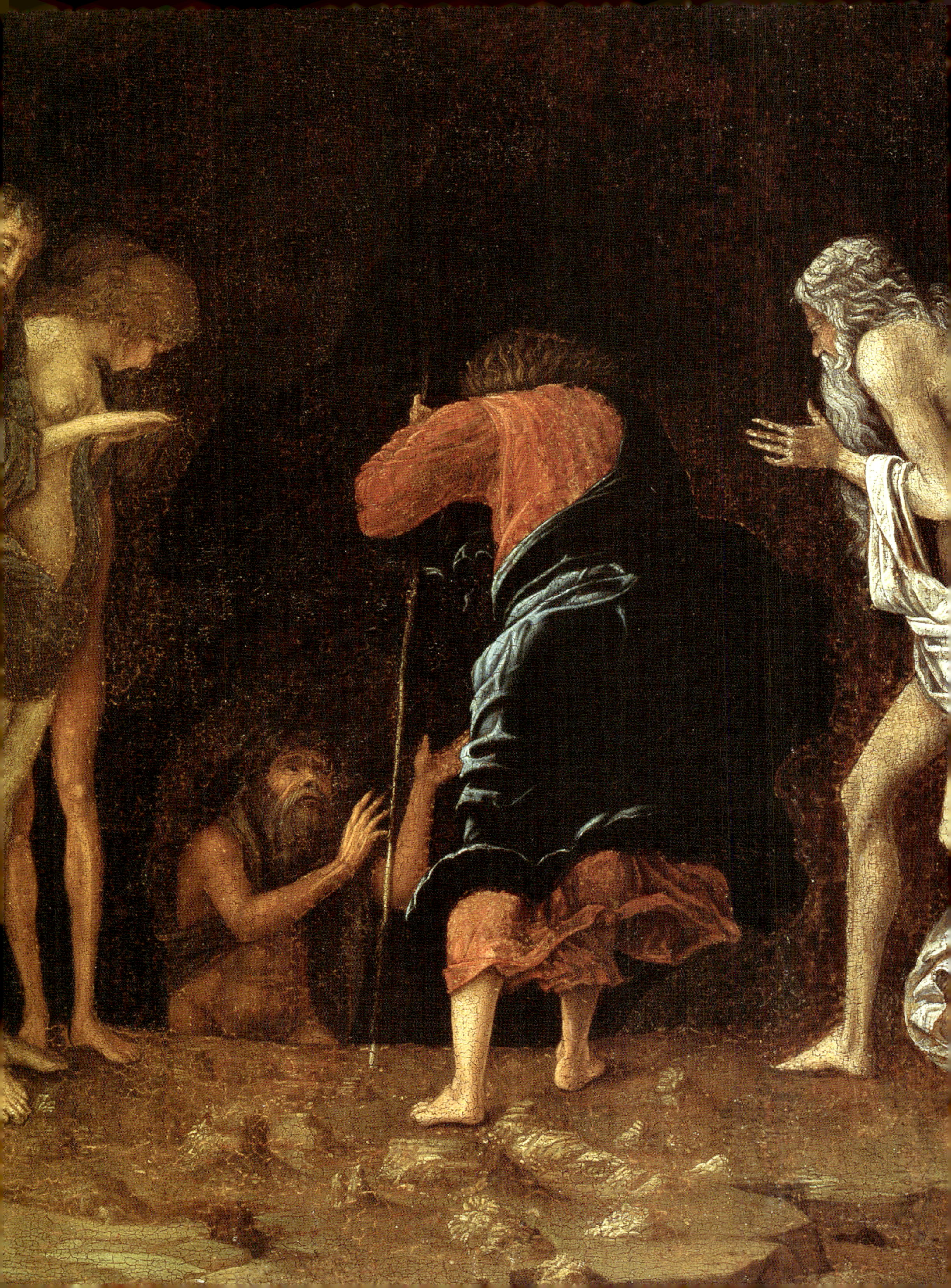

Chapter 13

Anastasis

The popular theme of Christ's descent into hell to rescue the souls of the dead, occurring between His own death and resurrection, arises in a text often attached to the apocryphal Acts of Pilate and preceding it in age. The two texts together were known during the medieval period as the *Gospel of Nicodemus*. In this account, the two sons of Simeon, the man who met Joseph and Mary in the temple (see Luke 2:25–35), offer an eyewitness report of Jesus' dramatic rescue of souls from the dark grasp of Hades. In the narrative, Simeon's sons had died, had gone to the world of departed spirits, had witnessed Jesus' destruction of the spirit prison and its gates, and had then been resurrected soon after Jesus rose from the dead (see Matthew 27:52–53).

The story of Jesus' descent inspired medieval painters to try to capture the event as one of the merciful consequences of Jesus' atonement. This moment of deliverance, enacted while Jesus' body lay in the tomb—and its artistic representation—is known as *anastasis*, though this Greek word in the New Testament properly refers to the resurrection of the dead.

In fulfillment of Isaiah's hope-laced prophecy that "they that dwell in the land of the shadow of death, upon them hath the light shined" (Isaiah 9:2), the light of the sun suddenly breaks into the dark realm of the dead where all departed spirits are imprisoned. This light signals the approach of Jesus in spirit form. But before He arrives, many of the prophets and patriarchs, including Adam and John the Baptist, declare that they had known and spoken about this moment. It is also evident from this scene that all the important inspired leaders from the past had gathered together with other righteous spirits in anticipation of Jesus' coming and knew that they were at last to be freed.

The story opens with Joseph of Arimathaea telling the high priests Annas and Caiaphas that not only Jesus but also many others have risen from the dead—in accord with Matthew 27:52–53, which ties the story to the New Testament account. According to Joseph, the sons of Simeon, now resurrected beings, were then in the town of Arimathaea where they were in a constant state of prayer. After being coaxed, these two sons later go to Jerusalem with Joseph and the others where, in a synagogue, they agree to write their death experiences independently of one another, though the two brothers had earlier been put under obligation not to recount what had happened in the realm of the dead. At the last, the two accounts were said to match in every detail, thus providing two identical testimonies. Their narratives, it is said, stand as the basis for the text.

For Christians, the story offered a sweet reassurance that the Resurrection would be universal, beginning with Jesus' raising of Adam from the dead. It also stood as proof that the words of the prophets would be fulfilled. The account also brings together a rainbow of references to stories from the ministry of Jesus that underscore His divine powers, such as His reviving of Lazarus from the dead. In addition, the account was an illustration that, in death, Jesus had mortally wounded the kingdom of Satan, which had previously maintained control over the peoples of the earth through disease,

Attributed to Andrea Mantegna (ca. 1431–1506), detail of *The Descent into Limbo*, ca. 1497, oil on panel, 28 x 22 inches. The Sarah Campbell Blaffer Foundation.

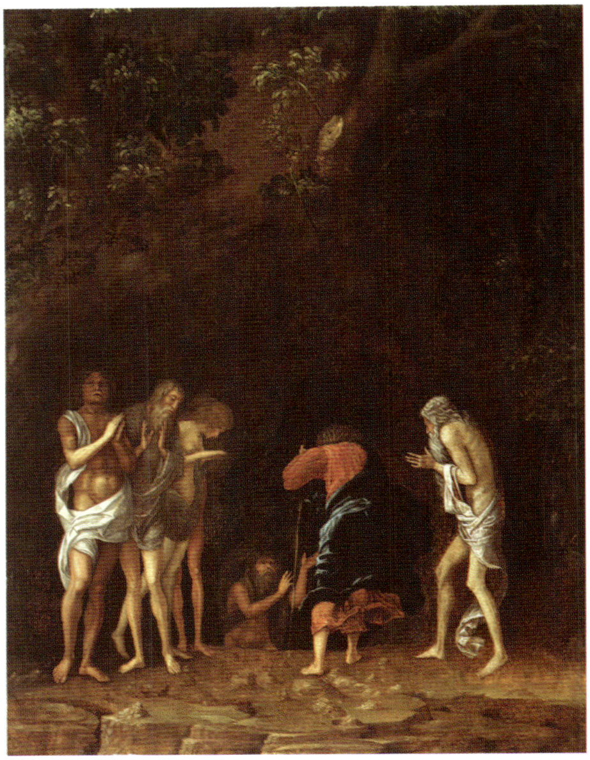

Figure 83. Attributed to Andrea Mantegna (ca. 1431–1506), *The Descent into Limbo*, ca. 1497, oil on panel, 28 x 22 inches. The Sarah Campbell Blaffer Foundation.

disability, and death. With the triumphant descent of Christ into hell, Satan is confined to hell and his power over those "bound in the chains of their sins" evaporates (*Gospel of Nicodemus* 20:3). For Jesus comes, forcing open the gates of hell in accord with the Psalm: "Lift up your heads, O ye gates; and be ye lift up, ye everlasting doors; and the King of glory shall come in" (Psalm 24:7).

A similar account lies in a modern scriptural report, which, like the story in the *Gospel of Nicodemus,* was tied to the atoning power of Jesus Christ. This account records a vision received by President Joseph F. Smith in 1918, now published as Doctrine and Covenants 138. The grounds for this story rest chiefly on two passages in the First Epistle of Peter in the New Testament. In writing of Jesus' suffering for sins, Peter declares that Jesus, "being put to death in the flesh, but quickened by the Spirit . . . went and preached unto the spirits in prison." Peter goes on to explain that "the gospel [was] preached also to them that are dead, that they might be judged according to men in the flesh, but live according to God in the spirit" (1 Peter 3:18–19; 4:6).

Though the scriptural ties differ, the ancient and modern accounts—the *Gospel of Nicodemus* and Joseph F. Smith's vision—share a set of common elements. First, Adam appears in a prominent light, as does Eve. Second, the patriarchs and prophets of the Old Testament era rate specific mention, including Abraham and Isaiah. Third, the righteous from all ages have gathered together in anticipation of their redemption, knowing that Jesus had suffered crucifixion and was coming to free them "from death and the chains of hell" (Doctrine and Covenants 138:23). Fourth, the assembled multitude was obviously in the light at Jesus' arrival because "the radiance from the presence of the Lord rested upon them" and the rebellious spirits were in "darkness," though this darkness may be understood as spiritual rather than as an absence of light (see Doctrine and Covenants 138:22, 24, 30).

What is different in the modern vision is that the spirits of the wicked were not freed at the visit of the crucified Jesus. Instead, they "were in darkness" (Doctrine and Covenants 138:30). In addition, "the Lord went not in person among the wicked and the disobedient who had rejected the truth" (Doctrine and Covenants 138:29). Rather, "from among the righteous" Jesus "appointed messengers, clothed with power and authority" who were commissioned to "proclaim liberty to the captives who were [still] bound, even unto all who would repent of their sins and receive the gospel" (Doctrine and Covenants 138:30–31). Further, unlike the *Gospel of Nicodemus,* the vision does not speak of Jesus breaking the strong gates of hell that kept the spirits of the dead imprisoned. In simple language, we read that "the Son of God appeared, declaring liberty to the captives who had been faithful" (Doctrine and Covenants 138:18). Moreover, nothing is said about Satan's fate, though it is understood that his power over the righteous has been brought to an end with Jesus' atoning sacrifice. Additionally, it becomes clear that one of the important purposes for building temples has to do with "the performance of ordinances therein for the redemption of the dead" (Doctrine and Covenants 138:54), that is, performing saving ordinances to which the dead otherwise had no access. These "ordinances of the house of God" make it possible for these spirits to be "redeemed, [and] . . . washed clean, [and] . . . receive a reward according to their works" (Doctrine and Covenants 138:58–59).

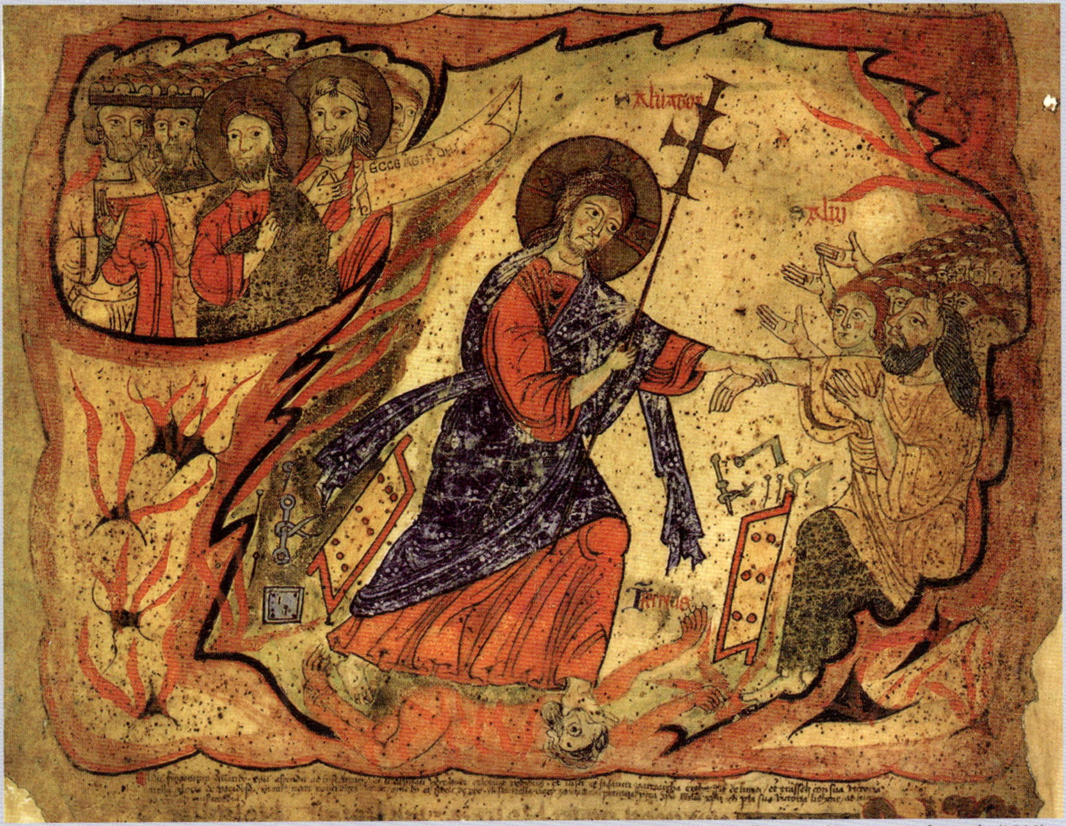

Figure 84. *The Harrowing of Hell*, from the *Exultet Roll: Codex Barberini Latinus* 592 (f. 4), ca. 1087, illuminated manuscript facsimile (1998), 32 3/8 x 10 3/4 inches (entire roll). Rare Books Division, Special Collections, J. Willard Marriott Library, University of Utah; © Biblioteca Apostolica Vaticana (Vatican).

The Descent into Limbo

Based on the apocryphal *Gospel of Nicodemus*, images of the Anastasis portray Christ's descent into hell to release the prophets and the patriarchs of the Old Testament (Figure 83). Also known as the Harrowing of Hell or Descent into Limbo, this doctrine emphasized Christ's victory over death and the devil. As recorded by Nicodemus, hell's "gates of brass were broken in pieces"[1] as Christ trampled Satan under His feet (Figure 84). Accordingly, artists often portrayed the doors of hell falling to the ground, crushing Satan and his demons. In Dürer's *Christ in Limbo*, Christ holds the banner of the Resurrection as He reaches out to liberate the righteous from Limbo (Figure 85). Adam and Eve are generally the first to be rescued, followed by Abel, clothed in fur skins. These images testify that, in "declaring liberty to the captives who had been faithful," Christ became the "Redeemer and Deliverer from death and the chains of hell" (Doctrine and Covenants 138:18, 23).

1. Hall, *Dictionary of Subjects and Symbols in Art*, 100.

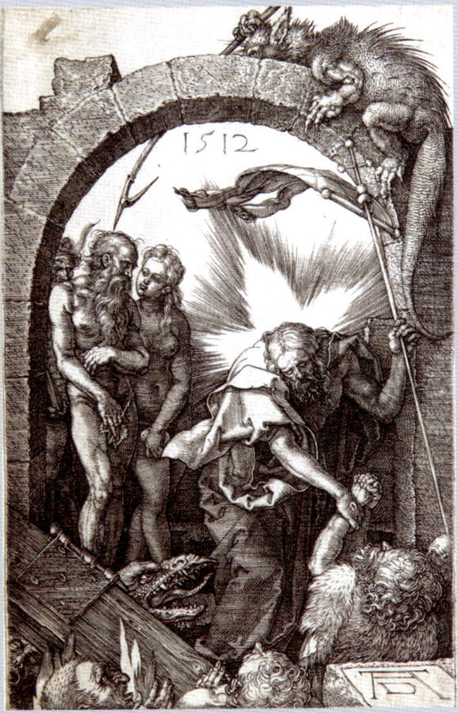

Figure 85. Albrecht Dürer (1471–1528), *Christ in Limbo*, from the *Engraved Passion*, 1512, engraving, 4 11/16 x 2 15/16 inches. Private collection of Shawn and Andrea Merriman.

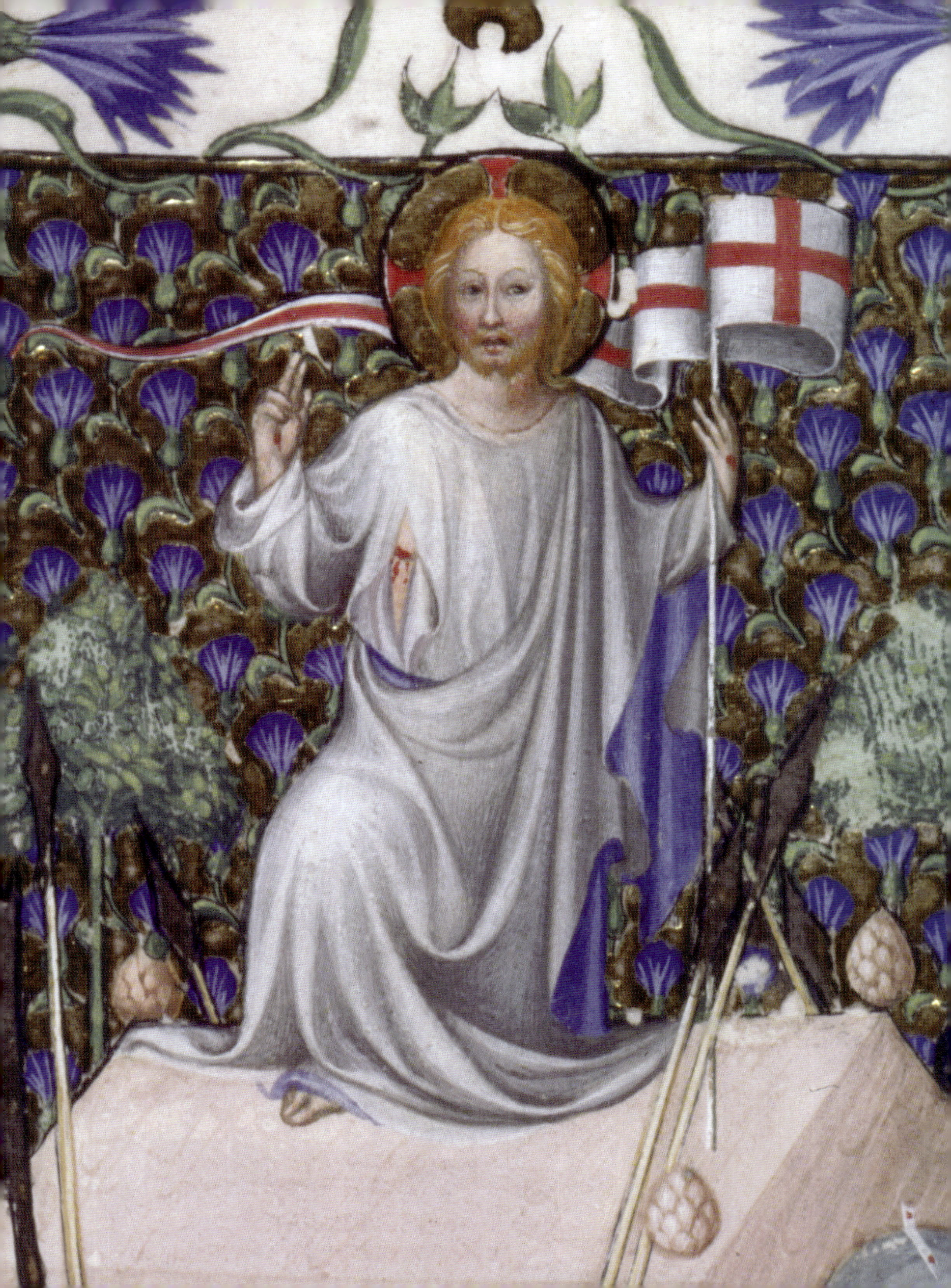

Chapter 14

Resurrection

Jesus of Nazareth has risen from the dead and ascended into heaven. This bold declaration by early Christian believers was a claim that others could not test because Jesus was no longer circulating in society as He once had. But His followers were steadfast in their insistence that Jesus had appeared to many, that they had seen and touched Him, that He had eaten with them, and that His eleven most trusted companions had seen Him ascend into heaven from the Mount of Olives. Their testimonies spoke of physical, palpable experiences with Him, complete with descriptions of what He wore, where He appeared, what He ate, and how He looked. It was an affirmation that would not go away.

The Resurrection

Perhaps the strongest reason to believe His followers' testimonies has to do with their plain reluctance at first to believe what they were seeing and touching. The Resurrection was not an event they would have made up, for they quickly dismissed the earliest reports, which came from women, whose "words seemed to them as idle tales, and they believed them not" (Luke 24:11). But when two of Jesus' closest mortal associates, Peter and James, the Lord's brother, affirmed that He had appeared first to one of them and then the other, doubtful followers had to take seriously the reality of the Resurrection.

The story grows out of the empty tomb where Jesus had been buried on a Friday afternoon. At the urging of Jewish authorities, the Roman governor, Pilate, had permitted the assigning of guards as a security detail at the tomb because these same authorities feared that Jesus' disciples would steal the body and then claim that He had risen from the dead, a clear indicator that the public was aware of Jesus' prophecy that He would conquer death.

Only Matthew reports the opening of the tomb. He records that "a great earthquake" struck, followed by the descent of "the angel of the Lord" who "came and rolled back the stone from the door" of the sepulchre and then, in an act of triumph, "sat upon" the stone (Matthew 28:2). The moment that the Risen Jesus stepped from the tomb remains unreported. But the accounts of witnesses who saw Him soon afterward constitute a massive mountain of testimony.

Old World Appearances

All of the Gospels hold that angels appeared to believing women at the tomb, the most prominent of whom was Mary Magdalene, who had come to the sepulchre to further prepare Jesus' body for burial because He had been entombed in haste. Again, it is only Matthew who rehearses that Jesus Himself met these women and sent them as His emissaries to the other disciples to instruct them to meet Him in Galilee, but not before they "held him by the feet, and worshipped him" (Matthew 28:9). Their witness was therefore physical, tangible.

In the Apostle Paul's grand catalogue of witnesses to Jesus' resurrection, he lists some of the most important of Jesus' appearances, including the one to himself, though he omits the appearances to the women, possibly because their word

Detail of *Resurrection*, from the *Prayer Book of Michelino da Besozzo* (f. 26v), ca. 1430, illuminated manuscript, 7 1/16 x 4 15/16 inches. The Pierpont Morgan Library, New York. MS M.944, f. 26v. Photograph © The Pierpont Morgan Library, New York.

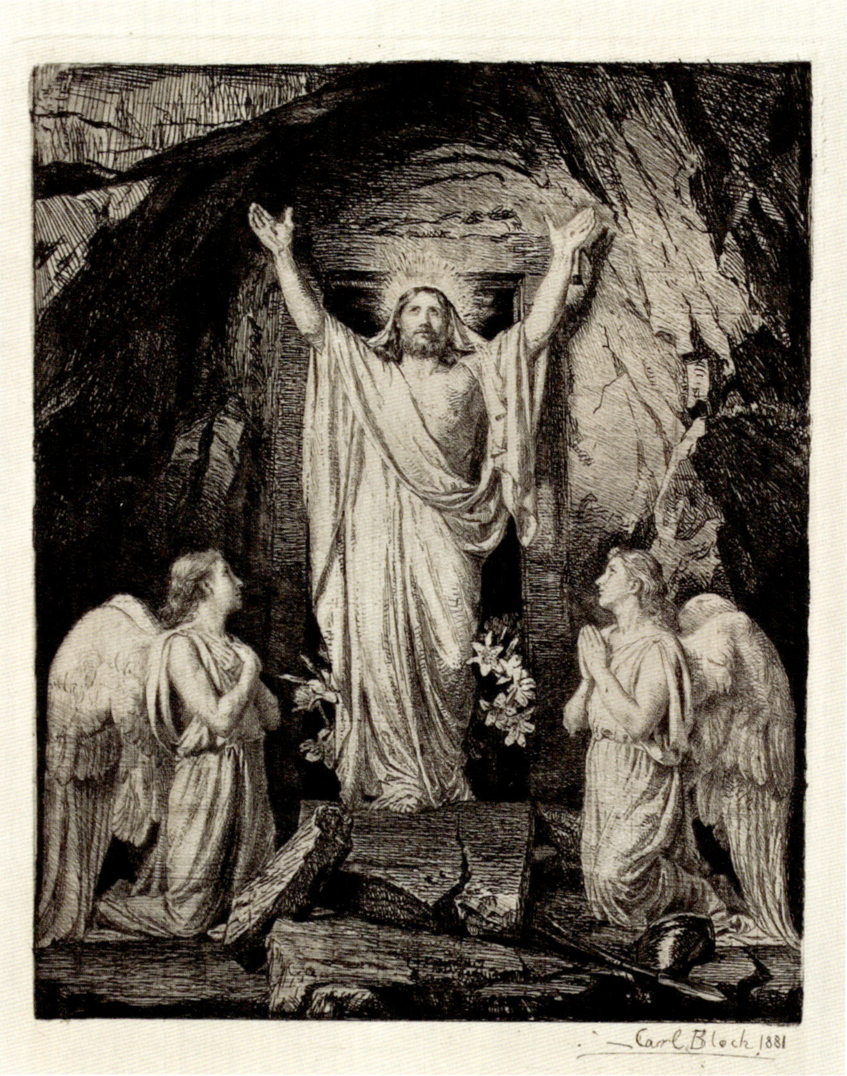

Figure 86. Carl Heinrich Bloch (1834–1890), *The Resurrection*, 1881, etching, 6 3/16 x 4 5/16 inches. Brigham Young University Museum of Art, purchased with funds provided by Robert and Lisa Wheatley.

would not carry weight in a legal case or hearing. In Paul's recounting, Peter stands first as the chief guarantor of the Resurrection: Jesus "was seen of Cephas [Peter], then of the twelve." Later, "he was seen of above five hundred brethren at once"—though we do not know the occasion—as well as by James, the Lord's brother, in a solo appearance (see 1 Corinthians 15:5–8). The sheer number of witnesses in Paul's rehearsal is both impressive and compelling.

Those who saw Jesus multiple times were the Eleven Apostles, for they were to be special witnesses to His resurrection. To be sure, they received word first from the women and then from Peter and the two who had accompanied the risen Jesus to the village of Emmaus (see Matthew 28:7–8; Mark 16:12–13; Luke 24:13–35). Though the apostles initially disbelieved the news, they were being prepared for what would follow. According to the Gospels, the first appearance to the Eleven occurred in Jerusalem the evening following Jesus' resurrection. Both Luke and John record that Jesus demonstrated His physical reality while He was present with them. By John's account, there was a second appearance in Jerusalem to the Eleven because Thomas had been absent on the first occasion (see John 20:24–29).

The next appearance was in Galilee, first at an appointed locale and then at the Sea of Galilee. According to Luke, Jesus appeared to the Eleven and taught them over a period of forty days, a season that came to a close with His ascension from the Mount of Olives. Both the number of appearances and the evident physicality of Jesus' person would have left a deep impression on the Eleven (see Matthew 28:16–20; Mark 16:14–20; Luke 24:36–52; John 20:19–29; 21:1–24; Acts 1:1–12).

The great extended blessing of Jesus' resurrection was that it opened the grave for all, a fact proved by the almost simultaneous resurrection of others. In his report of nature's response to Jesus' death, Matthew records that "the graves were opened; and many bodies of the saints which slept arose." But the action did not stop there. Witnesses were all-important: those who "came out of the graves after [Jesus'] resurrection . . . went into the holy city, and appeared unto many," thus establishing a pool of witnesses to a general resurrection that Jesus' rising had initiated (Matthew 27:52–53).

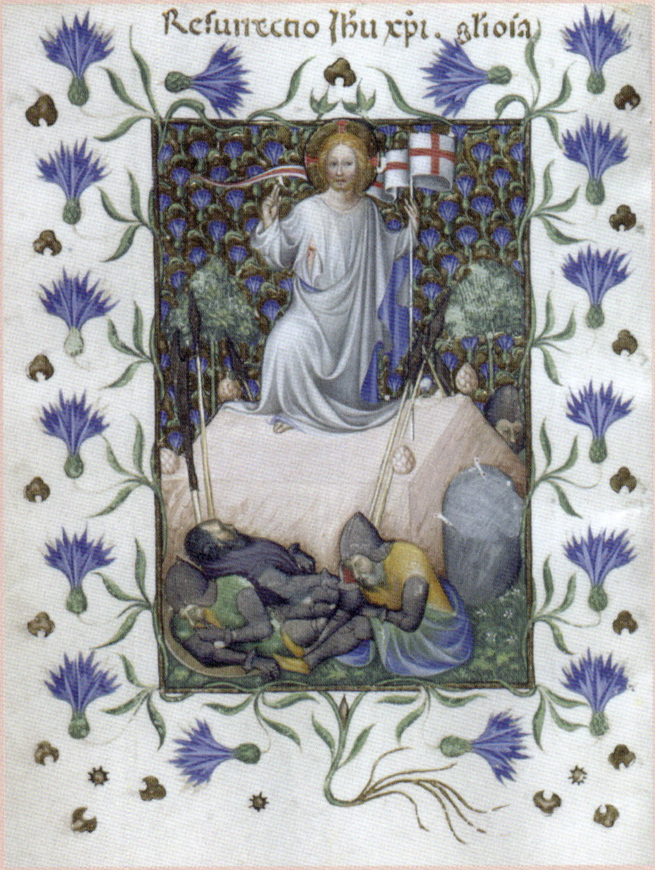

Figure 87. *Resurrection*, from the *Prayer Book of Michelino da Besozzo* (f. 26v), ca. 1430, illuminated manuscript, 7 1/16 x 4 15/16 inches. The Pierpont Morgan Library, New York. MS M.944, f. 26v. Photograph © The Pierpont Morgan Library, New York.

The Triumphant Christ

Christ's resurrection became a prominent focus in artistic representation by the late Middle Ages. In the majority of these images, Christ stands upright in the tomb or on the lid of the sarcophagus, clothed in a billowing white burial garment (Figures 86, 87, and 88). In figure 88, Albrecht Dürer places Christ on a closed tomb reminiscent of the Catholic practice of setting a statue of Christ on the altar at Easter[1] or referring to the emblems of the Eucharist as they are displayed on the altar. In figure 87, Christ gives a gesture of blessing and holds the banner with a red cross on a white cloth, symbolic of His triumph over death. The guards at the tomb are often seen in varying degrees of attentiveness. Some sleep, unaware of the miraculous resurrection, while others cower in fear at the appearance of the angels.

The eyewitness accounts of the resurrected Christ recorded in the scriptures are also related in artistic representations. In the Old World, Christ's appearance to Mary Magdalene (Figure 89), His presence at Emmaus (Figure 90), and His manifestation to the Apostles and the doubting Thomas (Figure 91) were all confirmations of His resurrected state. Yet there were other accounts from inhabitants in the New World who also saw and testified of Him. Their witnesses, documented in the Book of Mormon, are portrayed in the paintings of Minerva Teichert. In her mural *Destruction on the Western Continent* (Figure 92), the aftermath of the destruction following Christ's crucifixion is evidenced through the broken rock fragments, toppled columns, and surging waves. Gathered around the Mesoamerican temple, the survivors look heavenward to see the resurrected Christ descending into their midst. In another mural, Teichert depicts the institution of the sacrament among these ancient inhabitants (see 3 Nephi 18:3–4) (Figure 93). The radiant Christ stands at the apex of a pyramidal composition formed by the Nephites on the left and the Lamanites on the right. An unobstructed opening in front of the Savior makes Him visually accessible to viewers and invites their involvement in the sacramental ordinance.

1. Duchet-Suchaux, *Bible and the Saints*, 295.

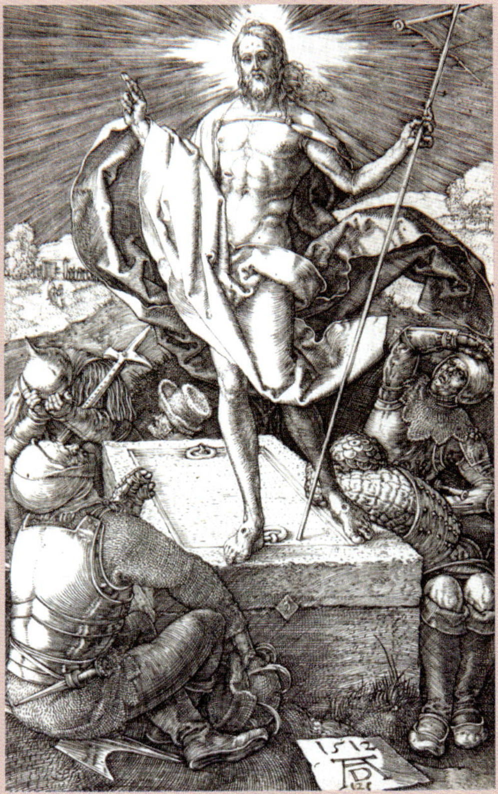

Figure 88. Albrecht Dürer (1471–1528), *Resurrection* from the *Engraved Passion*, 1512, engraving, 4 5/8 x 2 7/8 inches. Private collection of Shawn and Andrea Merriman.

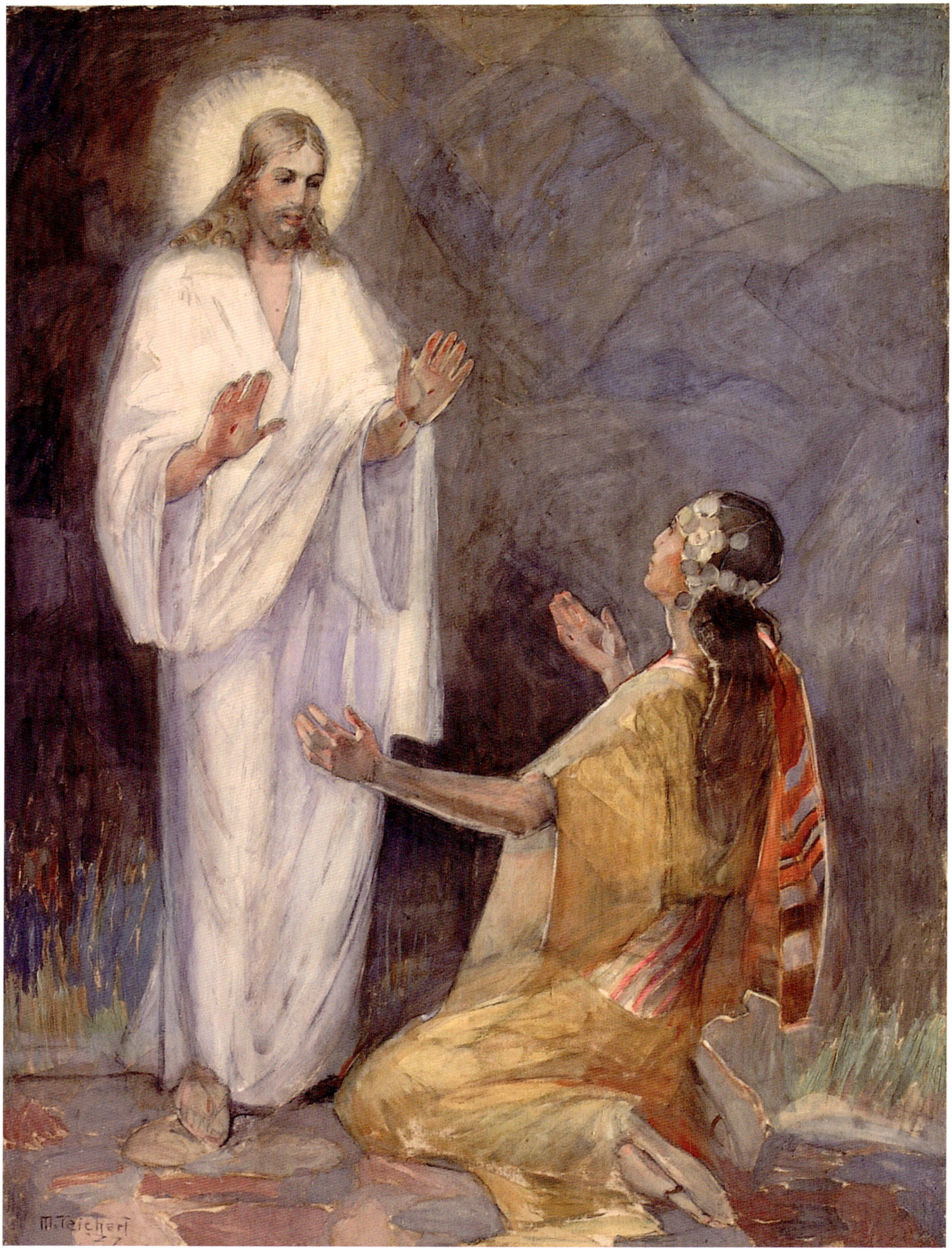

Figure 89. Minerva K. Teichert (1888–1976), *Touch Me Not*, 1937, oil on canvas, 76 1/2 x 59 3/4 inches. Brigham Young University Museum of Art.

Sadly but not unexpectedly, the denials and lies began soon thereafter. Those who were part of "the watch" at the tomb "came into the city" and told authorities "all the things that were done" when Jesus rose from the dead. To discredit these compelling testimonies, "the elders . . . gave large money unto the soldiers" on condition that they claim "His disciples came by night, and stole [the body] away." Matthew then sorrowfully reports that "this saying is commonly reported among the Jews until this day" (Matthew 28:11–13, 15).

New World Appearances

The Savior left a shining trail of witnesses not only among His followers in the Old World but also in the New. He had "other sheep . . . not of this [Old World] fold" who would "hear [His] voice" (John 10:16). As it turned out, they would also see Him and touch Him. As a result, they would come to hold the reality of Jesus' physical resurrection in their collective memories.

On a day many months removed from a devastating storm that had occurred in the New World simultaneously with Jesus' crucifixion, a crowd of about 2,500 gathered for a celebration at a temple in "the land Bountiful" (3 Nephi 11:1). There, in fulfillment of prophecy, the Savior appeared to the astonished gathering. Descending from heaven, the Resurrected Lord announced, "Behold, I am Jesus Christ, whom the prophets testified shall come into the world." Then He invited those in the multitude to "Arise and come forth unto me, that ye may thrust your hands into my side, and also that ye may feel the prints of the nails in my hands and in my feet, that ye may know that I am the God of Israel, and the God of the whole earth, and have been slain for the sins of the world" (3 Nephi 11:10, 14).

Not since Jehovah had descended onto Mount Sinai had such a large crowd witnessed the appearance of God. But there He stood, patiently offering

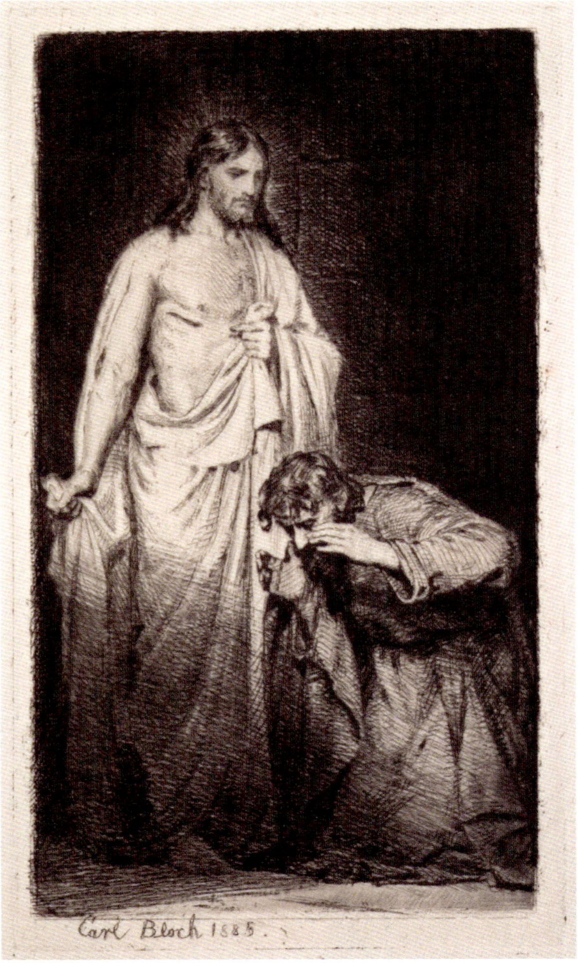

Figure 91. Carl Heinrich Bloch (1834–1890), *The Doubting Thomas*, 1885, etching, 4 3/8 x 2 1/2 inches. Brigham Young University Museum of Art, purchased with funds provided by Robert and Lisa Wheatley.

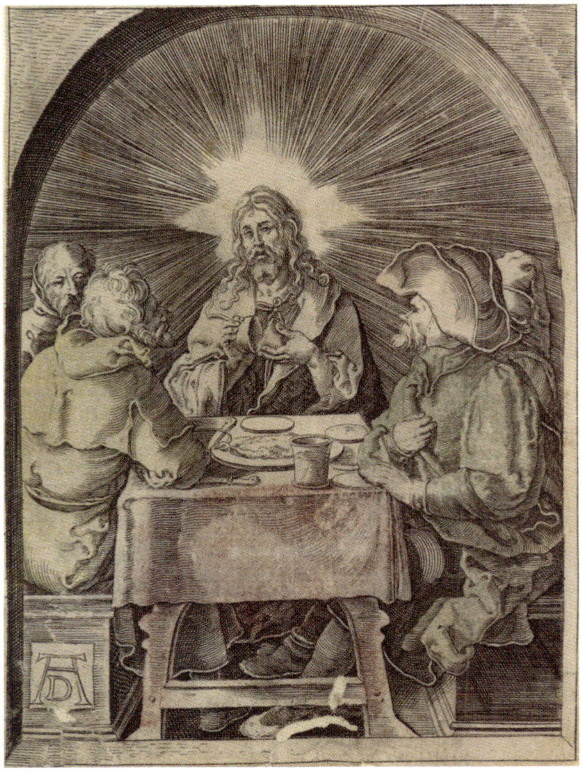

Figure 90. Anonymous, *Christ at Emmaus* (after Albrecht Dürer), ca. 1510, etching, 5 1/16 x 3 13/16 inches. Brigham Young University Museum of Art, purchase/gift from Mahonri M. Young Estate.

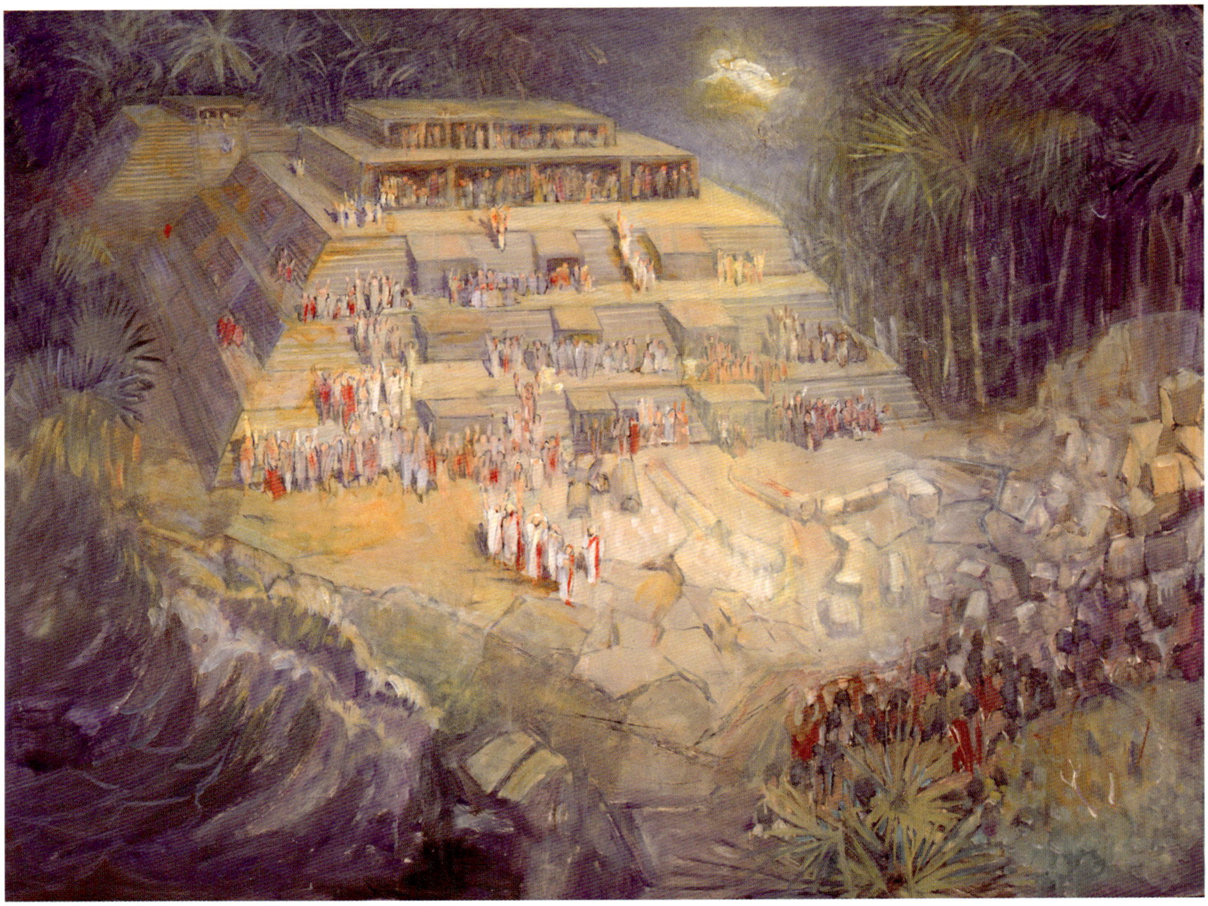

Figure 92. Minerva K. Teichert (1888–1976), *Destruction on the Western Continent*, ca. 1935, oil on masonite, 36 x 48 inches. Brigham Young University Museum of Art.

His resurrected body to be touched in the most perceptible of ways. Though He did not eat to demonstrate His physical reality, as He had among disciples in Jerusalem (see Luke 24:36–43), His willingness to allow Himself to be touched formed a sure witness of His tangible body. Unforgettable? By all means. Undeniable? Most assuredly.

The risen Jesus did not simply appear and then disappear. He spent three eventful days with followers in the New World. He organized them, He taught them, He healed them, He called down the powers of heaven upon them. His efforts were to bring a divine wholeness to these people. And in some ways, His words and actions offer an unobstructed view into His Old World ministry. For example, His sermon at the temple in Bountiful mirrors His Sermon on the Mount, putting to rest questions about whether Jesus delivered the Sermon on the Mount as a unified whole or whether it consists of strands of His teachings that Matthew brought together (see 3 Nephi 12–14; Matthew 5–7).

Even, and especially, the children in the multitude received special attention from the resurrected Lord. Near the end of the first day of His visit, the Savior commanded that the little children in the gathering be brought to Him. After offering a prayer, which was beyond words to repeat, He "took their little children, one by one, and blessed them, and prayed unto the Father for them." There followed a Pentecost-like experience, with "angels descending out of heaven as it were in the midst of fire" who "did minister unto [the children]" (3 Nephi 17:21, 24). It was plainly evident to all how much Jesus valued these little ones.

During the two following days, the risen Jesus again turned the attention of the gathering to the children. On the second day, "he did teach and minister unto the children of the multitude . . . and he did loose their tongues, and they did speak unto their fathers great and marvelous things, even greater than he had revealed unto the people." Then, on the third day, with the Savior's aid, the gathering "both saw and heard these children; yea, even babes did open their mouths and utter marvelous things" (3 Nephi 26:14, 16). For those three days, the air had been thick with palpable interaction between the heavenly and earthly.

And the number of witnesses had swelled. The first day, the crowd consisted of about 2,500 (see 3 Nephi 17:25). Because runners went from Bountiful to other settlements and homes and "noised abroad" the fact that the risen Savior would return the next day, people "did labor exceedingly all that night," and the next, "that they might be on the morrow in the place where Jesus should show himself," thereby becoming "an exceedingly great number" (3 Nephi 19:2–3). Evidently, no one counted the multitude. Or if a tally was made, it does not appear in the record. But we can safely estimate that the number of witnesses, including children who could remember, grew to several thousand.

There were other witnesses, whose numbers are not preserved. Five years before the birth of Jesus, a New World prophet known as Samuel the Lamanite had prophesied that at the resurrection of the Savior, "many graves shall be opened, and shall yield up many of their dead; and many saints shall appear unto many" (Helaman 14:25). Some of those who received such visitations must have resided too far away to reach Bountiful while the risen Jesus was still present. But their witness was so important that, when examining the written record of the terrible storm that had accompanied His death, the resurrected Lord pointed out that these appearances were not recorded, and He then "commanded that it should be written" (3 Nephi 23:13).

In sum, between Old and New World reports, the resurrection of Jesus Christ is one of the best documented occurrences in the history of the world. After two thousand years, it remains the center point of Christian faith and devotion.

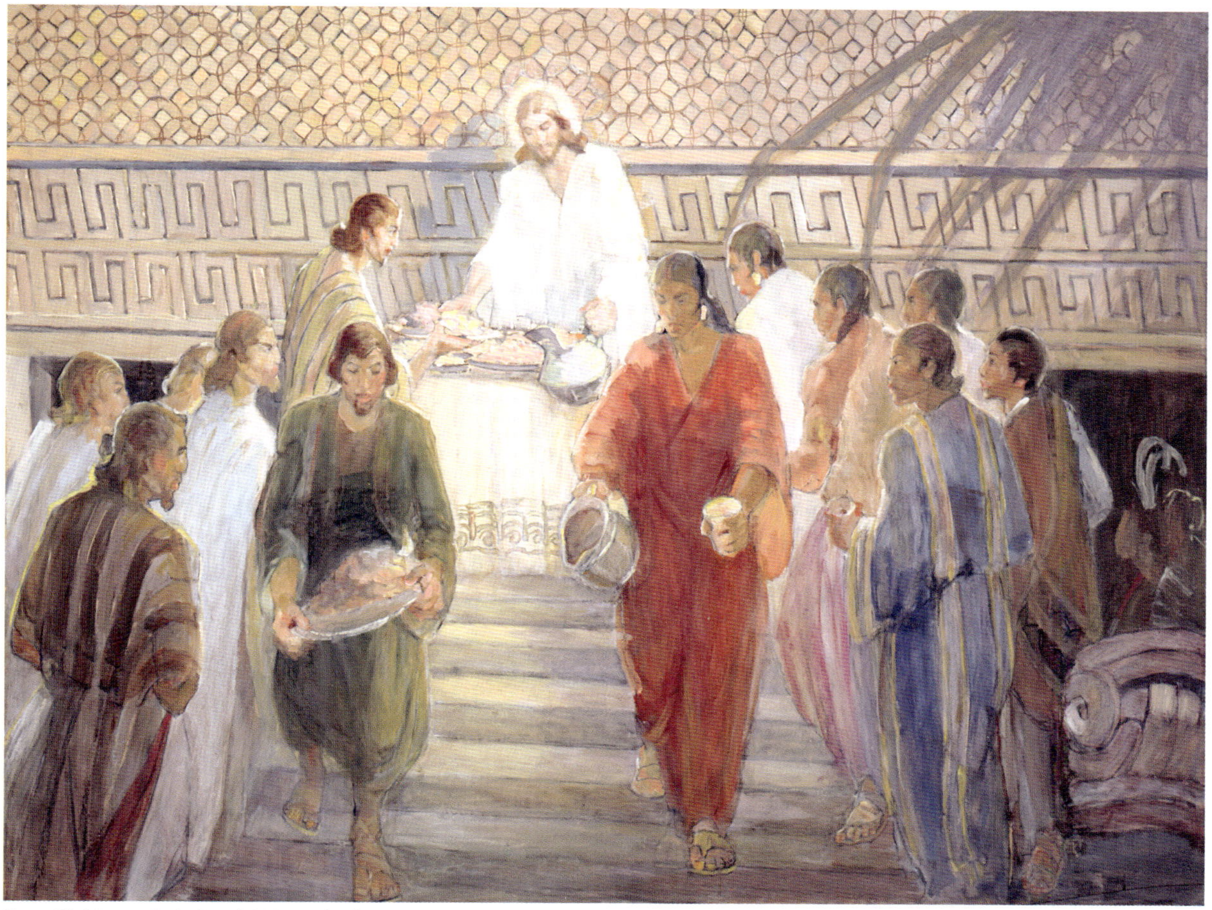

Figure 93. Minerva K. Teichert (1888–1976), *The Sacrament*, ca. 1935, oil on masonite, 36 x 48 inches. Brigham Young University Museum of Art.

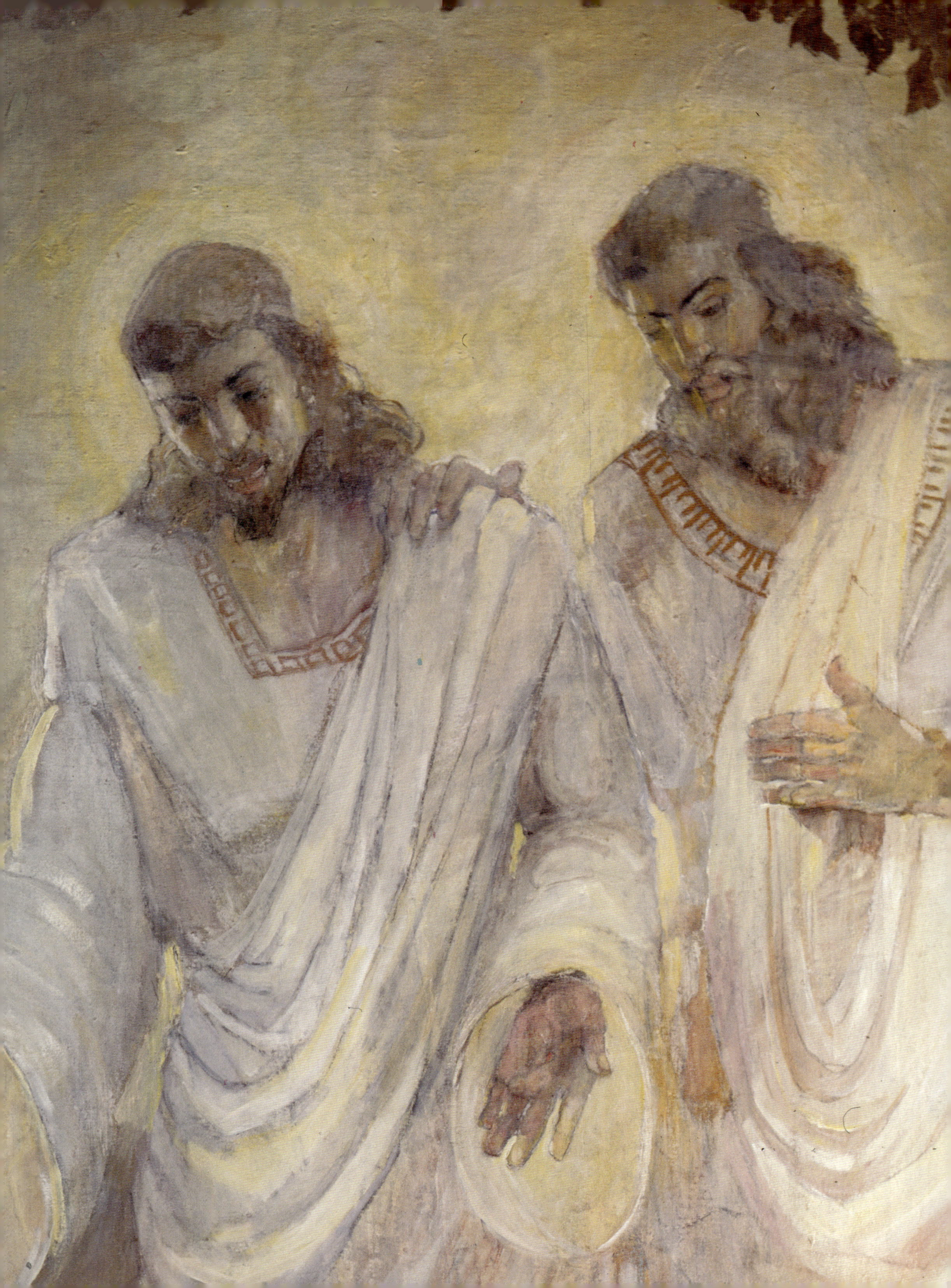

Chapter 15

The First Vision

The story of the Lord Jesus continues two thousand years after the close of the New Testament when an uncommon young boy with a very common name began a personal religious search that would change the world. Joseph Smith, we now know, was prepared and called by the Lord just as He had prepared and called Jeremiah and Paul (see Jeremiah 1:5; Acts 9:15–16) in earlier times.

Shortly after Jesus' resurrection and ascension, Peter prophesied about the "restitution of all things" that would occur in the last days (Acts 3:21; see also Luke 1:67–75). Those days suddenly burst upon the world in a quiet yet dramatic way in the early part of the nineteenth century in upstate New York.

The Birth and Early Life of Joseph Smith

Joseph Smith was born in 1805, just two days before the Christian world celebrated the birth of Jesus that year. It was a cold day in Vermont when the future prophet opened his eyes on the world. His mother and father celebrated the birth of their son without knowing what lay ahead for the young baby or for their family who would be swept up in events that would transpire in their own household.

During the next several years, the Smiths moved numerous times in Vermont and New Hampshire. Eventually, the family made a significant decision to move to western New York where they hoped to get another chance of making a home. Here they began working a tract of land of about a hundred acres.

Those years witnessed a remarkable period in American religious history, and events occurred in an equally remarkable place within that history. The fertile soil in upper New York state that promised security and stability did not compare with another fertile field the Lord had prepared—a field "already to harvest" (Doctrine and Covenants 4:4).

1820

Joseph Smith, from his birth on December 23, 1805, in the quiet hills of Vermont until the early spring of 1820, did not attract much notice. It was only after the Smith family arrived in New York that young Joseph witnessed a spiritual sunrise unexpected by anyone on earth but long part of the Lord's plan. When Joseph knelt in a wooded area near his log home to offer a sincere prayer, the courts of heaven listened, knowing it was time for a new day's dawn—a new dispensation.

Joseph described the events that led to the famous epiphany we know today as the "First Vision" as follows: "Some time in the second year after our removal to Manchester, there was in the place where we lived an unusual excitement on the subject of religion. It commenced with the Methodists, but soon became general among all the sects in that region of country. Indeed, the whole district of country seemed affected by it, and great multitudes united

Minerva K. Teichert (1888–1976), detail of *The First Vision*, oil on canvas, 102 x 78 inches. Brigham Young University Museum of Art.

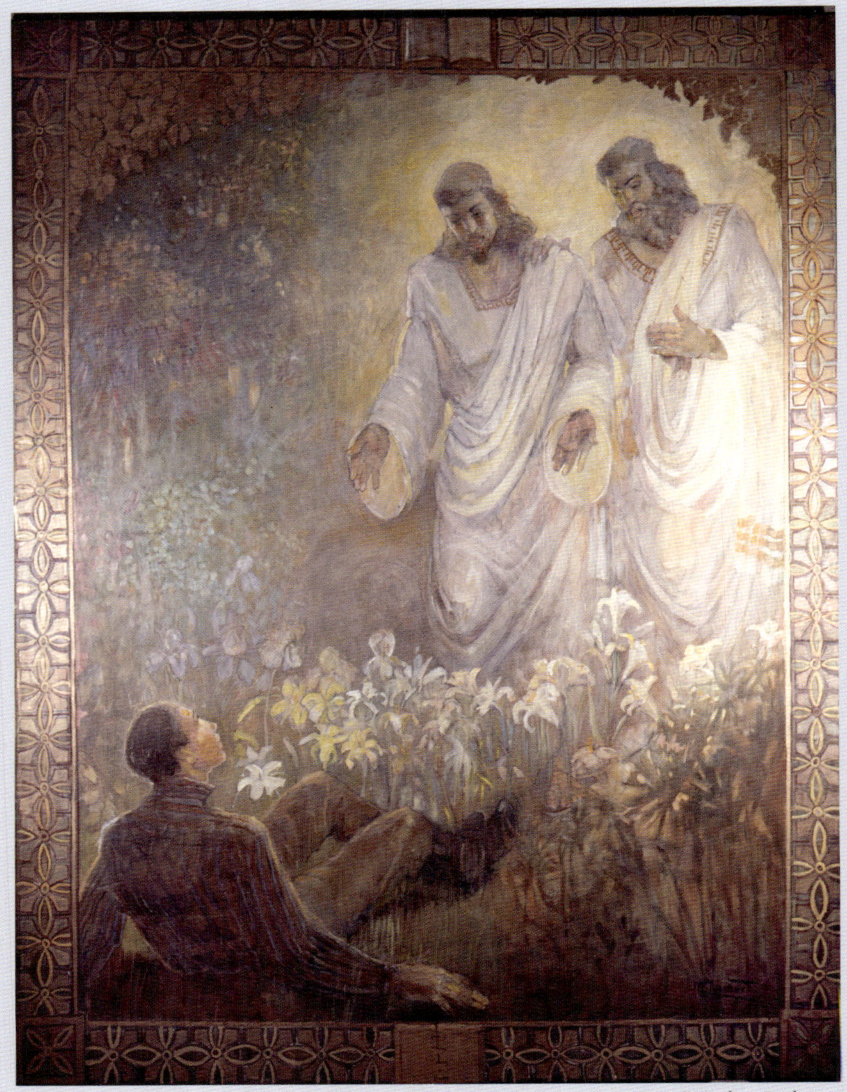

Figure 94. Minerva K. Teichert (1888–1976), *The First Vision*, 1934, oil on canvas, 102 x 78 inches. Brigham Young University Museum of Art.

"The Mormon Story"

The restoration of the gospel of Jesus Christ in "the dispensation of the fulness of times" (Ephesians 1:10) offers Latter-day Saint artists unique opportunities to testify of Christ. Minerva Teichert was one such artist. When given the mandate to tell "the Mormon story" by her teacher, American realist painter Robert Henri, she accepted the challenge.[1] For the next fifty years, she painted stories from the scriptures and scenes of heroic Mormon pioneers. Her large mural of *The First Vision* (Figure 94) captures the moment when the Prophet Joseph Smith saw "two Personages, whose brightness and glory defy all description, standing above [him] in the air" (Joseph Smith—History 1:17). God the Father places His hand upon Jesus' shoulder in a tender paternal gesture and introduces His Beloved Son to the young Joseph. Christ's outstretched hands reveal the marks of the Crucifixion. Later, Joseph would be visited by the angel Moroni who would reveal to him the gold plates containing "a record of God's dealings with the ancient inhabitants of the Americas."[2] The Prophet Joseph translated these sacred records and published them in 1830 as the Book of Mormon. Images of the gold plates and the Book of Mormon are found in the decorative border of the painting, emphasizing the importance of this book as a second witness of Christ.

1. Laurie Teichert Eastwood, ed., *Letters of Minerva Teichert* (Provo, UT: BYU Studies, 1998), 8.
2. "Introduction," in *The Book of Mormon: Another Testament of Jesus Christ*, trans. Joseph Smith, Jun. (Salt Lake City: The Church of Jesus Christ of Latter-day Saints, 1989).

themselves to the different religious parties, which created no small stir and division amongst the people, some crying, 'Lo, here!' and others, 'Lo, there!' Some were contending for the Methodist faith, some for the Presbyterian, and some for the Baptist" (Joseph Smith—History 1:5).

Interestingly, the Smith family was a microcosm of the larger American society because family members were divided by religious opinions. Although each was a deeply dedicated Christian, the family members had gravitated into three separate and distinct religious orbits. Joseph recalled that he was "in [his] fifteenth year" when his mother, Lucy, his brothers Hyrum and Samuel Harrison, and his sister Sophronia were "proselyted to the Presbyterian faith" (Joseph Smith—History 1:7). His father, Joseph Sr., and eldest brother Alvin, who had Universalist leanings, were distant from organized religious bodies and did not attend with Lucy, Hyrum, Samuel, and Sophronia. Joseph himself had "in process of time" become "somewhat partial to the Methodist sect" and "felt some desire to be united with them" (Joseph Smith—History 1:8).

Nevertheless, even though "during this time of great excitement" his "mind was called up to serious reflection and great uneasiness" and "though [his] feelings were deep and often poignant," he still kept himself "aloof from all these parties" (Joseph Smith—History 1:8). Young Joseph did continue to attend "their several meetings as often as occasion would permit." But in his confusion, he confessed that "it was impossible for a person young" as he was to "come to any certain conclusion who was right and who was wrong" (Joseph Smith—History 1:8).

Providentially, one of the Methodist preachers, George Lane, provided Joseph a text from the New Testament that would ultimately unlock the door and help the young man find the answers to the questions that weighed upon him. Joseph notes: "While I was laboring under the extreme difficulties caused by the contests of these parties of religionists, I was one day reading the Epistle of James, first chapter and fifth verse, which reads: *If any of you lack wisdom, let him ask of God, that giveth to all men liberally, and upbraideth not; and it shall be given him*" (Joseph Smith—History 1:11; emphasis in original).

While he was reading the text, the words burned into his heart. He recalled, "I reflected on it again and again" (Joseph Smith—History 1:12).

Joseph soon decided to put James' promise to the test and retired to a grove of trees near his home in Palmyra, New York. He notes: "So, in accordance with this, my determination to ask of God, I retired to the woods to make the attempt. It was on the morning of a beautiful, clear day, early in the spring of eighteen hundred and twenty. It was the first time in my life that I had made such an attempt, for amidst all my anxieties I had never as yet made the attempt to pray vocally" (Joseph Smith—History 1:14).

In what may have seemed like a simple act of faith, Joseph's sincere prayer caused the heavens to listen and respond. He tells us, "I saw a pillar of light exactly over my head, above the brightness of the sun, which descended gradually until it fell upon me." In the midst of that light, according to Joseph, "I saw two Personages, whose brightness and glory defy all description, standing above me in the air. One of them spake unto me, calling me by name and said, pointing to the other—*This is My Beloved Son. Hear Him!*" (Joseph Smith—History 1:16–17; emphasis in original).

Their appearance marked the beginning of "the dispensation of the fulness of times," when the Lord would "gather together in one all things in Christ, both which are in heaven, and which are on earth; even in him" (Ephesians 1:10). Truth rolled forth as the Father, speaking to Joseph, broke once and for all a heavenly silence: "*This is My Beloved Son. Hear Him!*" (Joseph Smith—History 1:17; emphasis in original). It was a boy prophet's introduction to the Lord and Savior of mankind.

A Comparison of the 1838 and 1832 Accounts of the First Vision

In the well-known and often-cited 1838 account published in the Pearl of Great Price, the story jumps from the Father's introduction to Joseph's making the now-famous inquiry, "Which of all the sects was right . . . and which I should join." However, a careful reading of the text suggests that something is missing from this 1838 account, an account written for non-Latter-day Saints, one that emphasizes the message most useful to them.

We pause on Joseph's recollection of the event in 1838 in which one of the personages, the Father, said to Joseph, "This is My Beloved Son. Hear Him!" Naturally, we may ask, "What did Jesus say to Joseph before Joseph began asking about which church to join?"

Another account, written in 1832, provides the answer. In this earlier retelling of the story, Joseph provided some information he decided to pass over in the very public 1838 account.

In this earlier and very personal account, Joseph notes that he "cried unto the Lord for mercy for there was none else to whom I could go and obtain mercy" (Joseph Smith's 1832 Diary). In addition to his wanting to know which church he should join, the 1832 account informs us that Joseph sought mercy, forgiveness, and the "God of Love."

Like the 1838 account, Joseph acknowledged in the 1832 narrative that the Lord answered his sincere prayer. He wrote, "The Lord heard my cry in the wilderness and while in the attitude of calling upon the Lord a pillar of light above the brightness of the sun at noon day came down from above and rested upon me" (Joseph Smith's 1832 Diary).

Most significantly, the personal report informs us what Jesus said after the Father commanded the young boy, "Hear Him!"

Joseph preserved the very first words of the Lord Jesus—the first words He had spoken on the earth after nearly two thousand years of silence: "Joseph my son thy sins are forgiven thee. Go thy way walk in my statutes and keep my commandments behold I am the Lord of glory I was crucified for the world that all those who believe on my name may have Eternal life" (Joseph Smith's 1832 Diary).

Although artists have visually captured the moment that the Father and Son appeared to Joseph Smith in the spring of 1820, nothing can capture the significance of the event quite like the words recorded by Joseph as he preserved the story with black ink on white paper.

Having received the personal assurance that his sins had indeed been forgiven, Joseph Smith then asked the next important question, "Which church should I join?" Again, the Lord spoke to Joseph. And the rest of the story, as they say, is history.

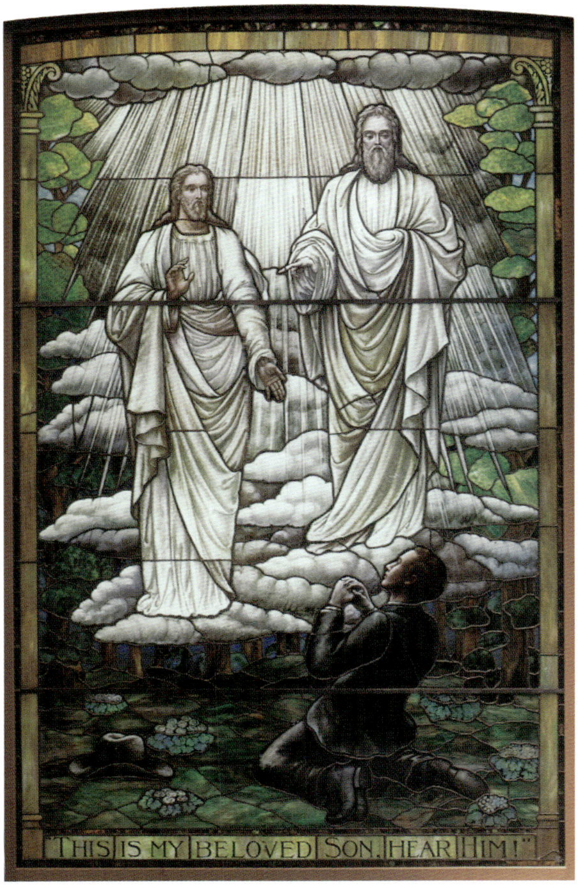

Figure 95. Anonymous, *Joseph Smith's First Vision*, 1913, stained glass, 84 x 60 inches. Museum of Church History and Art.

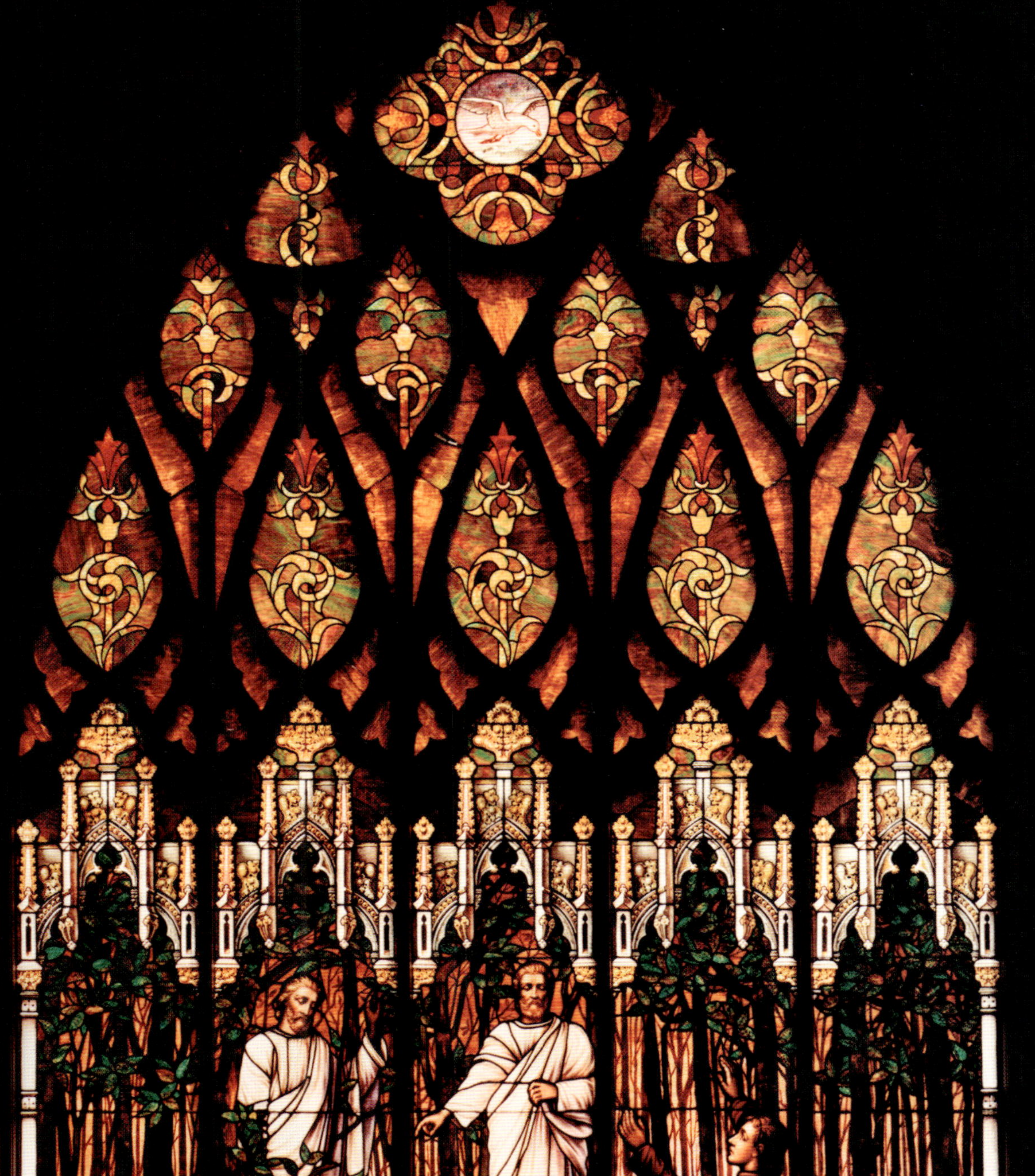

Figure 96. Lucy Thurston Kinney, *The First Vision*, 1908, stained glass window, 240 x 168 inches. T he Church of Jesus Christ of Latter-day Saints, Salt Lake Liberty Stake. Photography courtesy of John Telford.

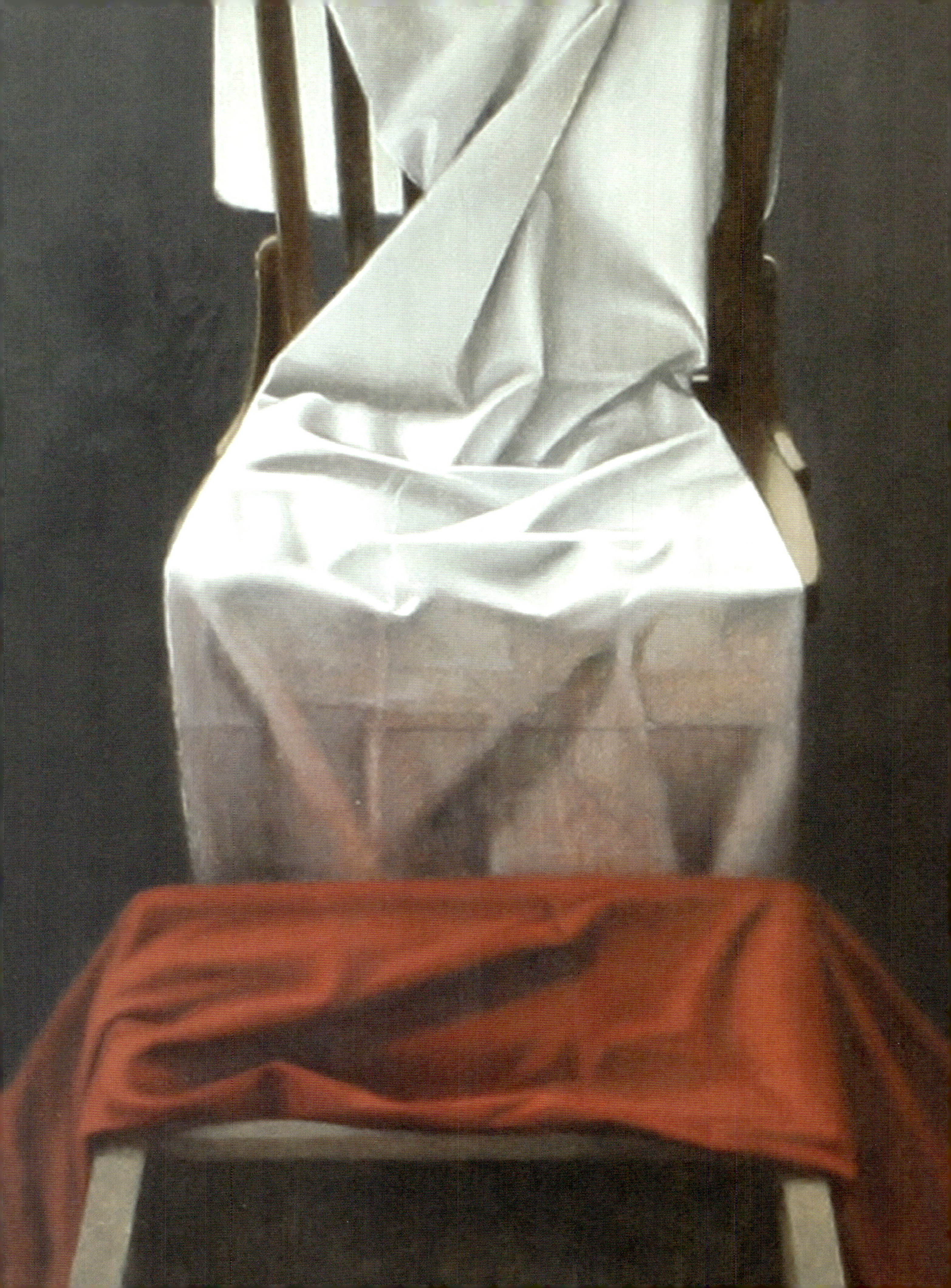

Chapter 16

Christ As Judge

In the middle of the synagogue, next to a pillar supporting the roof, stood a man with a withered right hand. The deformed man heard Jesus say to the assembled worshipers, "I will ask you one thing; Is it lawful on the sabbath days to do good, or to do evil? to save life, or to destroy it?" No one spoke. Then Jesus addressed the standing man, commanding him, "Stretch forth thy hand." Obediently, the man held out his crippled hand. In an instant "his hand was restored whole as the other" (Luke 6:9–10).

A reader's natural tendency is to focus on Jesus' stunning and compassionate miracle, the wondrous mending of a man's crippled hand, which restored him to full physical health. But disclosed to full view in this dramatic scene is Jesus the Judge. For in asking the question of His critics, "Is it lawful . . . ?" He has lifted up the ensuing miracle as a proof of His powers not only to heal but to perform such acts—with divine authority—on the Sabbath. In a sense, He has turned the synagogue into a courtroom wherein persons deal with questions about the legality of certain acts and then present their best evidence. In a related sense, by palpably and generously demonstrating that "on the sabbath days" it is appropriate "to do good," He has judged His critics' views on the Sabbath to be too narrow and dispassionate. This incident, wherein Jesus comes forward as Judge, anticipates at least two other occasions when He takes up essentially the same question, "Is it lawful . . . ?"—once when He intended to make a crippled woman whole and again when He was about to heal a man of dropsy in the home of a prominent Pharisee, each on a Sabbath day (see Luke 13:11–16; 14:1–6).

These instances point forward to Jesus in His role as Judge of all at the end of time. In the revealing words of the Apostle Paul, "We shall all [ultimately] stand before the judgment seat of Christ" (Romans 14:10). In his Gospel, John records Jesus' own words declaring this approaching event: "The Father . . . hath given [the Son] authority to execute judgment. . . . As I hear, I judge: and my judgment is just." This moment for judging "is coming, in the which all that are in the graves shall hear his voice" (John 5:26–30). Plainly, the authority to judge rests with Jesus, and the event will involve all who have lived in mortality (see 3 Nephi 27:14–15). The certifying pledge that Jesus will serve as Judge comes via the Resurrection: God "hath given assurance unto all men [of the judgment], in that he hath raised [Jesus] from the dead" (Acts 17:31).

And what will be the nature of this judgment in behalf of the newly resurrected? According to scripture, "God shall judge the righteous and the wicked" (Ecclesiastes 3:17). Said another way, "the Son of man . . . shall reward every man according to his works." But in addition to a person's works or actions, "every idle word that men shall speak, they shall give account thereof in the day of judgment" (Matthew 16:27; 12:36). More elements will play into this scene because "our thoughts will also condemn us," for God "is a discerner of the thoughts and intents of the heart" (Alma 12:14; Hebrews 4:12). Thus, a person's entire life stands open to judgment.

Ron Richmond (b. 1963), detail of *Exchange No. 8*, 2003–2004, oil on canvas, 60 1/8 x 60 3/16 inches. Brigham Young University Museum of Art, purchased with funds provided by Lew and Gail Burnham.

The Changing Image of Christ

Over the centuries, visual and textual representations of Christ have reflected shifts of emphasis in Christian thought. Beginning as monograms and symbols in the catacombs, depictions of Christ have ranged in scope from a youthful Good Shepherd to omnipotent Lord of the Universe, from an innocent, almost helpless Child to an austere Judge of the World, and from a Suffering Christ to Victorious Redeemer. For instance, during the Byzantine era when Christianity became the Roman Empire's official religion, Christ's image became that of an imposing ruler, taking on the imperial attributes of halo, purple robe, and throne. His likeness, portrayed in small panel paintings called *icons*, was often set against a gold or silver background, signifying His divine majesty. These icons were thought to have miraculous powers, such as the ability to forgive sins, heal infirmities, or bring victory in battle. *Christ Pantocrator* (Figure 98) exemplifies the Byzantine-style icon tradition, which was perpetuated in Russia through the nineteenth century.

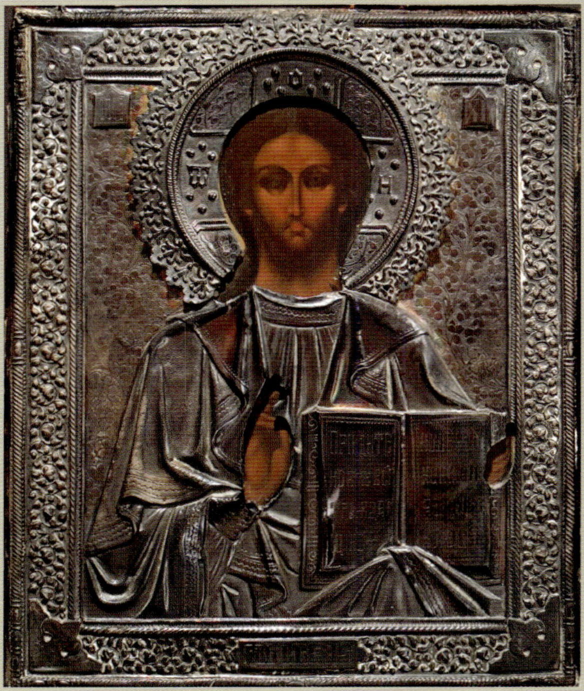

Figure 98. Russian icon, *Christ Pantocrator*, 1893, tempera and silver on panel, 10 1/2 x 8 14/16 x 1 1/8 inches. Brigham Young University Museum of Art, gift of Mr. and Mrs. Richard B. Oliver.

In the twentieth and twenty-first centuries, conceptual works have supplemented more traditional renderings by focusing on ideas, rather than on objects or narrative representations. Often the figure of Christ is not even present in such works; signs and symbols replace the human form, as in Ron Richmond's painting, *Exchange No. 8* (Figure 97). Referencing the Atonement and the Judgment, the chairs and cloths represent the manifold roles of Christ as Advocate, Judge, Intercessor, and resurrected Savior. The intense colors of the draped fabric call to mind the words of Isaiah: "Come now, and let us reason together, saith the Lord: though your sins be as scarlet, they shall be as white as snow; though they be red like crimson, they shall be as wool" (Isaiah 1:18).

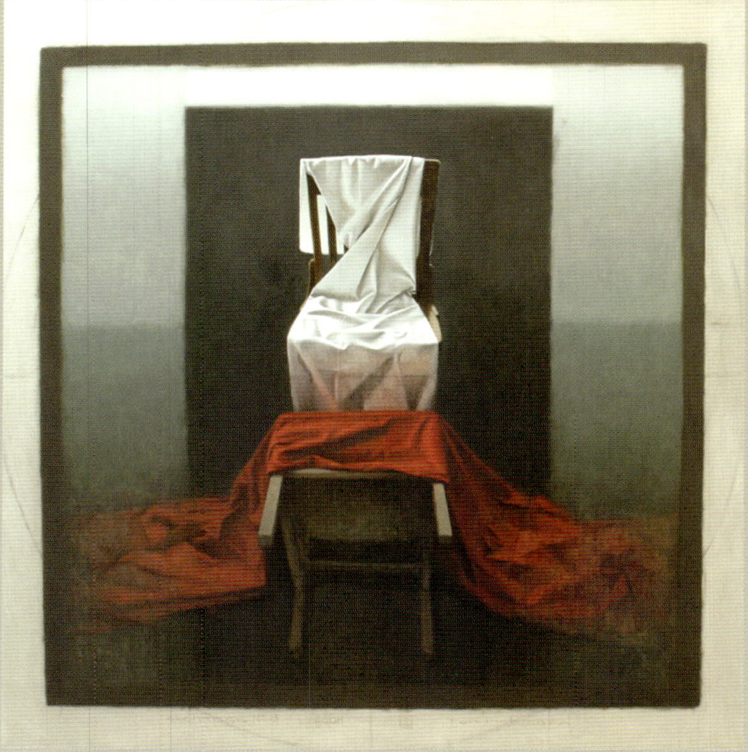

Figure 97. Ron Richmond (b. 1963), *Exchange No. 8*, 2003–2004, oil on canvas, 60 1/8 x 60 3/16 inches. Brigham Young University Museum of Art, purchased with funds provided by Lew and Gail Burnham.

Despite apparent differences in representation, *Christ Pantocrator* and *Exchange No. 8* mirror one another in their composition and tone. The metal halo surrounding Christ's head in the icon is echoed by the faint circle circumscribing the composition in *Exchange No. 8*. Both representations of Christ appear as frontal, static, iconic images that are simultaneously austere and approachable. When juxtaposed, these two works complement one another, both portraying the essence of godliness.

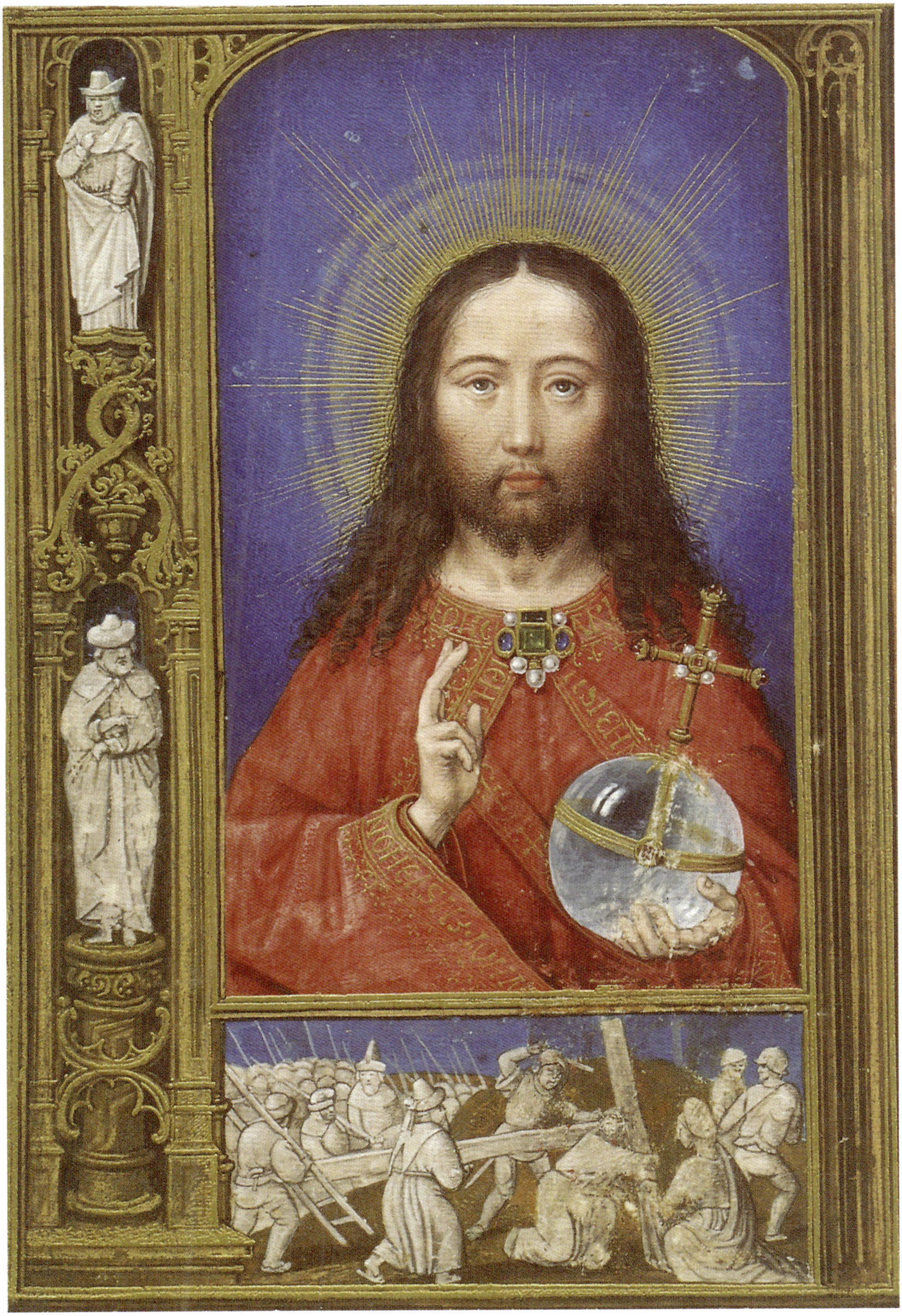

Figure 99. *Bust of Christ with Orb*, from *Le Livre d'Heures aux Fleurs* (f. 7), 1516, illuminated manuscript facsimile (1991), 6 1/2 x 4 1/2 inches. Rare Books Division, Special Collections, J. Willard Marriott Library, University of Utah; after the Fine Art Facsimile edition by Faksimile Verlag Luzern.

But not all will face Jesus' withering justice. For God promises "whosoever repenteth, and hardeneth not his heart, he shall have claim on mercy through mine Only Begotten Son, unto a remission of his sins; and these shall enter into my rest" (Alma 12:34). In fact, these persons will have access to the advocacy of the Savior because "he ever liveth to make intercession for them" with the Father, and will appear "in the presence of God for us" (Hebrews 7:25; 9:24; see also Doctrine and Covenants 45:3–5).

In a special category stand those who lived and died without an awareness of God's laws. An angel has affirmed that the Savior's "blood atoneth for the sins of those who have . . . died not knowing the will of God concerning them, or who have ignorantly sinned" (Mosiah 3:11; also Moroni 8:22; Doctrine and Covenants 137:7–9). Moreover, little children who die are shielded from judgment by Jesus' atonement (see Moroni 8:8, 11–12; Doctrine and Covenants 137:10). Hence, judgment for such persons will differ from those who have come out "in open rebellion against God" (Mosiah 2:37). In this connection, the purpose of preaching the gospel "to them that are dead" is "that they might be judged according to men in the flesh" (1 Peter 4:6; see also the chapter "Anastasis").

The Savior's judgment, as He reminds us, will gather "all nations: and he shall separate them one from another," not by nationalities but by individual responses to His messages of compassion and His invitations to behave in a kindly manner (see Matthew 25:31–36). Mercifully, He will judge and send people not simply into one of two places, heaven or hell, but, as Paul declares, into places of glory that are perfectly suited to an individual's ability to bear that glory (see 1 Corinthians 15:40–44; Doctrine and Covenants 76:91–98). Moreover, others will join Him in the task of judging, an aspect that art has featured but little, including the Twelve Apostles in the Old World who, He declares, will "sit upon twelve thrones, judging the twelve tribes of Israel" (Matthew 19:28), and the twelve disciples in the New World whom He chose and who will be "judges of this [New World] people" (3 Nephi 27:27; see also Mormon 3:19).

What will be the basis of these judgments? Scripture speaks of several. In one scene, John the Revelator sees "the dead, small and great, stand before God; and the books were opened . . . and the dead were judged out of those things which were written in the books, according to their works" (Revelation 20:12; see also Daniel 7:10). These books "refer to the records which are kept on the earth [and] . . . kept in heaven" (Doctrine and Covenants 128:7). But this is not all. In a number of passages that refer to the inner person, the Lord stands forth as one who tries or tests "the reins and the heart" (Jeremiah 11:20; 17:10; Psalms 7:9; 26:2). In this connection, Isaiah declares that the Judge "shall not judge after the sight of his eyes, neither reprove after the hearing of his ears"; rather, "with righteousness shall he judge" (Isaiah 11:3–4). Plainly, the Lord's judgment will rest on what He perceives inside each person, on what lies in the hearts of those who stand before Him.

Because of His majesty and righteousness, aspects that art portrays in the Judge, many will not want to come before Him at "the great and last day." Rather, those who are condemned by their consciences and their actions will wish, as did Alma the Younger, that they might be "banished and become extinct both soul and body, that [they] might not be brought to stand in the presence of . . . God, to be judged of [their] deeds" (Alma 36:15; see also 3 Nephi 26:4). This aspect of the Judgment is alluded to elsewhere in scripture. For we read that the dead "shall be brought to stand before the Lamb of God" for judgment, almost as if all are either escorted or carried physically to "be arraigned before the bar of Christ the Son," there to face the just Judge (see Mormon 9:2; Alma 11:44).

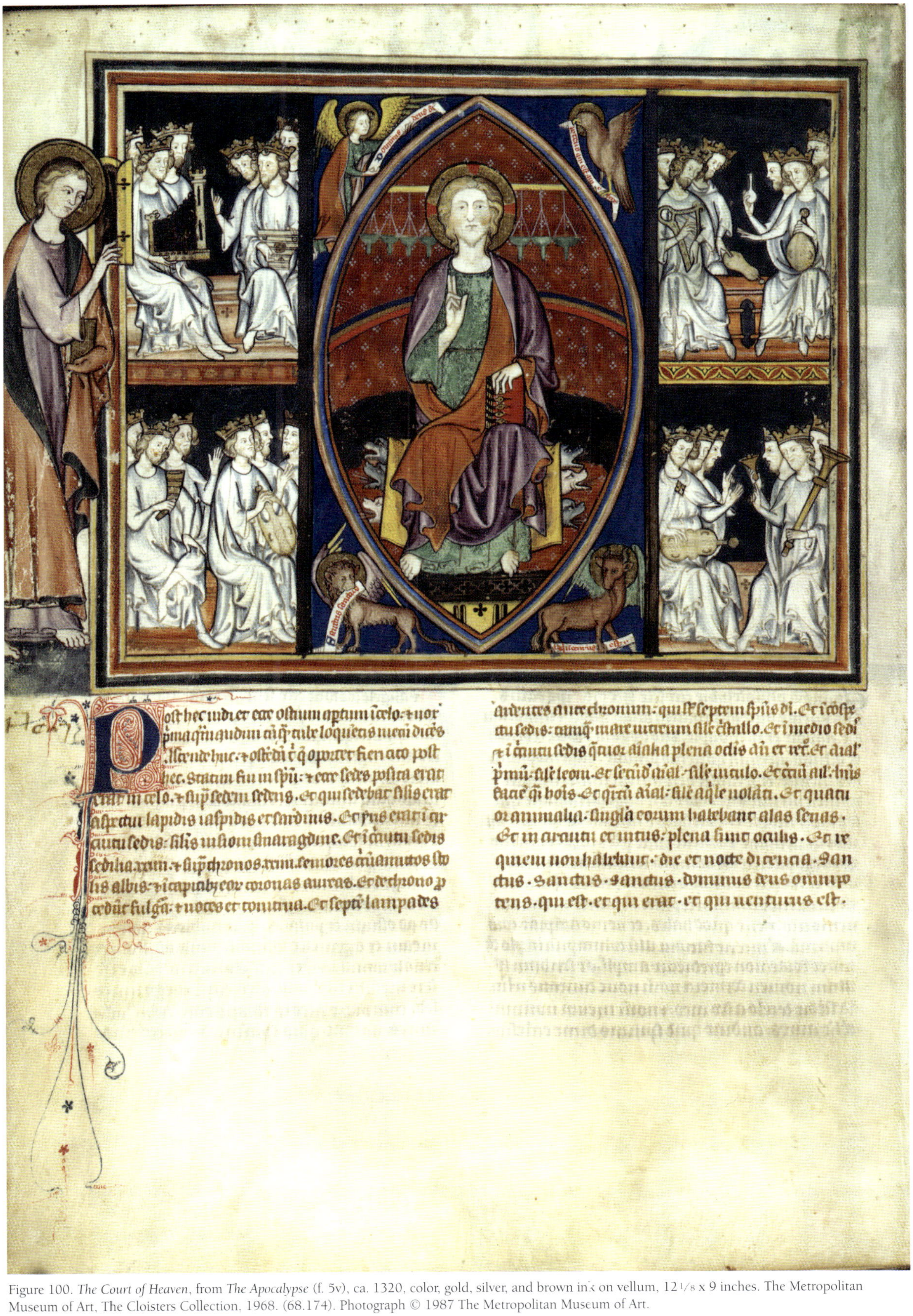

Figure 100. *The Court of Heaven*, from *The Apocalypse* (f. 5v), ca. 1320, color, gold, silver, and brown ink on vellum, 12 1/8 x 9 inches. The Metropolitan Museum of Art, The Cloisters Collection, 1968. (68.174). Photograph © 1987 The Metropolitan Museum of Art.

Further Reading

Backman, Milton V. Jr "First Vision." In *Encyclopedia of Mormonism.* 5 vols. Edited by Daniel H. Ludlow et al. New York: Macmillan, 1992.

Ball, Terry B. "Gethsemane." In *The Life and Teachings of Jesus Christ.* Vol. 3, *From the Last Supper through the Resurrection.* Edited by Richard Neitzel Holzapfel and Thomas A. Wayment. Salt Lake City: Deseret Book, 2003.

Brown, Raymond E. *The Birth of the Messiah.* Garden City, N.Y.: Doubleday, 1977.

———. *The Death of the Messiah.* 2 vols. New York: Doubleday, 1994.

Brown, S. Kent. *From Jerusalem to Zarahemla: Literary and Historical Studies of the Book of Mormon.* Provo, Utah: BYU Religious Studies Center, 1998.

———. "Gethsemane." In *Encyclopedia of Mormonism.* 5 vols. Edited by Daniel H. Ludlow et al. New York: Macmillan, 1992.

———. *Mary and Elisabeth: Noble Daughters of God.* American Fork, Utah: Covenant Communications, 2002.

———. "The Twelve." In *The Life and Teachings of Jesus Christ.* Vol. 2, *From the Transfiguration through the Triumphal Entry.* Edited by Richard Neitzel Holzapfel and Thomas A. Wayment. Salt Lake City: Deseret Book, 2006.

———. *Voices from the Dust: Book of Mormon Insights.* American Fork, Utah: Covenant Communications, 2004.

Bruce, F. F. *The Gospel of John.* Grand Rapids, Mich.: Eerdmans, 1983.

———. *New Testament History.* Garden City, N.Y.: Anchor Books, 1972.

Bushman, Richard Lyman. *Joseph Smith, Rough Stone Rolling: A Cultural Biography of Mormonism's Founder.* New York: Alfred A. Knopf, 2006.

Draper, Richard D. "From the Annunciation through the Young Adulthood of the Lord." In *The Life and Teachings of Jesus Christ.* Vol. 1, *From Bethlehem through the Sermon on the Mount.* Edited by Richard Neitzel Holzapfel and Thomas A. Wayment. Salt Lake City: Deseret Book, 2005.

Hall, John F. *New Testament Witnesses of Christ: Peter, John, James, and Paul.* American Fork, Utah: Covenant Communications, 2002.

———. "The Roman Province of Judea: A Historical Overview." In *Masada and the World of the New Testament.* Edited by John F. Hall and John W. Welch. Provo, Utah: Brigham Young University, 1997.

Hauglid, Brian M. "Luke's Three Parables of the Lost and Found: A Textual Study." In *The Life and Teachings of Jesus Christ.* Vol. 2, *From the Transfiguration through the Triumphal Entry.* Edited by Richard Neitzel Holzapfel and Thomas A. Wayment. Salt Lake City: Deseret Book, 2006.

Hennecke, Edgar, and Wilhelm Schneemelcher, eds. *New Testament Apocrypha.* 2 vols. Philadelphia: Westminster Press, 1963–64.

Holzapfel, Jeni Broberg, and Richard Neitzel Holzapfel. *Sisters at the Well: Women and the Life and Teachings of Jesus.* Salt Lake City: Bookcraft, 1993.

Holzapfel, Richard Neitzel. "Jesus in the Wilderness: Baptism, Fasting, and Temptations." In *The Life and Teachings of Jesus Christ.* Vol. 1, *From Bethlehem through the Sermon on the Mount.* Edited by Richard Neitzel Holzapfel and Thomas A. Wayment. Salt Lake City: Deseret Book, 2005.

———. *A Lively Hope: The Suffering, Death, Resurrection, and Exaltation of Jesus Christ.* Salt Lake City: Bookcraft, 1999.

———. "The Transfiguration." In *The Life and Teachings of Jesus Christ.* Vol. 2, *From the Transfiguration through the Triumphal Entry.* Edited by Richard Neitzel Holzapfel and Thomas A. Wayment. Salt Lake City: Deseret Book, 2006.

Holzapfel, Richard Neitzel, and David Rolph Seely. *My Father's House.* Salt Lake City: Bookcraft, 1994.

Huntsman, Eric D. "Before the Romans." In *The Life and Teachings of Jesus Christ.* Vol. 1, *From Bethlehem through the Sermon on the Mount.* Edited by Richard Neitzel Holzapfel and Thomas A. Wayment. Salt Lake City: Deseret Book, 2005.

———. "Galilee and the Call of the Twelve Apostles." In *The Life and Teachings of Jesus Christ.* Vol. 1, *From Bethlehem through the Sermon on the Mount.* Edited by Richard Neitzel Holzapfel and Thomas A. Wayment. Salt Lake City: Deseret Book, 2005.

Jackson, Bernard S. "The Trials of Jesus and Jeremiah," *BYU Studies* 32/4 (1992): 63–77.

Jackson, Kent P. "The Crucifixion." In *The Life and Teachings of Jesus Christ.* Vol. 3, *From the Last Supper through the Resurrection.* Edited by Richard Neitzel Holzapfel and Thomas A. Wayment. Salt Lake City: Deseret Book, 2003.

———. "The Olivet Discourse." In *The Life and Teachings of Jesus Christ.* Vol. 2, *From the Transfiguration through the Triumphal Entry.* Edited by Richard Neitzel Holzapfel and Thomas A. Wayment. Salt Lake City: Deseret Book, 2006.

James, Montague Rhodes. *The Apocryphal New Testament,* corrected ed. Oxford: Oxford University Press, 1953.

Jarman, Dean. "Judgment." In *Encyclopedia of Mormonism.* 5 vols. Edited by Daniel H. Ludlow et al. New York: Macmillan, 1992.

Jefford, Clayton N. "Pilate, Acts of." In *The Anchor Bible Dictionary.* 6 vols. Edited by David Noel Freedman, et al. New York: Doubleday, 1992.

Jeremias, Joachim. *Jerusalem in the Time of Jesus.* Philadelphia: Fortress Press, 1969.

Judd, Frank F. Jr. "The Parables of Matthew 13: Revealing and Concealing the Kingdom of God." In *The Life and Teachings of Jesus Christ.* Vol. 2, *From the Transfiguration through the Triumphal Entry.* Edited by Richard Neitzel Holzapfel and Thomas A. Wayment. Salt Lake City: Deseret Book, 2006.

———. "The Setting of the Sermon on the Mount." In *The Life and Teachings of Jesus Christ.* Vol. 1, *From Bethlehem through the Sermon on the Mount.* Edited by Richard Neitzel Holzapfel and Thomas A. Wayment. Salt Lake City: Deseret Book, 2005.

Largey, Dennis L. et al., eds. *Book of Mormon Reference Companion.* Salt Lake City: Deseret Book, 2003.

Marshall, I. Howard. *The Gospel of Luke: A Commentary on the Greek Text, The New International Greek Testament Commentary.* Grand Rapids, Mich.: Eerdmans, 1978.

Matthews, Robert J. *A Burning Light: The Life and Ministry of John the Baptist.* Provo, Utah: Brigham Young University Press, 1972.

Maxwell, Neal A. "The New Testament: A Matchless Portrait of the Savior," *Ensign* 16/12 (1986): 20–27.

McConkie, Bruce R. *Doctrinal New Testament Commentary.* 3 vols. Salt Lake City: Bookcraft, 1965–73.

McConkie, Joseph Fielding, Robert L. Millet, and Brent L. Top. *Doctrinal Commentary on the Book of Mormon.* Vol. 4. Salt Lake City: Bookcraft, 1992.

Morris, Leon. *The Gospel According to John.* Grand Rapids, Mich.: Eerdmans, 1971.

———. *Luke: An Introduction and Commentary.* Grand Rapids, Mich.: Eerdmans, 1988.

———. *Luke: An Introduction and Commentary.* Rev. ed. Grand Rapids, Mich.: Eerdmans, 1988.

Nyman, Monte S., and Charles D. Tate Jr., eds. *The Book of Mormon: 3 Nephi 9–30, This Is My Gospel.* Provo, Utah: BYU Religious Studies Center, 1993.

Pike, Dana M. "Before the Jewish Authorities." In *The Life and*

Teachings of Jesus Christ. Vol. 1, *From Bethlehem through the Sermon on the Mount.* Edited by Richard Neitzel Holzapfel and Thomas A. Wayment. Salt Lake City: Deseret Book, 2005.

Ritmeyer, Leen, and Kathleen Ritmeyer. *The Ritual of the Temple in the Time of Christ* Jerusalem: Carta, 2002.

Robinson, Stephen E., and H. Dean Garrett. *A Commentary on the Doctrine and Covenants.* 4 vols. Salt Lake City: Deseret Book, 2000–2005.

Schürer, Emil. *The History of the Jewish People in the Age of Jesus Christ,* rev. ed. 3 vols. Edited by Geza Vermes, Fergus Millar, and Matthew Black. Edinburgh: T & T Clark, 1973–87.

Seely, David Rolph. "The Last Supper According to Matthew, Mark, and Luke." In *The Life and Teachings of Jesus Christ.* Vol. 3, *From the Last Supper through the Resurrection.* Edited by Richard Neitzel Holzapfel and Thomas A. Wayment. Salt Lake City: Deseret Book, 2003.

Skinner, Andrew C. "The Arrest, Trial, and Crucifixion—A Lesson in Loyalty." In *Studies in Scripture.* Vol. 5, *The Gospels.* Edited by Kent P. Jackson and Robert L. Millet. Salt Lake City: Deseret Book, 1986.

———. *Gethsemane.* Salt Lake City: Deseret Book, 2002

Talmage, James E. *Jesus the Christ.* Salt Lake City: Deseret Book, 1963.

Taylor, Joan E. "The Garden of Gethsemane: Not the Place of Jesus' Arrest." *Biblical Archaeology Review* 21/4 (July/August 1995): 26–35, 62.

Wayment, Thomas A. "The Triumphal Entry." In *The Life and Teachings of Jesus Christ.* Vol. 2, *From the Transfiguration through the Triumphal Entry.* Edited by Richard Neitzel Holzapfel and Thomas A. Wayment. Salt Lake City: Deseret Book, 2006.

———. "The Woman Taken in Adultery and the History of the New Testament Canon." In *The Life and Teachings of Jesus Christ.* Vol. 2, *From the Transfiguration through the Triumphal Entry.* Edited by Richard Neitzel Holzapfel and Thomas A. Wayment. Salt Lake City: Deseret Book, 2006.

Welch, John W. "The Factor of Fear in the Trial of Jesus." In *Jesus Christ, Son of God, Savior.* Edited by Paul H. Peterson, Gary L. Hatch, and Laura D. Card. Provo: Utah: BYU Religious Studies Center, 2002.

———. *Illuminating the Sermon at the Temple and Sermon on the Mount: An Approach to 3 Nephi 11–18 and Matthew 5–7.* Provo, Utah: FARMS, 1995.

———. "Latter-day Saint Reflections on the Trial and Death of Jesus." *Clark Memorandum* (Fall 2000): 2–13.

———. "Miracles, Maleficium, and Maiestas in the Trial of Jesus." Forthcoming.

———. *The Sermon at the Temple and the Sermon on the Mount: A Latter-day Saint Approach.* Salt Lake City: Deseret Book, 1990.

Wells, M. Gawain. "The Savior and the Children in Third Nephi." *Journal of Book of Mormon Studies* 14/1 (2005): 62–73.

Wilkinson, John. *Jerusalem As Jesus Knew It.* London: Thames and Hudson, 1978.

Wright, Donald N. "Judgment Day, Final." In *Encyclopedia of*

Index

Adoration of the Magi, 17
Adoration of the Shepherds, 6, 8
Adoration of the Shepherds, The, 11
Agony in the Garden, from the *Engraved Passion,* 66
Anastasis, 91–93
Angel Appearing to the Shepherds, The, 8
Annunciation, The, xii, 2
Annunciation, The, from the *Life of the Virgin,* 3
Annunciation to the Shepherds, 9
Annunciation, Visitation, and Nativity, from *Der Ingeborg Psalter de Danemark,* 5
Apocalypse, The, 113
Apollo and Daphne, Master of, xii, 2
Artistic conventions, 39

Bait, 48
Baptism, 28
Baptism, artistic portrayals of, 26
Baptism of Christ, from the *Book of Hours,* 27
Baptism of Christ, from the *Codex Etschmiadzin,* 26
Baptism of Christ, The, 24, 26
Bearing of the Cross, from the *Engraved Passion,* 78
Betrayal of Christ, from the *Engraved Passion,*
Birth, as a theme of the New Testament Gospels, 7–8
Bloch, Carl Heinrich, ii, 36, 38, 41, 47, 62, 64, 83, 89, 96, 99
Book of Hours, 27
Books of Hours, 59
Bust of Christ with Orb, from *Le Livre d'Heures aux Fleurs,* 111

Christ and the Samaritan Woman among Ruins, 34
Christ and the Tempest, 40
Christ and the Woman Taken in Adultery, 47
Christ at Emmaus, 99
Christ Before Caiaphas, from the *Engraved Passion,* 72
Christ Before Pilate, from the *Engraved Passion,* 72
Christ Crowned with Thorns, from the *Engraved Passion,* 73
Christ Driving the Money Changers from the Temple, 54
Christ Entering Jerusalem, 50, 52
Christ Healing the Sick at Bethesda, 36, 38
Christ Healing the Sick (The Hundred Guilder Print), 41
Christ in Limbo, from the *Engraved Passion,* 93
Christ in the Garden of Gethsemane, 62, 64
Christ in the House of Simon the Pharisee, 49
Christ Nailed to the Cross, 79
Christ Pantocrator, 110
Christ Preaching (La Petite Tombe), 32
Christ Taking Leave of His Mother, from the *Life of the Virgin,* 53
Christ with a Crown of Thorns, ii
Codex Etschmiadzin, 26
Collaert, Guilliam, 45
Come Follow Me, 42, 44
Counter-Reformation art, 80–82
Court of Heaven, The, from *The Apocalypse,* 113
Cross, symbolism of the, 77
Crucifixion, artistic portrayals of, 80–82
Crucifixion, from the *Engraved Passion,* 84
Crucifixion, The, 83
Crucifixion, The—A Triptych, 76, 81

Das Turin-Maïlander Stundenbuch, 56, 58, 67
Daughter of Jairus, The, 41
Denial of Peter, 70, 74
Der Ingeborg Psalter de Danemark, 5, 59
Descent from the Cross by Torchlight, The, 82
Descent into Limbo, The, 90, 92
Destruction on the Western Continent, 100
Doubting Thomas, The, 99
Dürer, Albrecht, 3, 33, 53, 66, 68, 72, 73, 78, 82, 84, 85, 88, 93, 97

Ecce Homo, 75
Ecce Homo, from the *Engraved Passion,* 73
Engraved Passion, 66, 68, 72, 73, 78, 84, 85, 88, 93, 97
Entombment, from the *Engraved Passion,* 88
Entombment, The, 89
Exchange No. 8, 108, 110
Exultet Roll: Codex Barberini Latinus, 93

Fastolf, Master of Sir John, 27
First Vision: Joseph Smith's account of, 103, 105; artistic portrayals of, 104; comparison of 1832 and 1838 accounts of, 105–6
First Vision, The (Kinney), 107
First Vision, The (Teichert), 102, 104
Flagellation, from the *Engraved Passion,* 72
Flight into Egypt, 21
Flight into Egypt, from the *Stundenbuch der Maria von Burgund,* 22

Index

Garden of Gethsemane, artistic portrayals of, 67
Ghirlandaio, Ridolfo, 14
Goltzius, Hendrik, 86
Goodliffe, Kent, 89
Gospel Harmony of Eusebius, 12, 61
Gospel of Nicodemus, 91–93
Guttenberg, Christoph Friedrich Hörmann von und zu, 40

Harrowing of Hell, 93
Harrowing of Hell, The, from the *Exultet Roll: Codex Barberini Latinus*, 93
Harwood, James Taylor, 42, 44
Head of Christ, x
Herbert, John Rogers, 18, 20
Holy Family (Mazzola), 13
Holy Family (Primaticcio), 15
Home: as a symbol of the Annunciation, 2; as a theme of the New Testament Gospels, 8–9, 11

Jegher, Christoffel, 29
Jesus Christ: annunciation to Mary, 1–5; birth of, 7–9, 11–12, 16–17; early years, 19; flight into Egypt, 19–20; in the temple as a young boy, 20–21; relationship with Joseph, 21, 23; artistic response to lack of detail about youth, 22; baptism of, 25–27; temptation to change stones to bread, 27–28; temptation to cast himself off the pinnacle of the temple, 28–29; temptation to rule earthly kingdoms, 29; parables of, 31–32; Sermon on the Mount, 32, 34; and the woman at the well, 34; sermon on the Mount of Olives (Olivet Discourse), 34–35; power over human diseases, 37–38; power over natural elements, 38, 40; power over death, 40–41; calling of the Twelve Apostles, 43; casting out of the unclean spirit, 43; transfiguration of, 46–47; and the woman taken in adultery, 47–48; washing of feet by woman in need of forgiveness, 48–49; triumphal entry into Jerusalem, 51, 54–55; teaching in the temple, 55; Last Supper, 57–58, 60–61; prophecies of impending death, 57–58; in the Garden of Gethsemane, 63, 66, 69; hearing before Jewish authorities, 71–72; Peter's denials of, 72, 74; trial before Pontius Pilate, 74–75; Crucifixion, 77, 79, 84; burial of, 87, 89; descent into hell to rescue the souls of the dead, 91–92; resurrection of, 95; Old World appearances as a resurrected being, 95–96, 99; New World appearances as a resurrected being, 99–101; Joseph Smith's First Vision of, 103, 105–6; as Judge, 109, 112; changing artistic imagery of, 110
John, artistic portrayals of, 45
John the Theologian, 44
Joseph Smith's First Vision, 106

Kinney, Lucy Thurston, 107
Krajewski, Jan, 28
Krajewski, Krzysztof, 22

L, Monogrammist, 10
Lamentation of the Virgin, 86
Lamentation over Christ, from the *Engraved Passion*, 85
Large Passion, 82
Last Supper, artistic portrayals of, 59
Last Supper, from *Das Turin-Maïlander Stundenbuch*, 56, 58
Last Supper, from the *Gospel Harmony of Eusebius*, 61
Last Supper and Washing of the Disciples' Feet, from *Der Ingeborg Psalter de Danemark*, 59
Lazarus' raising, in Protestant Reformation art, 33
Lecterns, as symbols of the Annunciation, 2
Le Livre d'Heures aux Fleurs, 65, 111
Lemoyne, François, 17
Le Sueur, Eustache, 6, 8
Life of the Virgin, 3, 53
Lilies, as symbols of the Annunciation, 2
Limbo, artistic portrayals of the descent into, 93
Luke, artistic portrayals of, 45

Madonna and Child, 14
Man of Sorrows image type, 81
Mantegna, Andrea, 90, 92
Maria von Burgund Reading the Book of Hours with Mary in the Background, from the *Stundenbuch der Maria von Burgund*, 12
Mark, artistic portrayals of, 45
Mary, artistic portrayals of, 14–15, 53
Mary Magdalene, artistic portrayals of, 45
Mary with the Child Jesus, 15
Matthew, artistic portrayals of, 45
Mazzola, Giuseppe, 13
Miracle of the Loaves and Fishes, 39
Mount Olive, Flagellation and Way of the Cross, from *Das Turin-Maïlander Stundenbuch*, 67
Mount Olive, from *Le Livre d'Heures aux Fleurs*, 65

Narrative cycles, 73
Nativity, 10
Nativity, The, 10
Nativity scenes, symbolism of, 10

Our Savior Subject to His Parents at Nazareth, 18, 20

Pann, Abel, 15
Paul, artistic portrayals of, 45
Peter, artistic portrayals of, 45
Pilate Washing His Hands, from the *Engraved Passion*, 73
Poynter, Sir Edward John, 30, 32
Prayer Book of Michelino da Besozzo, 94, 97
Presentation, from the *Gospel Harmony of Eusebius*, 12
Primaticcio, Francesco, 15
Prodigal son, in Protestant Reformation art, 33
Prodigal Son Amid the Swine, 33
Prodigal's Return, The, 30, 32
Protestant Reformation art, themes in, 33

Raimondi, Marcantonio, 11, 23
Raising of Lazarus, The, 39
Rembrandt, Circle of, x
Rembrandt Harmenszoon van Rijn, 8, 14, 32, 33, 34, 39, 41, 54, 82
Rescue of the Lost Lamb, 35
Resurrected Christ, artistic portrayals of, 97
Resurrection, from the *Engraved Passion*, 97
Resurrection, from the *Prayer Book of Michelino da Besozzo*, 94, 97
Resurrection, The, 96
Return of the Prodigal Son, The, 33
Richards, J. Kirk, 24, 26
Richmond, Ron, 108, 110
Road to Calvary, The, 80

Sacrament, The, 101
Sacred moments, as a theme of the New Testament Gospels, 11–12, 16
Saint, 44
Saint Joseph with Jesus, 22
Saints Peter and Paul, 45
Scheffer, Ary, 70, 74
Śledź, Roman, 79
Sleigh, Bernard, 76, 81
Smith, Bruce H., 48
Smith, Joseph: birth and early life of, 103; First Vision, 103, 105–6
Springinklee, Hans, 10
St. Mark, 44
St. Peter, 45
Stoss, Workshop of Viet, 44
Stundenbuch der Maria von Burgund, 12, 22
Suffering Christ image type, 81

Tassaert, Octave, 80
Teichert, Minerva K., 9, 16, 21, 35, 39, 50, 52, 98, 100, 101, 102, 104
Temptation of Christ, 29
Three Wise Men, The, 16
Through Death Came Life, 89
Titian, Workshop of, 75
Title Page: The Mocking of Christ, from the *Large Passion*, 82
Touch Me Not, 98
Transfiguration, 46

Vanni, Francesco, 49
Virgin and Child with the Cat and Snake, The, 14
Virgin Mary, artistic portrayals of, 14–15, 53

Yaroslav School, 44
Young Christ Preaching in the Temple, 23